CHRISTIAN BEGINNINGS REVISITED

CHRISTIAN BEGINNINGS REVISITED

REVISITED

Jesus, his Disciples and the Evangelists
Fresh Perspectives on Old Puzzles

William Mennie

To order additional copies of this book, contact:
Xlibris Corporation
1-888-795-4274
www.Xlibris.com
Orders@Xlibris.com
48577

CONTENTS

PART III: THE MISSIONARIES

ACKNOWLEDGEMENTS

I owe an enormous debt of gratitude to my wife Andrée for unfailing support and helpful assistance, and to my daughter Yolande whose help in preparing the manuscript and getting it published was invaluable.

FOREWORD

Innumerable scholars, theologians and others have studied the historical evidence about Jesus and his disciples. What more can be said? Actually, quite a bit more. New information and new insights are continuing to shed light on some very old puzzles and contradictions. Many myths emerged over the centuries that may or may not contain some truth. Perhaps the most useful approach is to focus entirely on writings that were probably composed within 80 years of Jesus' death. In particular, we should look for clues that point to early material likely to have been written by disciples who actually walked with Jesus during his lifetime.

INTRODUCTION

When the Jewish people of Palestine rose in rebellion against the Roman army nearly 2000 years ago (66 C.E.), a small religious movement, founded 30 to 40 years earlier in the name of a man called Jesus, was in disarray.

"The Way" was a Kingdom of God group, a missionary church launched from Jerusalem where its leader Jesus had been crucified. Inspired by Jesus' teachings and by mystical revelations received after his death, a small band of disciples, instilled with a potent mix of traditional Hebrew and neo-platonic ideas, reached out to the surrounding world. But as they proselytized, their hopeful messages started to diverge over issues related to God's Plan and intentions. Along with progress came discord. Jewish, Greek and Roman authorities persecuted them, and by the early sixties C.E., their first leaders such as James, brother of Jesus, Simon Peter and Paul of Tarsus were dead. Their anguish increased as they experienced the horrendous consequences of the Roman-Jewish War, including the destruction of the Temple and the city of Jerusalem.

Modern scholars have come to realize that the four canonical Christian gospels attributed to Mark, Matthew, Luke and John were written after the Roman-Jewish War by author-editors who had not been disciples of Jesus during his lifetime. Claiming to "bear witness," each of them wrote "good news" books using orally transmitted information, earlier written materials, and their own poetic imaginations influenced by Hebrew scriptural tradition and a keen sense of connection to divine revelation. Mark dates from about 70 C.E., followed by Matthew and Luke ten to twenty years later, and John circa or after 100 C.E.

All four author-editors were affected by the sequelae of the Roman-Jewish War, especially the increasing influence of the teachings (if not the writings) of the deceased Paul of Tarsus, who neither walked with Jesus nor experienced the War.

Broadly speaking, the first three gospels known as the synoptics share an underlying common narrative, a matching interpretive framework, and a consistent set of religious teachings by Jesus. Most scholars agree that the authors of Matthew and Luke borrowed from Mark for much narrative and story material, and from Mark and a lost Sayings Gospel known as Q for the words of Jesus. The hypothesized Q Gospel (based on common sayings in Matthew and Luke, not Mark), expressed teachings that were not inconsistent with Hebrew scriptural tradition, and could be publicly taught in Palestine. It may have been written in part by the disciple Matthew (who did not write the Gospel of Matthew).

If Mark was the other major written source for the gospels of Matthew and Luke, where did Mark's story material come from? A traditional answer has been the disciple Simon Peter, and indeed Peter is featured as chief witness to many of the events described by Mark. But the extent to which lost written notes by Peter may have contributed is moot. There remains a suspicion that the deceased Peter was enrolled by the author of Mark to bolster some of his own inventions.

Clearly Mark had other sources than Peter, as exemplified by strong verbal agreement in certain passages of the texts of Mark and John. The "Signs" Gospel hypothesis proposed by some scholars offers a common source explanation for an early lost narrative gospel used by both author-editors, which described "signs" or miracle events. More evidence now available (see Part 1) permits a four-part reconstruction of what this text may have consisted of: endorsement of Jesus as the Messiah by important Israelites, self-endorsement by Jesus through public "signs," martyrdom by God's will, and vindication from God through post-crucifixion "appearances" of Jesus to his disciples. I have renamed it the lost narrative gospel of "Early John," used, revised, and rearranged in vastly different ways by canonical author-editors Mark, Luke and John.

A major source for Mark's words of Jesus has been uncovered by the 20th century discovery in Egypt of a translated (from Greek to Coptic) ancient text of the sayings Gospel of Thomas. More than 80% of Mark's sayings and parables parallel more primitive and enigmatic Thomas versions, which lack traces of later 2nd and 3rd century influences. Both Mark and Thomas feature "secret" teachings to inner-group disciples, but differ in respect to gnosis or knowledge of a spiritual realm of God within each human being. The named author of the very early Thomas text (preceding Mark) is the disciple Judas Thomas, who walked with Jesus.

The Gospel of John ("Later John"), although gnostic-influenced, presents words of Jesus which are *not* derivative from Thomas, Q or Mark. The author-editor remoulds previous ideas into his own idiosyncratic divine personhood for Jesus, identified as the divine Redeemer co-existent with God from the Beginning of creation. He refers to Thomas as Thomas Didymos (the Twin), the "doubting Thomas" who initially fails to comprehend the physical resurrection of Jesus, in contrast to the unnamed "disciple whom Jesus loved," who identifies the resurrected Jesus with the words "It is the Lord" (John 21:7).

Surprisingly, "the disciple whom Jesus loved" is specified as the author of the Gospel of John (John 21:24), and by implication as the person initially believed by the disciples to be Jesus' choice as leader during his temporary absence (John 21:23). The Thomas Gospel explicitly assigns that leadership role to James Justus (presumed brother of Jesus). Hence the strong possibility that this James was the author of the hypothetical "Early John" Gospel, parts of which are embedded as narrative framework in the Gospel of John.

*　　*　　*

Naturally the above assertions require convincing evidence to support the hypothesis of an as yet undiscovered lost gospel which was successfully suppressed in the years following the Roman-Jewish War, but which was the original narrative account giving rise to the others. Part I of my book is an in-depth exploration of the most relevant gospel material pertinent to elucidation of the "Early John" Gospel. The inferred story differs significantly from any of the canonical texts, and permits resolution and explanation of many contradictions and discrepancies contained in them.

Three propositions are the core of my book:

1. *That the actions of Jesus are best inferred from the lost Gospel of "Early John,"
   embedded partly in canonical gospels and probably written by James, brother
   of Jesus.* This early source reflected a Hebrew scriptural understanding of
   the personhood of Jesus as a new kind of Messiah of Israel. Canonical
   writers later altered the story in various ways to bring it in line with a
   Pauline interpretation of Jesus' identity, and to deflect implications of
   anti-Roman sedition.
2. *That the teachings of Jesus are best reflected in the found Gospel of Thomas
   and the lost inferred Gospel of Q1.* These early sources connect to an
   interpretation of the Kingdom of God, promoted by the "Hellenist"
   disciples of Jesus, particularly Judas Thomas.
3. *That the post-crucifixion "appearances" of Jesus to his disciples (excepting to Mary of
   Magdala) are accurately summarized by Paul in 1 Corinthians, and confirmed by
   embedded material in canonical gospels sourced from "Early John."* The formation
   of "The Way" of (or to) God in Jerusalem, and the establishment of apostolic
   authority, were a direct consequence of these reported visions.

Part II of my book is a reconstruction of the life of Jesus, based on the findings in Part I, which takes into consideration two very early contrasting depictions, neither of which fits the canonical descriptions.

1. The Jesus of Thomas is a Gnostic Teacher of Wisdom (Hellenist), focused on the divine Spirit of God within himself.
2. The Jesus of "Early John" is a new type of traditional Messiah of Israel (Hebrew), chosen by God acting from without.

Using the Thomas Gospel and inferred "Early John" Gospel to shape our perception, we may think of Jesus as a charismatic wandering Holy Man, Hebrew-trained but gnostically-influenced, who taught a divinely ordained idealistic Kingdom of God, in competition with a more traditional Hebrew apocalyptic reformer, John the Baptist. The arrest and execution of John by King Herod Antipas catapulted the teacher Holy Man Jesus into a more activist political stance as he sought ways to forestall violence by bridging differences between "Hebrews" and "Hellenists," between hinterland people and the Herodian establishment, and between Essenes and the Temple cult. Mediated by the Holy Spirit within Jesus, the "feeding of the multitude" was a milestone communal sharing event bringing together the followers of Jesus and the deceased John. Subsequent incidents in the Temple at the Feast of Tabernacles in Jerusalem, perhaps intended to demonstrate a larger scale non-commercial sharing model of the Kingdom of God, degenerated into a "failed insurrection," from which Jesus escaped "to the place where John at first baptized" (John 10:40). Later, Jesus returned to Jerusalem to rescue his brother James from the family tomb, rejuvenate his supporters, and turn himself over to the Roman authority resulting in his own death from crucifixion at the time of the Passover feast.

In reconstructing the above version of events, I have argued that Jesus' "spiritual twin," Judas Thomas, and his biological brother (or half-brother) James, were key players. Judas Thomas was his trusted disciple, gnostically-oriented, recipient of insider information on God's Kingdom (the Thomas Gospel) and arranger of the "turnover" of Jesus to Roman authorities at Jesus' own request (the "Early John" Gospel). Brother James seems to have been instrumental in key occurrences during the lifetime of Jesus, in managing the early years of the Jerusalem Church, and in writing the lost gospel of "Early John."

The confirming evidence is strong that Jesus existed historically, that he strove to teach and implement some extraordinary ideas, that his disciples were deeply affected by his very special charismatic personality, and that they experienced post-crucifixion revelatory visions of his living spiritual personhood.

Part III is a reinterpretation of events during the early years after the crucifixion of Jesus.

Thomas and his fellow "Hellenists" provided the Gnostic image of a spiritual "always living" Jesus in ongoing communication with his "elect" followers. He seems to have preserved in writing the Gnostic neo-platonic elements of what the "living Jesus" said, particularly as related to spiritual life after death, words which may have stimulated the post-crucifixion mystical revelatory experiences of the disciples.

James was the probable leader (canonical gospels notwithstanding) in interpreting the post-crucifixion revelations that confirmed Jesus' identity and mission as Messiah of Israel in accordance with the Hebrew scriptures. His lost "Early John" Gospel probably expressed the conviction that an earthly Kingdom of God would incorporate Gentiles into a new idealized Essene-like Gnostic lifestyle operating within a Jewish-type sacerdotal structure. James was a mediating figure between Gnostic spirituality and the continuity of Hebrew customs and scriptural tradition; the glue that kept things from falling apart pending the return to Earth of Jesus Messiah.

Then came the phenomenon of Paul of Tarsus, expressed in his famous epistles, which offered a third stream of competing ideas about Jesus as fully divine Son of God.

The outcome of the Roman-Jewish War changed everything. The Hebrew-oriented Jerusalem Church had shattered. The Hellenized Gnostic version weakened. The Pauline understanding seemed vindicated. New energy came from the perception that God had punished the Jewish people, as a sign of forthcoming action to overthrow evil and implement the Divine Plan for humankind. The importance of the written word became paramount, as new writers struggled to explain the story and teachings of Jesus in accordance with the will of God.

LIST OF MAJOR WRITINGS

The major writings are composed of two distinct groups.

The first group comprises four collections written within thirty years of the death of Jesus prior to the Roman-Jewish War. Three of them may be ascribed to disciples of Jesus who knew him during his lifetime.

The **Gospel of Thomas** is a recently discovered collection of sayings attributed to Jesus, composed as a private document for inner-group disciples.

The **Gospel of Q—Layer 1** is another collection of Jesus' sayings hypothesized by scholars as being embedded in the canonical gospels of Matthew and Luke. It seems intended for instruction of the general population.

Thomas and Q1 deal with the "words" of Jesus. Both gospels reflect an optimistic non-judgmental spiritual vision of an ideal Kingdom of God, open to everyone without distinction.

The **Gospel of John—Layer 1** (Gospel of "Early John") is an inferred narrative gospel embedded in the canonical Gospel of John, with some elements found also in Mark and Luke. It is directed to the Jewish population, and focuses on the personhood of Jesus and historical events. I am proposing it as an enlargement of the concept of the "Signs" Gospel already recognized by many scholars as being embedded in the Gospel of John. Jesus is interpreted as the divinely ordained Messiah of Israel who will return "in glory" to reorder the world.

The **Epistles of Paul** are a canonical collection of letters focused on the personhood of the resurrected Jesus Christ. In Paul's scenario, God has replaced the old Mosaic covenant with the Jewish people by a new covenant applicable to all humankind. The resurrection of Jesus as Son of God confirms and symbolizes the new arrangement, which foresees the triumph of God over Satan. Faith in Jesus Christ replaces membership in the Jewish community as a criterion for belonging to the Kingdom of God.

The second group of five writings date from 40 to 80 years after the death of Jesus, and include the four canonical gospels, as well as Q-Layer 2.

The **Gospel of Mark,** according to my interpretation, consolidates selected material from the Thomas Gospel and some lost notes of Simon Peter, with a drastically revised version of the "Early John" Gospel. The underlying ideas have linkages to the teachings of Paul. The intended audience seems to be Diaspora Jewish populations and Gentiles.

The **Gospel of Q-Layer 2** is an inferred collection of sayings and doings of Jesus embedded in the canonical gospels of Matthew and Luke, and mixed with Q1 but written later.

The **Gospel of Matthew** consolidates material from the Markan and Q gospels, plus additions and strong emphasis on Old Testament scripture. The main audience seems to be Diaspora Jews.

The **Gospel of Luke** also consolidates material from the Markan and Q gospels, plus wider sources that include the "Early John" Gospel. The author continues his story in Acts of the Apostles, which describes post-crucifixion events, and his audience seems to be primarily Gentile.

The **Gospel of John** (which I refer to as "Later John") is a drastically revised version of the Gospel of "Early John," (quite distinctive from the three synoptic gospels of Mark, Matthew and Luke) which contains its own evolved interpretation of Jesus. The audience is primarily Gentile.

PART I

THE WRITINGS

CHAPTER 1

THE SAYINGS GOSPEL
OF THOMAS

In December 1945, an Arab peasant in Upper Egypt named Mohammed Ali al-Sammon, while digging in the ground near the town of Nag Hammadi, found a large earthenware jar containing a bundle of very ancient papyrus manuscripts, today known as the Nag Hammadi Gnostic Library. Included were a wide range of Gnostic writings, philosophical speculations and apocryphal stories written in the Coptic language circa 350-400 C.E., having been translated from the Greek texts written centuries before. Among the manuscripts was a Coptic translation of the Greek version of the *Gospel of Thomas*, previously known to scholars only from a few scattered fragments.

Gnostic Writings[1]

Gnostic belief systems were a strand of religious thought that emerged among pagans, Jews and Christians as counterpoint to the prevailing orthodoxies early in the first millennium. Essentially, they revolved around the concept of "gnosis" (intuitive self-knowledge) or the discovery of God within oneself. The orientation was neo-platonic, with Jesus playing a central role in Christian versions, as God's emissary who brings revelation of "gnosis" necessary for salvation.

Until recent decades, information on Gnostic writings came mainly from 2nd century Christian opponents who denounced its ideas about God and Jesus as heresy, particularly the non-acceptance of the physical resurrection and second coming of Jesus Christ. The Nag Hammadi discovery has confirmed the existence of ancient Gnostic literature seemingly aimed at disputing the interpretation of Jesus' identity and teaching that had emerged from orthodox texts and letters. In part, the discovered Gnostic documents purport to reveal secret revelations from Jesus to named disciples which explain the divine realm in terms radically divorced from Hebrew scriptural tradition. Some of this is mystical communication from Jesus after his death. Other texts, such as the separately discovered Gospel of Judas, deal with events related to the crucifixion of Jesus, which may reach back to very early alternative traditions. References to Pauline and Johannine ideas and other indicators in them locate all these writings well into the 2nd and 3rd centuries.

The Gospel of Thomas, however, is something else, because it seems to have very little connection to second century polemics, and much connection to the first century, as discussed below. The text is a collection of 114 purported sayings and parables of Jesus, similar in its structure both to Old Testament collections (e.g. Proverbs, Wisdom of Solomon), and Hellenistic collections of sayings by philosophers. Jesus is presented as a sage who puts forth his teachings within a framework of ideas that seem far removed from the presuppositions of the canonical gospels and the traditional scriptures of Israel. And yet much of the text resonates with words and phrases located also in the canonical gospels.

The Contents of Thomas [2]

According to the Nag Hammadi version, the Thomas Gospel begins: "These are the secret (or hidden) sayings which the living Jesus spoke and which Didymos Judas Thomas wrote down." It thus differs radically from the canonical gospels not only in its structure as a simple collection of sayings, but also as a *secret* gospel of teachings, intended for a small inner group of disciples, and not for the general public. Most of the sayings are preceded only by the words "Jesus said," although some are set out as responses to questions from specific named disciples or from his disciples in general.

The subject matter of Thomas is the "mysteries" of the Kingdom of God, which is the divine realm of the "Light of the Father within." The Kingdom of God equates with the mysterious world of the Spirit, which is an emanation from God the Father. Beyond material creation rests the pre-created holistic reality of the Light of the Father, the supreme transcendent male deity.

Fortunately, the female principle of Wisdom (Sophia) is part of God's emanation, whence comes the spark (or light) from the world of Spirit that resides within each created human individual. The "light within" belongs to the "undivided" spiritual realm where "the end will be where the beginning is" (Thomas 18).

The central message from Thomas is that the Kingdom of God is timeless, spiritual, always present, and already here. For example:

Thomas 3—" . . . Rather the Kingdom is inside of you, and it is outside of you"

Thomas 51—His disciples said to him, "When will the repose of the dead come about, and when will the new world come?" He said to them, "What you look forward to has already come, but you do not recognize it."

Thomas 113—His disciples said to him, "When will the kingdom come?" Jesus said, "It will not come by waiting for it. It will not be a matter of saying 'here it is' or 'there it is.' Rather, the Kingdom of the Father is spread out upon the earth, and men do not see it."

According to the Jesus of the Thomas Gospel, participation or entry into the Kingdom (i.e. mystical identification with the Spirit), is achieved by recovering one's original spiritual "undivided" self, (unencumbered by differences between physical and non-material, male and female, etc.). Such participation is available to everyone through a child-like intuitive inner-directed process. "Whichever one of you comes to be a child will be acquainted with the Kingdom" (Thomas 46).

The Kingdom within is reached by the process of gnosis (or knowledge), "when you come to know yourselves." And at that point "you will understand that you are children of the living Father" (Thomas 33). Equipped with this knowledge of their divine origins, members of the Kingdom achieve true understanding of the life of the spirit. Material needs become "spiritualized" and power, hierarchy and hatred start to fade away. For practical purposes, entry into the Kingdom implies an alternative mode of living in the world, spelled out in various cryptic aphorisms relating to food, clothing, shelter, travel and other matters of daily existence. Features of this lifestyle include itinerancy, optimism, loving relationships, voluntary poverty, "depreciation of the flesh," and an anti-conventional social attitude.[3]

By becoming "children of the living Father," disciples "cast off" the material world, and join the enduring mystical world of the Spirit. Baptism is a metaphor for "casting off"; removal of clothes and washing symbolize escape from the material body. Baptismal nakedness also symbolizes re-birth like a newborn baby, and androgyny as in a child.

The importance of spreading the Kingdom is stressed. "It will not come by watching for it" (Thomas 113). Beginning like a grain of mustard seed, the Kingdom, according to Jesus, will grow into a large plant—if the seed falls on tilled soil (Thomas 20). So the disciples must "proclaim from your rooftops" (Thomas 33) to promote the flow of the Spirit. But, of course, proselytization brings about contact with dissenting individuals and groups. There is little point in bringing the message to Gentiles, for instance: "Do not give what is holy to dogs, lest they throw them on the dung heap" (Thomas 93). The scribes and the Pharisees "have taken the keys of knowledge and hidden them. They themselves have not entered, nor have they allowed those who want to enter to do so" (Thomas 39). The parable of the invited guests is directed against commercial preoccupations: "Buyers and merchants will not enter the places of my Father" (Thomas 64). Even close friends and relatives may not understand: "No prophet is accepted in his own village; no physician heals those who know him" (Thomas 31). Therefore, "it is dissension which I have come to cast upon the world" (Thomas 16), and the Kingdom must be strong and vigilant to protect its own growth (Thomas 21, 35 and 103).

Despite the above passages, violence is ruled out. "Jesus said: The Father's Kingdom is like a person who had good seed. His enemy came at night and sowed weeds among the good seed. The person did not let them pull up the weeds, but said to them, 'No, or you might go to pull up the weeds and pull the wheat along with them! For on the day of the harvest the weeds will be conspicuous and will be pulled up and burned'" (Thomas 57). Thus, Jesus excludes removal of "weeds" by human action, leaving the matter up to God, but his response does seem to open up the possibility of divine apocalyptic judgment "on the day of the harvest." Similarly, in the parable of the leased vineyard (Thomas 65), Jesus seems to sympathize with the exploited peasantry, while simultaneously warning against the consequences of violence against landlords.

In regard to traditional Mosaic Law, Jesus seems to take positions against fasting and eating rituals (Thomas 14); against circumcision (Thomas 53); and against Temple culture (Thomas 71). At the same time, Thomas situates Jesus on non-rebellious ground vis-à-vis Rome in Thomas 100: "They showed Jesus a gold coin and said to him 'Caesar's people demand taxes from us.' He said to them 'Give Caesar the things that are Caesar's, give God the things that are God's, and give me what is mine.'"

The Identity of Jesus

In the Thomas Gospel, Jesus is a Teacher of Wisdom, who by "knowing himself" has reached the "hidden truth" of the Kingdom of God. Having achieved gnosis, Jesus knows himself as a son of God, a spiritual being incarnated in the flesh. "Jesus said: I took my stand in the midst of the world, and in flesh I appeared to them . . ." (Thomas 28).

The words of Jesus (often enigmatic as befits "hidden truth") contain revelation of that truth, referred to as the "bubbling spring" of wisdom. The receiver of the words is invited to seek insight into himself and God. "Jesus said: Whoever drinks from my mouth *will become like me*, I myself shall become that person, and the hidden things will be revealed to that person" (Thomas 108; emphasis mine). There seems to be no special distinction between Jesus and other enlightened children of God. They come from the same place, and will return to the same place. "Jesus said: If they say to you, where have you come from, say to them, 'We have come from the light, from the place where the light came into being by itself . . . '" (Thomas 50). "And he said: Whoever discovers the interpretation of these sayings will not taste death" (Thomas 1).

"Jesus said to his followers, 'compare me to something and tell me what I am like.' Simon Peter said to him, 'You are like a *just messenger*.' Matthew said to him, 'You are like a *wise philosopher*.' Thomas said to him, 'Teacher, *my mouth is utterly unable to say what you are like*.' Jesus said, 'I am not your teacher. Because you have drunk, you have become intoxicated from the bubbling spring that I have tended.' And he took him and withdrew and spoke three sayings to him. When Thomas came back to his friends, they asked him, 'What did Jesus say to you?' Thomas said to them, 'If I tell you one of the sayings he spoke to me, you will pick up rocks and stone me, and fire will come from the rocks and consume you' "(Thomas 13; emphasis mine).

The enigmatic answer of Jesus on his own identity seems to imply a mystical comprehension or self-understanding as a spiritual entity directly linked to divine authority. Jesus has achieved gnosis. Everyone else may also achieve gnosis and enter the Kingdom. But it is important to note that John the Baptist has *not* achieved gnosis. In the only direct reference to John in the Thomas Gospel (Thomas 46), Jesus says: "From Adam to John the Baptist, among those born of women, no one is so much greater than John the Baptist that the person's eyes should not be averted. But I have said that whoever among you becomes a child will know the Kingdom and will become greater than John." What does this mean? Apparently it means that members of the Kingdom "will not taste death," will recover their original "undivided" self, and return to God. By inference, presumably, all other human beings including John the Baptist will "taste death" and remain divided from God.

Death and Resurrection

In Thomas 12, the disciples say "We know that you are going to leave us," which implies that Jesus gave advance warning of his departure to his inner-group disciples and also fits the Markan story (see Chapter 5). But whether this meant withdrawal to a solitary life, imprisonment, or death is not specified. Nowhere does the Thomas Gospel refer to crucifixion or resurrection. Nevertheless, it is made clear that like all who have discovered the Kingdom of God, Jesus "will not taste death." He is referred to as the "living Jesus," and God is referred to as the "living Father."

Essentially, the Thomas understanding is that death is simply a "casting away" of the physical body as part of the process of rejoining one's original spiritual "undivided" self with its source, the Light of God the Father. Those who belong to the Kingdom of God will die physically, but "will not taste death." What happens to Jesus will happen also to the rest of them. This "democracy" of death means that the ability to mystically merge with God in recovering one's original "undivided" spiritual self is available to everyone. The conventionally powerless "nobodies" of society have equal access through an inner-directed process of enlightenment. "Fortunate are the poor, for yours is heaven's kingdom" (Thomas 54). The real poverty is exclusion from the spiritual Kingdom of God. "But if you do not know yourselves, then you dwell in poverty and you are in poverty" (Thomas 3).

Disciples, Apostles and Family of Jesus

The disciples of Jesus are portrayed in the Thomas Gospel as questioners seeking to understand the revelation of wisdom contained in the words of Jesus. Particularly notable is that the questioning disciples include women as well as men. The named women are Mary and Salome. The named men are Peter, Matthew and Thomas. Whereas "the disciples" are mentioned many times, the total number is never indicated.

In Thomas 13, Peter's understanding of Jesus as a "just messenger" is suggestive of a traditional Jewish prophet. Matthew's idea that Jesus is like a "wise philosopher" suggests a Greek or Hellenistic perception of Jesus. Paradoxically, Thomas' inability to use words to describe Jesus implies his superior mystical knowledge of Jesus, and justifies his apparent spiritual twinship with Jesus, implied by his nickname, and doubly emphasized by the words Thomas Didymos (twin in Aramaic and twin in Greek). Jesus takes Thomas aside to give him secret knowledge apparently unacceptable to the other disciples.

Thomas' special status as scribal interpreter of the words of Jesus is accompanied by the designation of James as future leader when Jesus "leaves his disciples" (Thomas 12). Only the future leadership of "James the Just" (or Righteous) is mentioned; there is no mention of the appointment of apostles (whether twelve or any other number).

In regard to the family of Jesus, the Thomas Gospel quotes Jesus as assuring his disciples that his brothers and mother have no special status. "He said to them, 'Those who do the will of my father are my brothers and my mother. They are the ones who will enter my father's kingdom'" (Thomas 99). This also implies, however, that his earthly family members can qualify as his spiritual brethren as part of a new spiritual family that encompasses all human beings who follow God's will.

The Crucial Issue of Dating

It is quite easy to suppose that the Thomas Gospel may have been the work of a later unnamed writer, who attributed the text to the disciple Thomas. In fact, many modern scholars have argued that it is a late Gnostic construction worked out in the second century C.E. Quite clearly, many of the Thomas sayings and parables parallel similar material in the canonical gospels, relating to entry into the Kingdom, lifestyle implications and spreading of the message. By contrast, the more enigmatic gnostic-type statements are conspicuous by their presence in Thomas and their absence in Mark, Matthew and Luke.

But scholars realize also that the Thomas version of various sayings by Jesus is frequently more primitive or original than the comparable elaborated texts found in the synoptic gospels. Moreover, the absence of any traces of a storyline or narrative framework in Thomas argues against derivation.

In the case of the Gospel of Mark, careful study shows that more than 80 percent of the sayings and parables of Jesus contained in Mark (excluding "signs" and prophecies) are also contained in Thomas (see Appendix 1). In most instances Mark provides an elaboration, a reinterpretation, and a story context for a more primitive version in Thomas. It is particularly noteworthy that the material used by Mark that seems derivative from Thomas does not include any of the gnostic-oriented mystical sayings that illuminate Thomas' neo-platonic theosophy. Accordingly, a plausible hypothesis advanced by some scholars is that an early version of Thomas lacking Gnostic orientation was used by Mark well before an overlay of Gnostic ideas was added to Thomas at a much later date by other writers. The conclusion would be that minimally at least, the Thomas sayings and parables included in Mark must have been written down some time prior to the composition of Mark's Gospel.

But the overlay of non-traditional Gnostic ideas in Thomas about the spiritual ever-present Kingdom of God, serves to inform the lifestyle sayings and vision expressed in the rest of Thomas. Without such "explanatory" statements about salvation through gnosis, the rationale for the other Jesus sayings is less clear. Mark, on the other hand, has a very different perspective to "explain" the particular sayings that he has used (see Chapter 5). Insofar as Mark opposed "salvation through gnosis," he was motivated to omit any Thomas sayings that were incompatible with his own understanding. This can be seen most clearly in respect to Mark's omission of the three key "kingdom is already here" sayings in Thomas (Thomas 3, 51 and 113).

Another highly significant point is that most of the Gnostic writings found in the Nag Hammadi collection include indications of familiarity with one or the other of distinctive canonical gospel or Pauline ideas. But the Thomas Gospel lacks confirmatory evidence of such derivative connections.

The conclusion follows that *both* Gnostic mystical sayings and other elements of Thomas were written prior to 70 C.E. when Mark wrote his gospel. Also, the Johannine gospel, the Gospel of Luke and the letters of Paul contain important traces of gnostic-type ideas, as will be shown later in Chapters 4, 8 and 9. In particular, the negative Johannine depiction of the disciple Thomas provides confirmatory clues about his Gnostic position. Furthermore, the Thomas saying on the leadership question (Thomas 12), implies a very early date following the death of Jesus. "The followers said to Jesus 'We know that you are going to leave us. Who will be our leader?' Jesus said to them, 'No matter where you are, you are to go to James the Just, for whose sake heaven and earth came into being'" (Thomas 12). Which is not to deny that there may have been later editing, or that some of the reported sayings of Jesus may derive directly from the scribal Thomas as much as from Jesus.

Who Wrote the Thomas Gospel?

According to the Nag Hammadi version, the Thomas collection begins as follows: "These are the *secret* sayings which the *living Jesus spoke*, and which Didymos *Judas* Thomas wrote down" (emphasis mine).

The author is Thomas, reported by Mark to be one of the twelve specially selected disciples (Mark 3:18), with no further reference. The Gospel of John, however, mentions Thomas several times. In fact, the selection by John of "doubting Thomas" as the chief witness to the physical resurrection of Jesus (John 20:24-29) is a dramatic high point of John's Gospel, all the more powerful in contrast to Thomas' Gnostic "non-resurrection" collection of the sayings of Jesus.

It turns out that Thomas is the Hellenized spelling of the Aramaic word "Toma" which means "twin." Mark's gospel uses only this nickname for identification. An implication might be that Mark wished to conceal the real birth name, since his Greek-speaking readership would not be aware of the Aramaic meaning of Thomas. On the other hand, the Johannine Gospel adds redundantly the Greek word for twin "Didymos" when he mentions Thomas, thus calling him "twin twin." Apparently this author, too, wants to conceal his birth name while feeling obliged to recognize his status of "twin."

The question arises as to whether the use of the nickname "Twin" refers to an actual birth relationship, or whether it means only that the individual bears a close physical (or psychological) resemblance to another person. It could also mean, symbolically, that the person shares a special status or understanding, presumably with Jesus. A strong case can be made for this latter interpretation. As scribal recorder of the words of Jesus, Thomas' special insight and relationship could bestow an acceptance by others as a "spiritual twin" of Jesus (see also Chapters 9, 14, and 20).

A logical inference might be that Thomas is the "second Judas" among the disciples referred to in the gospels of Luke and John. In the Lukan case, the second Judas is referred to ambiguously as either the son or brother of James (Luke 6:16). In the Johannine case, the reference is to Judas (not the Iscariot) (John 14:22). Since Mark mentions a person named Judas as one of the brothers of Jesus (Mark 6:3), it becomes possible that Judas Thomas is an actual brother of Jesus.

Is Thomas therefore a real brother (even a twin) of Jesus, as well as a "spiritual twin"? The answer is no, because Thomas (without the name Judas) is mentioned side by side with Judas, son or brother of James in two listings of disciples by Luke (Luke 6:14-17 and Acts 1:13). Thomas is also separated from Judas (not Iscariot) in the Johannine gospel (John 14:5 and 22). Moreover, why would Thomas refer to the brothers of Jesus as "standing outside" if he was one of them (Thomas 99)?

Concluding Comment

The Thomas Gospel seems to be the first creative scribal response to the teachings and activities of Jesus. The disciple Thomas assembles his best recollection of highlights of the special teachings of Jesus to a small inner-group of disciples. Thomas may have put his own spin on the words of Jesus, but the collection of sayings provides a base from which his followers can *live* the words of Jesus, which constitute a special revelation from God.

These words of Jesus do not deal directly with the burdens of oppression faced by Jewish people living under Roman rule, for example "Give Caesar the things that are Caesar's" (Thomas 100). Nor does Jesus condemn directly Mosaic Law, ritual practices or the Temple cult; but his attitude towards circumcision (Thomas 53), food (Thomas 14) and the physical Temple (Thomas 71) show a neo-platonic sensibility toward scriptural traditions. The Thomistic sayings are consistent with the image of a Teacher of Wisdom who bypasses traditional theology to focus on a "changing of ways" aimed at achieving spiritual harmony with God the Father. They are consistent also with the image of an itinerant "walkabout" teacher, who counsels his followers to "Be passers-by" (Thomas 42). And yet this quiet relaxed teaching approach is accompanied by a timeless sense of the urgent importance of the present moment; "proclaim (the message) from your rooftops" (Thomas 33), the mustard seed falls on "tilled soil" (Thomas 20), and "the harvest is large but the workers are few. So beg the master to send out workers to harvest" (Thomas 73). Jesus seems aware that his confrontation with conventional wisdom in the Jewish polity will stir up trouble: "I have come to impose conflicts upon the earth: fire, sword, war" (Thomas 16).

Even so, the Thomistic Jesus makes no prophecies about the future, nor any special claim to divine status. There is no mention of the manner of his departure from this world, or of any sacrificial role as saviour of humankind. He is described as the "living Jesus," without any claim to titles such as Messiah, Son of God, or King of Israel. He is a Teacher of Wisdom. His true self is his spiritual self, which can, perhaps, appear to his followers in spiritual form after his death. But the important thing is the teachings rather than the special personhood of Jesus. His disciples have been shown how to enter the Kingdom of God, without special rituals or intermediaries. All who achieve enlightenment are children of God. The Kingdom of God equates with the Holy Spirit, which is continuously present and available, as a divine spark which can be activated in human beings.

What are we to make of a non-mythological Jesus purportedly remembered in prose by his "spiritual twin" the disciple Thomas? Did some anonymous scribe peruse the Gospel of Mark many decades later to extract and abbreviate without order or design, fragments of sayings by Jesus and mix them with Gnostic musings about God and man? If so, why did this scribe not provide any mythological explanation of Jesus, either in support of or as an alternative to the interpretation of his Markan source? Also, why is there no sign of Pauline ideas as is the case in most second-century Gnostic writings? The answer surely is that the author knew nothing of Mark's Gospel (which had not yet been written), or of Paul's epistles, and was writing down a first-stage early remembrance of the words of Jesus, his teacher and "spiritual twin," as a reference guide for other disciples.

---

[1]   See Pagels, Elaine, *The Gnostic Gospels*, Random House, New York, 1979; and Dart, John, *The Jesus of Heresy and History*, Harper and Row, San Francisco, 1988.

[2]   For the complete text of the Gospel of Thomas, see Meyer, Marvin W., *The Gospel of Thomas, The Hidden Sayings of Jesus*, New York, Harper Collins, 1992.

[3]   See Crossan, J.D., *The Historical Jesus*, Harper, San Francisco, 1991.

CHAPTER 2

THE LOST SAYINGS GOSPEL
OF Q—LAYER 1

When scholars in the 19th century began to look critically at the canonical gospels, a distinction was made between the Gospel of John, and the other three synoptic gospels that seemed to share a significant amount of narrative material. A consensus took hold that Mark was the earliest of the canonical gospels, and that both Matthew and Luke were dependent in part upon the Markan account as a source. It also seemed that another common source must have been available to Matthew and Luke, to explain certain material found in both of them, but not in Mark. Christian Weisse (1838) proposed the "two document hypothesis" that Matthew and Luke composed their gospels independently, but each relied on two common written sources: the Gospel of Mark, and another source that must have consisted mainly of sayings of Jesus. This latter document was termed "The Gospel of Q."[1]

Q is a hypothetical "lost gospel," parts of which are embedded in Matthew and Luke. No document corresponding to Q has yet been discovered, but during the past 150 years much progress has been made in ascertaining and interpreting its probable contents. Some scholars reject the Q hypothesis.

The Contents of Q[1]

Since Q is a hypothetical document, opinions vary as to its precise elements. In general, scholars limit it to material common to Matthew and Luke, but not found in Mark. Of course, Matthew and Luke may each have omitted various things from Q, and some Q material may be in only one or the other. And some material common to Mark, Matthew and Luke could also have been part of Q. Therefore, the original Q might well have comprised more than what scholars are able to define.

Essentially (as with the Thomas Gospel), the Q defined by scholars is a collection of purported teachings of Jesus, but unlike Thomas it has occasional elements of narrative context. A significant portion of the material consists of lifestyle sayings and instructions, but additionally there is a substantial apocalyptic and prophetic element. As pointed out by Mack[2], the initial impression for the scholar is of a motley collection of ad hoc sayings material lacking much in the way of compositional design.

Some scholars have proposed a layered approach, which includes an original "sapiential" layer (Q1), an apocalyptic layer (Q2), and later additions (Q3). Separation of these layers provides an explanatory framework for understanding the composition of the Q material. For present purposes, I focus attention on Q1, using a modified version of the text proposed by Burton L. Mack.[1]

The Q1 Layer[1]

The Q1 layer is a joyful exposition of the lifestyle philosophy of Jesus, presented in clusters of aphorisms that include picturesque images and memorable sayings of a counterculture lifestyle.

Here we find messages about the blessings of poverty; about the value of loving your enemies; about the hollowness of customary pretensions; about the foolishness of worry over clothing, food and other material things. As pointed out by B.L. Mack: "The perspective is that of the underdog, and the vision is that of those who can see through the emptiness, who already know that the emperor has no clothes."[3] "Q's challenge to its readers was to have another look at their world and dare to dance to a different tune."[4]

Examples of aphorisms are:

> How fortunate the poor; they have the Kingdom
> Can the blind lead the blind?
> A good tree does not bear rotten fruit
> Everyone who asks receives
> People are worth much more than the birds
> Life is more than food
> Everyone who glorifies himself will be humbled
> Whoever tries to protect his life will lose it.

Examples of the better way of living are:

Rejoice when reproached
Love your enemies
If struck on one cheek, offer the other
Give to everyone who begs
Judge not and you won't be judged
Don't be afraid
Make sure of God's rule over you
Sell your possessions and give to charity.

From passages such as these emerged the many beautiful elaborations contained in canonical Matthew and Luke, such as the sublime Sermon on the Mount and the Lord's Prayer. Clearly, the scribal author of the Q1 Sayings had captured much of the quality, poignancy and pungency of the teachings of Jesus that had lodged themselves in the memories of his followers. Q1 instructs people on the joy of experiencing the Kingdom of God in this world.

Q1 and the Thomas Gospel

Most scholars seem to agree that the Thomas and Q1 gospels are separate and independent sources of the "sapiential" or wisdom teachings of Jesus. Some consider the Thomas Gospel to be derivative from Q1, while a few think of Q1 as derivative from Thomas. Probably both writers had direct access to Jesus.

Since virtually all the Q1 sayings of Jesus have parallels in the Thomas Gospel, excepting perhaps the Lord's Prayer, it seems obvious the author of Q1 was familiar with most of its material. The ethical and lifestyle teachings from Thomas are elaborated in Q1, but the superstructure of the Gnostic belief system in Thomas is missing. Literary quality, poetic imagination and clarity of expression are more evolved than in the Thomas Gospel.

An important distinction is that Thomas was written as a private or "secret" document for use by the "inner group" of disciples, whereas Q1 seems to be intended as a public message addressed to everyone. This may explain why the Thomas Gospel includes information on the Gnostic superstructure of Jesus' teaching, as well as the practical ethical and lifestyle implications of participating in the Kingdom of God. Q1, on the other hand, is an instruction on behaviour, attitudes and action appropriate for spreading the Kingdom; information on the ultimate rationale for the recommended lifestyle is lacking. The Q1 motto seems to be to emphasize the positive, and focus on behaviour rather than theological argument with upholders of the status quo. The aim is to reach out to all the people with information on how to live in accordance with God's rule without directly challenging the traditional precepts of Judaism.

Who Wrote Q1 and What Was Its Purpose?

The primary clue as to the motivation and authorship of Q1 may be found by turning to Thomas 13, discussed in the previous chapter. This is the saying where Jesus asks specified followers to "tell me what I am like." The disciple Matthew responds with an imperfect answer that "You are like a wise philosopher." In other words, Thomas depicts Matthew as perceiving Jesus to be primarily like a Hellenistic teacher of wisdom. Is it not therefore remarkable that the selection of the wisdom teachings of Jesus in Q1 seem to be closely akin to the ideas of Hellenistic Cynic philosophy? Whereas Thomas includes a great deal of Gnostic mysticism in his collection, the Q1 author focuses mainly on Cynic-like lifestyle sayings. The Matthewan perception of Jesus as a wise philosopher (reported by Thomas) seems consistent with the possibility that Matthew is in fact the author of Q1.

Who was Matthew? According to Mark's gospel, he was one of the twelve specially selected disciples, but as with the disciple Thomas, Mark makes no further reference to him in his gospel. Could Mark have been deliberately obscuring the important scribal roles of both Thomas and Matthew, associated with the earliest collections of Jesus' wisdom sayings? Just as Mark can be suspected of suppressing information about Thomas, he may also be suspected of suppressing information about Matthew (see Chapter 5).

Most scholars agree that the Gospel of Matthew (written later than Mark) was not written by the disciple Matthew. It was written by an unnamed Jewish scribe, extremely learned in the Hebrew scriptures, who focused on reinterpretation of the story of Jesus as the fulfilment of God's will, as disclosed in ancient writings. At the time it was written, the disciple Matthew was either deceased or a very old man. The anonymous later author made extensive use of Q1, and quite possibly chose to attribute his gospel to Matthew because of Matthew's authorship of Q1. In effect, however, by using Matthew's name, he was enrolling Matthew as a witness against himself, by incorporating the Q1 sayings material into a completely different framework of understanding about Jesus (see Chapter 7).

As discussed elsewhere (Chapters 7 and 14), Matthew may have been a former tax collector, which could be consistent with a Hellenistic outlook, a scribal background and a good education. It also implies that a formerly wealthy Matthew was converted to a completely alternative lifestyle.

The author of Q1 is enthused by the remembered teachings of Jesus, which are taken for granted as being a revelation of divine wisdom. There is no indication from the inferred passages that the death of Jesus, his resurrection, or apocalyptic judgment form part of the message. Apparently, the significance of Jesus rests in his words—not his personhood.

When Was Q1 Written?

What is the justification for considering Q1 to be written earlier than the rest of the Q complex? Could it not have been written about the same time as Q2 (which was probably composed by a reader of the Gospel of Mark as I will show in Chapter 6)? Q2 seems to provide an apocalyptic explanatory framework for the Q1 sayings, which functions as an alternative to the gnostic-style framework of the Thomas Gospel. If Thomas is an integrated construction by a single author, could not the same be true for the Q Gospel?

There are several answers. First, there is a sharp contrast between the optimistic, positive tone of Q1 sayings of Jesus, and the darker negative outlook of the rest of the material (see Chapter 6); Q1 seems to reflect a non-violent period of joyful understanding and discovery of God's Kingdom. Also, it seems to function as a set of teaching messages for use by missionaries setting out to proselytize the general public. The words of Jesus, emanating from a compassionate God, will bring new hope to downtrodden human beings. Such one-sided optimism implies a very early stage of missionary activity—a selective outward expression of the "insider" teachings in the Thomas Gospel. A second point is that Matthew is a likely author of the Q1 material, and a correspondingly unlikely author of Q2 and the Gospel of Matthew, written 40 to 50 years after the death of Jesus. My proposed dating for Q1 goes back to the early years following the death of Jesus.

---

1   See Mack, Burton L., *The Lost Gospel*, Harper, San Francisco, 1993, and Kloppenberg, John, *The Formation of Q*, Fortress Press, Philadelphia, 1987.

2   Mack, op. cit, pp.105-107.

3   Mack, op. cit., p. 111.

4   Mack, op. cit., p. 105.

CHAPTER 3

THE LOST GOSPEL OF
"EARLY JOHN"

The Gospel of John (known as the fourth gospel), expresses its version of the teachings of Jesus within a narrative framework, as do the three synoptic gospels (Mark, Matthew and Luke). Together they form part of the official canon of the New Testament, despite large differences in both ideas and construction of events between John and the others. Some of the crucial elements in the Johannine gospel reflect the same sort of thinking as the synoptic writers, but there is little evidence of familiarity with the texts of Matthew or Luke. Most scholars agree that the Johannine gospel was completed later than the synoptics (circa 100 C.E.) and was aimed at a Greek-speaking Gentile community.

The orthodox view on authorship has been that a very elderly apostle John (son of Zebedee) wrote or dictated the material, which was then elaborated by another John (probably John the Divine, exiled to the island of Patmos by the Roman Emperor Domitian). Major factual variations from the synoptic writings have been explained either by the elderly John's fading memory, or by an oral tradition more interested in ideas than factual accuracy.

Consistent with the notion of an eye-witness account of events by the apostle John, are a considerable number of details that imply direct personal observation and argue for an authenticity factor. But contrariwise there is also an impression of internal contradictions in the Johannine gospel that suggest some later writing superimposed on an earlier text (or texts). The contradictions may be summarized as follows:

(1) Whereas some of the material contains details that only an eyewitness could have known, other parts are highly imaginative renderings that

could not have been witnessed directly (e.g. John 19:33-38 describes an explicitly private conversation between Pontius Pilate and Jesus, with no-one else present).

(2) Many passages indicate an author writing for a Gentile community that needs explanations about Jewish tradition (e.g. John 4:9 "The Samaritan woman said to him 'How is it that you, a Jew, ask a drink of me, a woman of Samaria? *For Jews have no dealings with Samaritans*'"—emphasis added). Contrariwise, some of the writing on Jesus' credentials as God's Messiah seems directed at a Jewish audience in Palestine; some phrases or terms would be meaningful only to Jewish readers.

(3) Jewish supporters of the credentials of Jesus such as John the Baptist and Nathaniel identify him in terms of traditional Jewish messianic expectations relating to the restoration of Israel as the Kingdom of God. On the other hand, a number of elaborate "self-explanations" spoken directly by Jesus focus on his essential divinity as the eternal Son of God and Saviour of the whole world.

(4) In stylistic terms, the many long beautifully poetic speeches of "self-explanation" by Jesus contrast strangely with the highly cryptic style of other passages.

(5) A major repetitive theme of hostility, opposition and misunderstanding contrasts sharply with another repetitive theme of widespread popular support and various endorsements of Jesus by important people.

(6) In a number of instances a later writer seems to be correcting errors or changing meaning, without replacing the offending passages (e.g. John 4:1 "Now when the Lord knew that the Pharisees had heard that Jesus was making and baptizing more disciples than John, *although Jesus himself did not baptize, but only his disciples*"—emphasis added).

(7) Recent scholarly research appears to indicate that some parts of the Johannine gospel were written originally in Aramaic, whereas other parts were drafted in Greek without any Aramaic antecedents.

(8) And finally, there seems to be tension between Simon Peter (Galilean outlook) and "the disciple that Jesus loved" (Judean outlook).

The Mark-John Connection

Many scholars have noted that although the Johannine author apparently was not familiar with the gospels of Matthew and Luke, he must have had access to Mark, because a few stories and descriptions read as if borrowed directly from Mark (e.g. cleansing of the Temple, feeding of the 5,000, and Jesus walking on the water). But why would he borrow precise wording from Mark for incidents which he presumably witnessed (unlike Mark), while ignoring or contradicting much of the rest of the Markan text? That Mark was borrowing from John seems impossible since John wrote his material 30 to 40 years after Mark.

But if those parts of John were written earlier by another writer, it becomes possible, even probable, that Mark was borrowing from that earlier text, as well as from other sources. I shall refer to that inferred earlier text as the "Early John" Gospel. The author-editor of the Gospel of John, "Later John," re-arranged the material and omitted significant parts. Mark also used "Early John" as a source, while making major changes in the story lines, and Luke had access to at least some parts of "Early John." Important clues about "Early John" are contained as well in the Epistles of Paul.

The Fig Tree Clue

The major narrative divergences between the Gospel of John and the synoptic gospels have puzzled scholars and theologians over the centuries.

> *According to the synoptics*—Jesus launches his public mission in Galilee after baptism by John. Eventually, he goes up to Jerusalem, enters to popular acclaim, "cleanses the Temple," announces the bread and wine Eucharist at the Passover supper, is arrested and tried by the Sanhedrin, and tried and crucified by the Roman governor.

> *According to John*—Jesus launches his public mission by "cleansing the Temple" in Jerusalem and baptizing in Judea, following endorsements by John the Baptist and other important persons. After descending into Galilee, he returns to Jerusalem a number of times for feasts such as the Feast of Tabernacles; he "feeds the multitude" in Galilee and then announces the bread and wine Eucharist. Later, he flees to the desert, "raises Lazarus," re-enters Jerusalem to popular acclaim at Passover time, and is arrested and crucified by Pontius Pilate, without a Sanhedrin trial or the Passover supper.

Recently, a clue to the discrepancies has been proposed by Bishop John Shelby Spong of the Episcopalian Church in the United States[1]: the story of Jesus cursing the fig tree (Mark 11:12-26). It occurs after the entry of Jesus into Jerusalem, and prior to his cleansing of the Temple.

According to Mark, Jesus is hungry one morning when going to Jerusalem from Bethany, on his way to the "cleansing of the Temple" just prior to the Passover feast. When unable to find figs on a fig tree in leaf, "for it was not the season for figs," Jesus curses the tree: "May no one ever eat fruit from you again." And "when they passed in the morning they saw the fig tree withered away to its roots."

Apparently, this odd story symbolizes the idea that the Jerusalem Temple failing "to produce good fruit" deserves destruction. But Mark is forced to acknowledge the inappropriateness of Jesus looking for figs in the Spring Passover season. The story would make sense only if it was September-October, the time of the harvest Feast of Tabernacles.

Take a closer look at the Markan text (Mark 11:12-26). There is a separation of the sentences on the "cursing of the fig tree" and the apparent next morning discovery of the "withering away of the tree." The latter part of the text states that "Peter remembered" the cursing as if the sighting of the dead tree had in fact been much later in time leading him to recall the cursing incident. If the withering of the tree had been the next morning, there would hardly be need to mention that "Peter remembered." The text does not explicitly say that the withering was observed the next morning; rather the wording "as they passed by in the morning" implies a later observation consistent with the real possibility that the withering was seen the following Spring at the Feast of Passover, while the cursing might have occurred at the Autumn Feast of Tabernacles. Such a natural occurrence could have been perceived as symbolically significant by Peter, but translated into a 24-hour symbolic miracle by Mark, and into an instantaneous miracle by Matthew (Matthew 21:19).[2] The story of the fig tree itself, apparently emanating from Peter, is not recorded in the canonical gospel of John.

If the fig tree story is a genuine recollection, does it mean that the related cleansing of the Temple incident occurred at the Feast of Tabernacles, and may have been so reported in the original "Early John" story? And if the cleansing of the Temple occurred at the Feast of Tabernacles, what does this say about the joyous entry into Jerusalem which Mark states took place on the day prior to the Temple cleansing? According to research by Bishop Spong, the festival of Tabernacles was characterized by processions of people waving palm branches, using Psalm 118 in the liturgy, shouting hosannah, and chanting "Blessed is he who comes in the name of the Lord."[3] Could it be that the original "Early John" document placed these two key events at the Feast of Tabernacles?

An important supporting clue is that the Johannine gospel reports that the crowd at the Passover "entry into Jerusalem" used "branches of palm trees" (John 12:12) as in a religious procession, whereas the synoptic gospels refer instead to tree branches spread on the road (e.g. Mark 11:8). The deletion of reference to waving palm branches suggests a conscious decision by Mark to eliminate information that linked Jesus' arrival in Jerusalem to the Feast of Tabernacles rather than the Passover Feast. "Later John" also moved this event to Passover but retained other parts of the Feast of Tabernacles story. If indeed both authors made such a change, we begin to have a rational explanation for much that is mysterious in both the Gospel of John and the Gospel of Mark.

None of the canonical gospels places the Jerusalem entry and Temple cleansing stories at the Feast of Tabernacles. But what about "Early John"? Could he have written a different story? What is a plausible picture of the contents of the "Early John" Gospel? For a full analysis the reader should refer to APPENDIX 2 and Chapters 5, 8 and 9 which deal with the reactions of Mark, Luke and "Later John" to their source document.

In this present chapter I will discuss the clues that point to a four-part early narrative gospel which begins with the discovery and endorsement of Jesus as the Messiah by important people, in particular John the Baptist. In the second part, Jesus explains himself mainly through public "signs," referred to by some scholars as the Signs Gospel. The third part consists of Jesus' tragic martyrdom, which paradoxically signifies God's endorsement, confirmed in the fourth part by Jesus' post-crucifixion appearances to his followers.

Endorsements of Jesus

The endorsements of Jesus, which set the stage for his public mission and martyrdom, are contained within Chapters 1 to 4 of the Johannine gospel. They include endorsement by important people, particularly John the Baptist, praise from new disciples, and public acclaim.

Changes and additions to the early text by "Later John" can be identified with reference to his later understanding of the identity of Jesus directed to a world-wide audience rather than to the people of Israel, and which include both major statements and stories, as well as special phrases or words that change the original meaning. The residue of embedded "Early John" material shows contrasting proselytization of the people of Israel.

Examples of major "Later John" additions are the beautiful gnostic-influenced introduction (John 1:1-18); the launching of Jesus' mission by cleansing the Temple which is a transfer from Feast of Tabernacles events (John 2:13-23); and most of the marriage of Cana incident, perhaps derived in part from Hellenistic myth (John 2:1-11).[4]

An example of a change of meaning by "Later John" is the repetition of the "Behold the Lamb of God" sighting of Jesus by John the Baptist in order to explain that he is "the Lamb of God who takes away the sin of the world," and "ranks before me for he was before me" (John 1:29-31). The source statement, presumably written by "Early John," is "Behold the Lamb of God" (John 1:36) implying Jesus' status as traditional sacrificial Saviour of Israel. The synoptic gospels do not use the concept, but Paul's Epistle to the Corinthians confirms that the idea of Jesus as Lamb of God preceded the "Later John" text: "For Christ, our paschal lamb has been sacrificed" (1 Corinthians 5:7).

In another major restatement of a conversation between Jesus and Nicodemus (John 3:1-21), "Later John" transforms the "Early John" explanation for being reborn to enter the Kingdom of God (John 3:1-6), into a completely different statement about eternal salvation through faith in the Son of God.

The embedded "Early John" story that remains after these and other inferred additions are removed, is focused on the endorsement or recognition of Jesus by leading prophets, shamans or teachers, and the recruitment of significant disciples. They describe Jesus as having a unique special relationship to God, superior to their own. Particularly interesting is that these endorsements seem to come from individuals representing diverse elements of the population of Palestine: Baptists, Samaritans and Galileans, as well as Hellenists, Pharisees and Officials (publicans).

John the Baptist's leading role in endorsing Jesus while downgrading himself is especially noteworthy. Not only does he insist on his own "unworthiness" relative to ancient prophets and Jesus (John 1:19-27), but as a prophet he ignores his own future martyrdom while forecasting that of Jesus in the titular phrase "Lamb of God." He depreciates his own water baptism relative to Jesus' baptism with the Holy Spirit (John 1:33), and prophesies that "He (Jesus) must increase but I must decrease" (John 3:30).

Note how two stories of a meeting between John the Baptist and Jerusalem priests, and of Jesus' baptizing campaign in Judea, serve as vehicles for John's endorsement of Jesus. Add-on corrections by "Later John" include such phrases as "the Pharisees sent them" (re: the Jerusalem priests—John 1:24), and "although Jesus himself did not baptize, but only his disciples" (re: Jesus was baptizing more disciples than John—John 4:2). The later editing implies the existence of an earlier text needing modification to match the later author's interpretation. Why are there no traces of the source story in Mark? Presumably because Mark suppressed it completely as being incompatible with his version of the role of John the Baptist, in which John baptizes Jesus, and Jesus himself does not baptize.

Nathaniel's endorsement of Jesus (John 1:43-51) is interesting because of the possibility that he was some sort of shaman associated with Essenes or Samaritans. It is the disciple Philip, evangelist to the Samaritans (Acts 8:4), who first brings the message to the sceptical Nathaniel. Seen "sitting under a fig tree," Nathaniel could well be a shaman, and the words of Jesus about him are highly complimentary, "Behold, an Israelite indeed, in whom is no guile," which could imply his lack of formal qualification as an Israelite. Perhaps this unusual use of the term "Israelite" derives from "Early John's" perception that Jesus considered Samaritans or Greeks to be fully acceptable as Israelites. Nathaniel responds by putting Jesus on a pedestal: "Teacher, you are God's son! You are King of Israel!"

Simon Magus, a leading Gnostic shaman in Samaria (see Acts 8:4-24), may also have been recorded by "Early John" as endorsing Jesus. Such an inference rests on weak evidence in John 4:1-42, and the story in Acts about Philip's later proselytization activities in Samaria. If so, the write-up has been smothered by the "Later John" story of the Samaritan woman (John 4:3-42). Some scholars argue that the "Samaritan woman" was actually Helen, the wife of Simon Magus.

The endorsement by Nicodemus, "a man of the Pharisees" (John 3:1), that "God is with Jesus" (John 3:2) is significant and the statement by the disciple Andrew "we have found the Messiah" even more so because "Later John" feels compelled to add "which means Christ" (John 1:41).

The fundamental question at issue in such inferred "Early John" passages is the identity of the Messiah (the Anointed One), the future ideal ruler to be sent by God to restore the Kingdom of Israel. The endorsements arise from the perception that the Holy Spirit (a concept of the Essenes)[5] resides within Jesus. John the Baptist expresses this in a vision of the Spirit (as a dove) descending on Jesus from heaven (John 1:32). The descent of the Spirit from above instead of the expansion of the Gnostic Spirit from within suggests that "Early John's" understanding has diverged from that of the Thomas Gospel.

"Early John's" emphasis has moved from the words of Jesus as the source of revelation (as in the Thomas and Q gospels) to the personhood of Jesus expressed in titles.

The audience for this material is clearly Jewish, and not Gentile as with "Later John." Moreover, the audience is not the inner-group disciples of Jesus as in Thomas, but various elements of the population of Israel.

Self-Explanation by Jesus (The "Signs" Gospel)

The Signs Gospel, or second stage "Early John" embedded mainly in Chapters 4 to 10 of the Johannine gospel, records some public actions by Jesus that bear witness to divine power within himself, appropriate to a Messiah of Israel anointed by God. This stage follows the earlier testimonials by significant individuals, which included reference to some private acts implying divine power. This follow-up material includes five major "signs" or miracle stories: feeding of the multitude of 5000, walking on water, healing of the paralytic, healing of the blind man, and the resurrection of Lazarus. Additionally, there are two other public "signs" which are: the entry of Jesus into Jerusalem riding on an ass, and the cleansing of the Temple.

On what basis can we infer that these seven stories originate with "Early John" rather than "Later John"? Mainly because Mark presents the same stories, with modifications (the Lazarus story is in "Secret Mark" and the rest in canonical Mark). But also because the first four of the above-mentioned "sign" stories in the Johannine gospel are written with escape hatches in the wording that permit the possibility of a natural explanation, whereas the parallel Markan stories are unambiguously miraculous (see Chapter 5). It would be counterintuitive for "Later John" to have "naturalized" Mark's miraculous versions; therefore, Mark must have "miraculized" the "Early John" versions. In the fifth case, Mark's "Secret Gospel" story of Lazarus (if authentic) seems plausible as a direct borrowing from "Early John," which makes the Johannine version of the story into a "miraculization" by "Later John" of the original story.

But there is much more to the "Signs Gospel" than the signs. Strong evidence points to highly important missing material carefully deleted by Mark, Luke and "Later John." Essentially, the "Signs Gospel" begins when Jesus leaves Judea to go to Galilee (John 4:1), because of the Pharisees according to the Johannine gospel, and "after John was arrested" according to Mark (Mark 1:14) and Luke (Luke 3:20). Where did Jesus go first? To Cana, after passing through Samaria (according to John); to Capernaum (according to Mark); to Nazareth (according to Luke).

In this part of the story, all three canonical writer-editors seem perturbed about their source material. "Later John" omits any reference to the arrest of John the Baptist, while apparently elaborating two miraculous "signs" stories located in Cana ("water into wine" John 2:1-11, and "healing of Herodian official's son at a distance" John 4:46-54); contrariwise Mark (who describes many miracles performed by Jesus) seems unaware of these particular events, or any visit to Cana. Instead, Mark mentions a visit by Jesus and his disciples to nearby Nazareth where Jesus is unable to perform great miracles, and is rejected by the local people (Mark 6:1-6). And yet Mark's story seems linked to the Johannine text by the editorial comment "For Jesus himself testified that a prophet has no honour in his own country" (John 4:44) inserted just prior to the Johannine mention of Jesus' arrival in Cana.

My speculative inference is that "Early John" had mentioned the unpopularity of Jesus in Nazareth as the reason for Cana being the site of important "signs," which, however, may have been worded to allow the possibility of some natural explanation. "Later John," however, decided to fully "miraculize" these two stories with careful attention to detail. Insofar as Mark may have decided that the Cana "signs" were not credible miracles, he focused on the Nazareth rejection of Jesus as the reason "he could do no mighty work there" (Mark 6:5). If there was a Cana scenario written by "Early John" (separated into two parts by "Later John," John 2:1-11 and John 4:46-54), a significant point is that Jesus was accompanied from Cana to Capernaum by his disciples, his brothers and his mother (John 2:12). Anything else that "Early John" may have written about Jesus in Galilee prior to "the feeding of the multitude" seems to have been deleted by "Later John."

What happened next in the narrative of "Early John" may be inferred by comparing Mark and "Later John" as to similarities and differences: what each omitted and what each retained.

The first clue is that immediately preceding the feeding of the multitude of 5,000, Mark presents a graphic story of the arrest and execution of John the Baptist; by contrast the Gospel of John provides no description of this momentous event. So if "Early John" wrote anything about it, it was deleted by "Later John."

Secondly, in his Passion Story which includes the entry into Jerusalem and the cleansing of the Temple, Mark also mentions an "insurrection" ("And among the rebels in prison, who had committed murder in the insurrection, there was a man called Barabbas"—Mark 15:7), that seems to have taken place in close conjunction with these events. If Mark's source was "Early John," a likely inference is that the dissension at the Feast of Tabernacles described in the Gospel of John (John 7:14-52), may have included an "insurrection," mention of which was suppressed by "Later John." Note also that Luke, in elaborating on Mark's reference to Barabbas, adds the information that the insurrection was "started in the city" (Luke 23:19).

Thirdly, in support of the insurrection hypothesis, we have a report in Mark that his opponents accuse Jesus of saying "I will destroy this temple that is made with hands, and in three days I will build another, not made with hands" (Mark 14:58). While Mark describes this as a false accusation, both Mark and "Later John" seem to be covering up and reinterpreting some such statement by Jesus. "Later John" reports Jesus as saying "Destroy this temple and in three days I will raise it up" (John 2:19), meaning that Jesus is referring to his body as a temple to be destroyed by others and raised up by himself (God) three days later, and that the entire cleansing of the Temple incident is simply a prophetic "sign" of this future event. From this, we may infer the possibility of a statement in the "Early John" text either by Jesus or by some of his followers, that the Temple of stones should be replaced by a "Temple of people."

Fourthly, working from Mark's Gospel, we may infer that his "Early John" source implied a connection between the beheading of John the Baptist by King Herod, and the next event which is the feeding of the multitude, an encounter between Jesus and his disciples and "5,000 men." The clue is the word "men," and following the symbolic shared "feeding," the subsequent effort of the crowd (described only in John) "to take him by force and make him king" (John 6:15). We may deduce that these people could have been mainly "lost sheep" followers of John the Baptist who were seeking a new leader, and had been much impressed by Jesus' version of the ancient "manna in the wilderness" story (about the falling of manna from heaven to feed the Israelites), with its signs of messianic hope. "This is indeed the prophet who is to come into the world" (John 6:14).

A further deduction from Mark is that Jesus negotiated with the crowd while sending his disciples away in a boat. The frightened disciples are later reassured by the "walking on water" incident (John 6:16-21 and Mark 6:47-51), and sometime after, the "Early John" narrative (suppressed by "Later John"), would show Jesus going up to Jerusalem with a "great multitude" as reported by Mark (Mark 10:46). But instead of heading for the Passover Feast, they would be going to the Feast of Tabernacles, a harvest celebration that would match the manna from heaven story theme from the "feeding of the multitude."

In contradiction to any such hypothesis, the Gospel of John says that subsequent to the feeding of the multitude, Jesus came up privately from Galilee to the Feast of Tabernacles in Jerusalem, after refusing to accompany his brothers who said to him "Leave here and go to Judea, that your disciples may see the works you are doing" (John 7:3). And Jesus replied: "'I am not going up to this feast, for my time has not yet fully come,' so saying he remained in Galilee" (John 7:8-9). The text admits explicitly that Jesus lied to his brothers. Why does the Johannine text emphasize that Jesus lied to his brothers and then went up to Jerusalem *by himself?*

To explain, it is necessary to postulate that the Johannine dialogue between Jesus and his brothers (John 7:1-10), is an insert, written by "Later John." Part of the evidence for this assertion (outlined further in Chapter 9), is "Later John's" writing patterns such as "For even his brothers did not believe in him"; "the world hates me because I testify of it that its works are evil"; and "my time has not yet come."

Why would "Later John" be so concerned about creating a scene to demonstrate that Jesus went up secretly to Jerusalem, and acted publicly only "about the middle of the feast" (John 7:14) and "on the last day of the feast" (John 7:37). A reasonable answer is that "Later John" had repositioned both the cleansing of the Temple and the entry into Jerusalem away from the Feast of Tabernacles to the Feast of Passover. And having made these changes to the "Early John" text, the author required an alternative scenario to account for Jesus' presence at the Feast of Tabernacles. Contrariwise, Mark simplified everything by deleting all references to Tabernacles.

The importance of Passover for "Later John" relates directly to his overall view of Jesus as the eternal Son of God who interacts with the world as the Passover Lamb of God. Thus, according to "Later John's" narrative, Jesus commences his mission by cleansing the Temple at Passover time, and closes his mission with the final entry into Jerusalem, again at Passover time. And to further complete the picture, Jesus reveals himself as the Bread of Life after feeding the multitude in Galilee, also at Passover time.

The repositioning of these crucial events (Jerusalem entry and Temple cleansing) by "Later John" had other consequences for his narrative structure. An important public sign by Jesus in Jerusalem presumably described in "Early John," is the healing of the paralytic ("take up your pallet and walk"—John 5:8) performed on the Sabbath day as a symbol of the resurrection of a crippled

Israel; this act becomes a basis for argument and dissension when Jesus stands up "about the middle of the feast." Because "Later John" has postulated that Jesus was "secretly" in Jerusalem at this time, he is forced awkwardly to transfer this *public* healing event to an earlier unspecified "feast of the Jews" (see John 5:1), thus disconnecting the event (John 5:19) from the public reaction to it (John 7:20-24). Similarly, another "Early John" sign at the Feast, the healing of the blind man so that "those who do not see may see" (John 9:39), is transferred to another Sabbath day at the Feast of the Dedication (John 10:22) in the winter.

My conclusion is that the "Early John Signs Gospel" featured a Feast of Tabernacles event that included the "signs" of Jesus' entry into Jerusalem and cleansing of the Temple. Further signs of the presence of the Holy Spirit and messianic hope included the healing of the paralytic and the healing of the blind man (which Mark transferred to Galilee), as well as the public teaching interventions by Jesus "about the middle of the feast" (John 7:14) and "on the last day of the feast" (John 7:37).

In such a context of multiple signs, the Johannine description of turmoil at the Feast of Tabernacles (John 7:14-52) becomes much more credible. For example, the accusation by some persons that Jesus "has a demon" may have been inspired by his immediately prior cleansing of the Temple, while the controversy over the healing of the paralytic also implies an immediately prior event. It would not be surprising if a "multitude" of previous John the Baptist supporters would be considered "accursed" by the authorities: "But this crowd, who do not know the law, are accursed" (John 8:48). And it would not be surprising if some of this crowd participated in some sort of insurrection, despite Jesus' obvious opposition to violence. Just as Jesus was bringing the Holy Spirit to these people when feeding the multitude in Galilee, his "riding on the donkey" may have been intended to pacify his own followers as much as to signal peacefulness to the Jerusalem authorities. In any case, whatever the intentions of Jesus, the Johannine text indicates that following the Feast of Tabernacles, he had to flee to the desert beyond the Jordan with his disciples, "to the place where John had first baptized" (John 10:40). The reason for this was "again they tried to arrest him, but he escaped their hands" (John 10:39). The main elements of an insurrection scenario are probably present in the lost original "Early John" write-up.

Whatever that write-up contained, the Johannine gospel shows Jesus as a leader whose works are intended to demonstrate the presence of the divine Spirit within him. As a result, Nicodemus, a Judean leader and Pharisee, endorses Jesus: "Rabbi, we know that you are a teacher come from God; for no one can do these signs that you do, unless God is with him" (John 3:2). Also responding to him are the common people of Judea: "When he was in Jerusalem . . . many believed in his name when they saw the signs which he did" (John 2:23) and "Yet many of the people believed in him; they said 'When the Messiah appears, will he do more signs than this man has done?'" (John 7:31). "And the authorities said: 'What are we to do? For this man performs many signs. If we let him go on thus, everyone will believe in him and the Romans will come and destroy both our holy place and our nation'" (John 11:47-48).

Caiphas, The High Priest, however, knows something that the others don't. "You know nothing at all, you do not understand that it is expedient for you that one man should die for the people" (John 11:50). Thus, for "Early John," the High Priest parallels John the Baptist's "Lamb of God" prophesy, in stating that "Jesus should die for the nation, and not for the nation only, but to gather into one the children of God who are scattered abroad" (John 11:52). Even the High Priest is a prophet who understands that Jesus is a sacrificial messiah martyr who will unite all the peoples of Israel.

The Martyrdom of Jesus

While the Johannine Passion story differs from the synoptic gospel accounts, it may be inferred that the "Early John" account differs even more. When we remove the entry into Jerusalem scenario from the Johannine gospel Passover Feast account, the implications are substantial and assist in clarifying the likely features of the "Early John" story. What remains of this "Early John" text is contained within Chapters 11 to 21 of the Johannine Gospel. Clues derive mainly from Mark, but also from Luke who seems to have had some access to the lost text (see Chapter 8). Koester is a modern scholar who emphasizes a common source for the Passion Stories in the gospels of Mark and John.[5]

My proposal for the essence of the suppressed "Early John" story is that Jesus *voluntarily* submits to *possible* martyrdom, as a consequence of the insurrection at the Feast of Tabernacles. Whether directly stated, or only implied in the "Early John" text, Jesus accepts responsibility for violent "seditious" actions by others undertaken in his name. As Roman governor, Pontius Pilate requires some form of punishment for the insurrection (Mark 15:7), as an expression of Roman power and warning to the population of Israel.

In the suppressed "Early John" version, the intended victim of the Roman response would be the rebel Barabbas along with some of his associates, and Pilate comes up to Jerusalem in a deliberate action to impress the Jewish people at Passover time of the folly of messing with Rome. Jesus unexpectedly surrenders himself on condition that his followers not be punished: "If you seek me, let these men go" (John 18:8), presumably including Barabbas and his fellows. Pontius Pilate, under some pressure, cancels the execution of Barabbas, and publicly orders punishment of Jesus to be followed by his release; the punishment includes flogging and a short period on the cross as a public humiliation and warning. But God intervenes to allow the death of Jesus so that he can be raised up or "resurrected," perhaps to return later in glory for the implementation of God's Kingdom. The key message would be that Jesus died because of God's will, and not because of Satan acting through Pontius Pilate.

Evidence for the above scenario is based on inferences from the "Later John" text, the Gospel of Mark, and the Gospel of Luke. Each of these three scribes revised and distorted the original write-up to conform to their own apologetic aims (see Chapters 5, 8 and 9).

The Passion Story in the Johannine gospel really begins with the private and quiet return of Jesus to Bethany near Jerusalem to perform a final sign of messianic hope i.e. being "born again." Confirmation that "Early John" contains some form of the "resurrection of Lazarus" story comes (somewhat shakily) from the discovery of the "Secret Gospel" of Mark (See Chapter 5), which has a variant version, suppressed from canonical Mark. Luke follows canonical Mark in suppressing the story, but his access to the "Early John" text is indicated by the "widow of Nain" story (Luke 7:11-17), the "Martha and Mary" story (Luke 10:38-42), and the story of Lazarus in the bosom of Abraham (Luke 16:14-31). Luke himself composes these stories but uses the names of protagonists and other elements derived from "Early John" (see Chapter 8).

Much of the original Lazarus story written by "Early John" may have been smothered by "Later John's" version of it as being a public sign that caused a Sanhedrin reaction, the entry into Jerusalem and the arrest of Jesus. Mark's "Secret Gospel" story presents it as a private event with unnamed protagonists, but Luke's borrowing of names from his source supports the involvement of persons named Lazarus, Martha and Mary in the "Early John" story. My inferred setting argues strongly in favour of a private event, intended as a sign of hope for young inner-group disciples and followers of Jesus (perhaps also as a "not to worry" message about his own forthcoming surrender to the Roman authorities). The staging of the event seems to indicate close family ties between Jesus and the family of Lazarus, with opposition from other disciples shown in both Secret Mark and Johannine versions. The rescue perhaps signified divine forgiveness through action by the Holy Spirit.

After Jesus withdraws quietly to Ephraim (Gospel of John), or "across the Jordan" ("Secret Mark"), the next Johannine gospel scene following the Lazarus event is the meal in Bethany. Here Mary of Bethany uses expensive lotion to anoint the feet of the returning Jesus, who is clearly preoccupied with his forthcoming ordeal in Jerusalem. "Let her alone, let her keep it for the day of my burial. The poor you have always with you, but you do not always have me" (John 12:7-8). Confirmation that the meal in Bethany is an "Early John" story comes from consideration of what Mark and Luke did with it. Mark alters important details and substitutes unnamed protagonists, but leaves the story in place at Bethany prior to the arrest of Jesus (Mark 14:3-9). Luke, on the other hand, moves elements of the story to an earlier time and place in Galilee (Luke 7:36-50), perhaps as a response to the contradictions between Mark's version and that of "Early John." The proof that "Early John" composed the original story (rather than "Later John") comes from the use by Luke of Johannine details suppressed by Mark: the repentant female sinner of Luke's version, anoints Jesus' feet with ointment and *wipes them with her hair* (Luke 7:38).

It is very likely that the scene of the Last Supper in "Early John" is simply a continuation of the meal in Bethany where Mary anoints Jesus. The washing by Jesus of his disciples' feet (mentioned only in the Johannine gospel) seems a logical follow-up of Mary's action on his own feet. Also, the Johannine gospel says nothing about the physical location of the Last Supper, and reference to it begins with the phrase "And during supper . . ." (John 13:2), as if it was a continuation of the text on the supper in Bethany (John 12:1-8). Moreover, at the end of supper Jesus "went forth with his disciples across the Kidron valley" (John 18:1), which makes sense as a move toward Jerusalem from Bethany, rather than the reverse direction as specified in the synoptic gospels. Why would Jesus go outwards from Jerusalem to the Garden of Gethsemane, away from those he expects to meet who also go out from Jerusalem to find him?

The Johannine gospel, as edited by "Later John," situates the Last Supper on the evening before the Passover (John 13:1), is unclear as to the number of disciples present, and makes no reference to the New Covenant (see Chapter 9). Mark's fundamental premise, on the other hand, is that the Last Supper was an inner-group gathering on Passover day, at which Jesus announced the New Covenant (see Chapters 4 and 5). Mark moves the Last Supper forward by one day, explicitly locates it in Jerusalem, and in separating it from the Bethany meal, apparently moves the latter backward by one day to "two days before the Passover" (Mark 14:1). Luke agrees with Mark about the dating of the Last Supper, but shows his discomfort with the Bethany story by deleting it. "Later John," however, perceives the Bethany meal and its protagonists as an integral part of the Lazarus story and of a new explanation for the entry into Jerusalem scenario which he had transferred from the Feast of Tabernacles to the Feast of Passover. Concerning the Bethany story he writes: "When the great crowd of the Jews learned that he was there, they came, not only on account of Jesus but also to see Lazarus, whom he had raised from the dead" (John 12:9). In transforming the Lazarus story into a public event, "Later John" had to separate the Bethany story from the private Last Supper, and have it take place "six days before the Passover" (John 12:1). This fitted a highly public entry into Jerusalem story, where Jesus is welcomed the day after the Bethany meal by a great crowd that had heard about the resurrection of Lazarus.

According to the Johannine gospel, Jesus is arrested by Roman soldiers, and brought directly to the High Priest Annas for interrogation on the same night as the Last Supper, prior to the Passover Feast. Nothing much happens, Jesus professes innocence, and is struck by one of the officers. Mark and Luke confirm the meeting with the High Priest, without mentioning his name, and emphasize mocking and beating by the officers. They add on a trial of Jesus by the assembled Sanhedrin (Council of Jerusalem). Mark compresses the trial into the evening of Jesus' arrest, and Luke tries to make it more plausible by scheduling it for the following day. Jesus is condemned directly for blasphemy in Mark, and reviled somewhat less directly in Luke. The Lukan version is likely to have been more closely derivative from "Early John" than Mark; "Later John" suppresses the trial by the Sanhedrin (see Chapters 5, 8 and 9).

What did the "Early John" text have to say about the role, attitude and reaction of the inner-group disciples to the arrest of Jesus? Perhaps not very much. The surviving Johannine text reports that Jesus asked one of his disciples at the Last Supper to go out saying "What you are going to do, do quickly" (John 13:27). When soldiers and officials came to arrest him, he said: "If you seek me, let these men go" (John 18:8). And when they took Jesus to the Court of the High Priest, he was accompanied by two disciples (Simon Peter and another disciple).

The Johannine gospel, along with all the synoptic gospels, describes two themes of denial and betrayal of Jesus, expressed in the persons of the disciples Simon Peter and Judas Iscariot.

Denial of being a disciple of Jesus seems a credible part of a put-down of Simon Peter by the "Early John" writer, even though Peter's denial makes good tactical sense under the circumstances. In the context of the "Early John" account, Peter's real sin was to oppose God's will by continuing the violence of the insurrection when he drew his sword and cut off the right ear of Malchus, the High Priest's slave (John 18:11). The insurrection itself was the true betrayal of Jesus.

Betrayal of Jesus by Judas Iscariot, however, could not have been part of the "Early John" story. The reason is that the betrayal by Judas Iscariot is fictional material first created by Mark, as will be explained in Chapter 5. My inference is that "Early John" referred to a disciple named Judas acting as emissary in contacting the arresting authorities at the request of Jesus. The words in John 13:27-30 "Jesus said to him 'What you are going to do, do quickly'" and "he immediately went out" probably indicate only that a disciple named Judas was his emissary to the Roman authorities in the "Early John" story.

The author of "Early John" interpreted these and subsequent events in retrospect as the fulfilment of God's will that Jesus be martyred as a sign leading to his exaltation in Heaven and eventual future return "to gather into one the children of God" (John 11:52). "Later John," however, wholeheartedly accepted the Judas betrayal scenario, adding more details of his own, for reasons outlined in Chapter 9.

The next part of the story is the trial of Jesus before Pontius Pilate, and some scholars agree that there is a common source underlying the very different accounts in the Markan and Johannine gospels. I would add that there are also clues about the contents of this common source in Luke's Gospel.

Essentially my thesis is that "Early John" described a scenario in which Pontius Pilate interacts with a group of "chief priests and officers" (John 19:6); there is no explicit mention of a "crowd" of people in the Johannine gospel. It would seem that "Later John" introduced the term "Judeans" to imply that the "chief priests" represented all Jewish people. It was Mark who introduced the word "crowd" to imply popular support for the priests and officers who wanted Jesus crucified.

Again we have a situation where suppression of "Early John" material by "Later John" and Mark is offset by Luke's use of his alternative "Early John" source. It becomes clear from Luke's text that both "Later John" and Mark were carefully suppressing references to Jesus' involvement in the insurrection. So much so, that in the Johannine text, when Pilate asks the priests "What accusations do you bring against this man?" they reply insolently "if this man was not an evildoer, we would not have handed him over" (John 18:30). Similarly, Mark reports that "the chief priests accused him of many things" (Mark 15:3), without any further amplification.

Luke is not happy with such vague generalities, so he writes "And they began to accuse him, saying 'we found this man perverting our nation, and forbidding us to give tribute to Caesar, and saying that he himself is Christ a King . . . he stirs up the people, teaching throughout all Judea, from Galilee even to this place'" (Luke 23:2-5). In other words, the Sanhedrin accuses Jesus of sedition against Rome, and of "stirring up the people." The reference to "all Judea" is indicative of an "Early John" connection to these words.

In my hypothesized "Early John" version, the Sanhedrin priests accuse Jesus of claiming to be King of the Jews. Pilate talks privately to Jesus in the praetorium, and then renders his verdict, recorded in Luke: "I will therefore punish him and release him" (Luke 23: 16 and 22), explained by the "custom that I should release one man for you at Passover" (John 18:39). "But they all cried out together, 'take away this man, and release to us Barabbas'" (Luke 23:18). Perhaps this meant that the priests and officers wanted Barabbas to be physically punished and released, and that Jesus should be "taken away" (i.e. imprisoned). In any case, according to Luke, Pilate repeated his decision (Luke 23:20), and according to John "they cried out *again* 'Not this man, but Barabbas'" (John 18:40, emphasis mine).

The significant point is that in the Johannine text, there is no identification of "they," and no indication that "they" had cried out *before*. Something has been deleted, and quite possibly the deleted material (which may have been included in Luke) suggests that the priests and officers favoured physical punishment and release of Barabbas and a prison term for Jesus. It is very unlikely that they would have supported a crucifixion on Passover day. Pilate, however, proceeds to punish Jesus with flogging and a short period of crucifixion, agreeing that Jesus will be taken down from the cross the same day without his legs being broken (John 19:31-33), and then presumably released.

"Later John" makes the preposterous suggestion that Pilate handed Jesus over to the Judeans for crucifixion "Then he handed him over to them (the chief priests) to be crucified" (John 19:16). Mark does not go this far, although he claims that Pilate ordered the crucifixion "wishing to satisfy the crowd" (Mark 15:15). Mark does make a revealing slip as he copies from "Early John": "And the soldiers led him away inside the praetorium and *they called together the whole battalion*" (Mark 15:16, emphasis mine). In other words, the Romans undertook a massive show of force to prevent any aggressive action to rescue Jesus by a hostile anti-Roman population.

All the texts on the Passion Story include details that seem derived from references in ancient scripture, to show that events occurred "according to the scriptures." Undoubtedly, some of this was in the "Early John" text. The quiet ending in the Johannine text seems consistent with "Early John's" inferred theme of endorsement by God. "When Jesus had received the vinegar, he said, 'It is finished,' and he bowed his head and gave up his spirit" (John 19:30). As the Lamb of God, Jesus was a true son of God, accepting sacrifice as a step toward implementation of God's Kingdom in Israel. "Early John" finds endorsements even from enemies. Pontius Pilate himself recognized that Jesus was not guilty of sedition against Rome. And the High Priest Caiphas also recognized the martyrdom of Jesus when he said: "It is expedient . . . that one man should die for the people and that the whole nation should not perish." "Later John" chose to retain "Early John's" statement, despite his knowledge of the later destruction of Israel in the Jewish war with Rome. "Caiphas . . . being high priest that year prophesied that Jesus should die for the nation, and not for the nation only, but to gather into one the children of God who are scattered abroad" (John 11:48-52). Here is a clear reference to Jesus as a sacrificial Messiah destined to unite the Jewish Diaspora with people of the homeland in a new Kingdom of God in Israel.

Post-crucifixion Appearances of Jesus: Vindication from God

The logic of the hypothesized "Early John" Gospel is that something must have been included about divine action from God to "raise up" Jesus as vindication and endorsement of his unique personhood and mission.

Jesus had taught, according to the Thomas Gospel, that those who enter the Kingdom of God "will not taste death." Each member of God's Kingdom will cast off his body and return his spiritual self to its source in God the Father.

But all four canonical gospels went further than this in interpreting the resurrection of Jesus as a cosmological event signifying the coming advent of God's

Plan for humankind. The "living Jesus," now reunited with God in Heaven, had confirmed this through post-crucifixion appearances to his disciples and leaving behind an empty tomb.

In the Johannine gospel, there are two Empty Tomb stories, both of them featuring a woman named Mary of Magdala. The *first story* shows that Mary alone before dawn discovers that the gravestone has been removed, and runs to report to Simon Peter and "the other disciple" that "They have taken the Lord out of the tomb and *we* do not know where they have laid him" (John 20:2). The two disciples go to the tomb and verify the absence of the body of Jesus. In the *second story*, Mary enters the tomb, encounters two angels, asks where is the body of Jesus, and encounters a vision of Jesus (she does not touch him), who tells her he is "ascending to my Father and your Father" (John 20:17). She then reports to "the disciples" that "I have seen the Lord."

Once again, there is evidence that "Later John" divided one source story in two, to enable his own elaboration and revision of the second part. One clue is the apparently missing element of his first story, that Mary must have entered the tomb in order to confirm that "they have taken the Lord out of the tomb." Perhaps the reference to Mary's presence "while it was still dark" was intended to account for her failure to enter. Another hint is the repetition of her thought in both stories that Jesus' body had been moved; and a third is the use of "we" in the first story which contradicts the assertion that Mary was alone. But the best evidence of what the original "Early John" story contained comes from the versions of Mark and Luke.

Mark mentions three women, including Mary of Magdala, visiting the tomb "when the sun had risen," observing the rolled-away stone and entering the tomb. Thereafter he contradicts everything in the two Johannine stories. One young man (instead of two angels) explains that Jesus has risen, "goes before you into Galilee, there you will see him as he told you," and instructs the women to tell his disciples, particularly Peter. The women flee and "said nothing to anyone" (Mark 16:1-8).

Clearly Luke was unhappy with Mark's story, and revised it to include selected elements from "Early John," plus details of his own. An unnumbered group of women visit the tomb "at early dawn," note the rolled-away stone, and enter; they encounter two men who remind then that Jesus had told them about his resurrection on "the third day." They proceed to inform the disciples, some of whom (including Peter) visit the tomb and find nothing. In effect, Luke denies the Markan version, as well as the Johannine story of Mary's visionary encounter with the risen Jesus.

My conclusion is that the "Early John" source story probably contained the following elements: visit to the tomb by Mary of Magdala and other women "at early dawn on the third day," the rolled-away stone, entry into the tomb where they encounter two men but no body of Jesus, a visionary encounter with Jesus by Mary alone, perhaps stimulated by the two men's statement that Jesus had risen, communication by the women to the disciples, and a visit by Peter and "the other disciple" to the tomb, which confirms the disappearance of the body of Jesus. For Mary, it does not matter that Jesus' "cast off" body has disappeared from the tomb; she now knows that his spiritual self continues to live.

Our first canonical source of information on post-crucifixion appearances by Jesus is a letter from Paul of Tarsus. His first Letter to the Corinthians provides an independent reference to five appearances of Jesus to Peter and James individually, as well as to "the twelve," the apostles as a group and "500 brethren" (1 Corinthians 15:3-7). This account "was received" by Paul, presumably during visits to Peter and James, thus implying a common understanding of the events among them.

What is the evidence of such appearance stories in "Early John," since the story of the post-crucifixion appearances of Jesus in the canonical gospels seems to bear little resemblance to what Paul reported?

A valid answer is that some details of Paul's list of appearance stories are embedded in the Gospels of Mark, Luke and "Later John." By using Paul's information as a framework, it becomes possible to uncover clues which indicate that these scribes were using source information from an "Early John" text that closely matched what Paul wrote about the appearances. The most extraordinary finding is that Mark made use of such material, while simultaneously omitting to describe any post-crucifixion appearances by Jesus. What Mark did was to "retroject" the post-crucifixion appearances described in "Early John," back into the lifetime of Jesus, as follows:

1. the private appearance to Peter becomes the "transfiguration" story (Mark 9:2-13);
2. the appearance to twelve inner-group disciples becomes the "recruitment of disciples" story (Mark 1:16-20);
3. the appearance to "500 brethren" becomes the second "feeding of the multitude" story (Mark 8:1-1);
4. the private appearance to James is suppressed, but the Parousia (return of Jesus) message is retained and changed (Mark 13);
5. the appearance to all the apostles and accompanying missionary message is reconstituted as the appointment of the twelve (Mark 3:13-19).

My hypothesis as to how and why Mark undertook such an astounding change to the "Early John" source story is explained in Chapter 5 of this book, and further evidence is considered in Chapters 8 and 9, where Luke and "Later John" seem to include parts of the information for some of their post-crucifixion appearance stories. My own inference is that the stories in Mark's Gospel constitute evidence that "Early John" described post-crucifixion appearances of Jesus in his gospel.

Here are the main elements of what was probably written by "Early John," along with modifications by canonical writers:

1. Peter is the first to experience a private vision of Jesus, presumably in Galilee (and is unaware or unaccepting of Mary's earlier private vision). This happens on a mountain, where he may or may not have been accompanied by other disciples who did not share the vision. Mark retrojects this to the lifetime of Jesus, recording it as "the Transfiguration," with Peter accompanied by James and John, sons of Zebedee; however, only Peter converses with the transfigured Jesus, and Jesus says to tell no-one until "the Son of Man has risen from the dead" (Mark 9:1-8). Luke adds significant information to the Markan story (presumably from "Early John"), that the three of them were asleep, and experienced a "waking vision," which involved an obscuring cloud and "not knowing what he said" (Luke 9:28-36).

2. A group of disciples, perhaps seven in number (twelve according to Paul), experience the spiritual presence of Jesus in association with an extraordinary catch of fish while fishing on Lake Galilee; it reminds them of their commitment to spread the Kingdom of God. Mark retrojects this story as two sequential recruiting events by Jesus of brothers Simon and Andrew, and brothers James and John, at the start of his mission in Galilee (Mark 1:16-20). Luke combines these two recruiting stories into one, plus the miraculous catch of fish and other embellishments that suggest an "Early John" source (Luke 5:1-11). "Later John" retains the same story as a post-crucifixion event with seven disciples and a miraculous catch of fish, plus other important modifications (John 21:1-23).

3. A much larger group of followers (500 according to Paul) have a collective experience of the spiritual presence of Jesus when re-assembling for a repeat "feeding of the multitude" in Galilee. Mark retrojects this event to the lifetime of Jesus as a second "feeding" story (Mark 8:1-10). Luke omits it as an unlikely event during Jesus' lifetime, and as inconsistent with his own version of post-crucifixion appearances. "Later John" also ignores it.

4. The disciple James has a private vision of Jesus, which includes a message that Jesus will return "before the present generation passes away." Mark

retrojects this to the lifetime of Jesus as a private prophecy by Jesus to "Peter and James and John and Andrew" (Mark 13). Luke follows Mark, but turns it into a public prophecy (Luke 21), separated from the post-crucifixion vision event which occurs on the road to Emmaus (Luke 24:13-32). "Later John" attempts to correct the prophecy in the light of Jesus' failure to return as predicted (John 21:20-23).

5. A group of followers meet in Jerusalem, where they experience the spiritual presence of Jesus directing them to go out into the real world as apostles of the Kingdom of God in preparation for his return. Mark retrojects this to the lifetime of Jesus, where he appoints twelve apostles in Galilee "to preach and cast out demons" (Mark 3:13-18). Luke repeats a similar delegation of authority by Jesus during his lifetime (Luke 6:12-17 and 9:1-6), but also provides a post-crucifixion story of delegation of authority, presumably sourced in part from "Early John" (Luke 24:13-53). "Later John" writes his own version of this Jerusalem meeting (John 20:19-29).

Disciples, Apostles and Family of Jesus

The Johannine gospel describes disciples and followers of Jesus, as does the Thomas Gospel, without using the term "apostle." It does refer to "the twelve" as a chosen inner group of disciples (John 6:70 and 20:24), but lacks any story about the commissioning of the chosen group during the lifetime of Jesus, or any list of names of the chosen twelve.

Of great significance is the fact that Luke has two listings of apostles, one when Jesus was alive (Luke 6:14-17), and another post-crucifixion list (Acts 1:13). The first list is clearly derived from Mark with some modifications that suggest an alternative source. The second list also has the corrections from a presumed alternative source, but has other changes that distinguish it from the first list. The interesting point is that the changes in the second list are consistent with information on specified disciples in the Johannine gospel, leading to a hypothesis that Luke used an "Early John" post-crucifixion list of apostles, while retaining some modifications of his own based on Mark. The analysis is complicated, and we defer details to chapters 5, 8 and 9. The end result is an inferred "Early John" list of twelve apostles associated with the post-crucifixion appearance of Jesus in Jerusalem to "all the apostles" (reported by Paul), that brought about their appointment and accompanying mission. Explanation of the names in the inferred "Early John" list can be found in chapters 5, 8 and 9.

Luke's List (Acts 1:-13)	Inferred "Early John" List
1) Peter	1) Simon Peter
2) John	2) John
3) James	3) James
4) Andrew	4) Andrew
5) Philip	5) Philip
6) Thomas	6) Judas Thomas
7) Bartholomew	7) Nathaniel
8) Matthew	8) Matthew
9) James, the son of Alphaeus	9) James Justus (the Just)
10) Simon the Zealot	10) Joseph, of James Justus
11) Judas, of James	11) Simon Iscariot
12) Matthias (elected to replace Judas Iscariot)	12) Judas, of Simon Iscariot

Such a hypothesis provides an explanation for the absence of the term "apostle" in the Johannine gospel. In the "Early John" scenario, the inner group followers of Jesus were termed "disciples" until the final post-crucifixion appearance, when a selected group were commissioned as "apostles." At this final stage of his story, "Early John" may have presented a list of the chosen twelve apostles, which served as a model for the later lists presented by the synoptic gospel writers. The "Early John" list was suppressed by "Later John" as part of the latter's complete revision of post-crucifixion events. One of his motives was to more effectively suppress evidence that members of Jesus' earthly family were among the first apostles (see Chapter 9). "Later John" did not deny the existence of brothers, sisters, and parents of Jesus. On the contrary, he made explicit mention of the mother and brothers of Jesus, as unnamed persons. But he carefully avoided linking their family status with the names of the protagonists in the drama of the life and death of Jesus.

In so doing "Later John" was following the lead of "Early John," who also seems to have been concerned about suppressing the role of the family of Jesus. Even more so! For although "Early John" seems to have mentioned unnamed brothers accompanying Jesus in Galilee (John 2:12), he may have used alternative names at other times that would conceal their presence in the story. Why would he do this? One answer is the teaching of Jesus against family attachments, that membership in the Kingdom of God pre-empted family connections in favour of brotherhood under God the Father.

Another answer is that the credibility of any "Early John" resurrection story might be compromised by witnesses acknowledged to be members of Jesus' earthly family.

What is the evidence that "Early John" avoided naming family members? There would be very little, if it were not for the fact that Mark's Gospel names Jesus' mother as Mary, and lists the names of his four brothers as James, Joses, Judas and Simon (Mark 6:3). Mark connects these named brothers and mother to Jesus' inability to perform miracles when rejected by the people of Nazareth, his hometown. Did this story and the names come from Mark's "Early John" source? There is nothing in the Johannine gospel to confirm it and Luke's deletion of the names from his own text suggests that he preferred the "no name" approach found in his alternative "Early John" source. Probably Mark obtained the names from his Simon Peter source (See Chapter 5), but they represented an embarrassment, which Luke eliminated from his own text.

Luke's embarrassment points towards his preference for an "Early John" approach that covered up all explicit references to the names and roles of Jesus' earthly family. Only when it came time to name the twelve disciples commissioned as apostles at the post-resurrection appearance in Jerusalem, did "Early John" include their names on a list. The evidence for such a list comes from Luke's second list of apostles (Acts 1:13), its comparison with Mark's list and "Later John's" concealment efforts (see chapters 5, 8 and 9).

My contention that "Early John" made few references to family members of Jesus rests on the hypothesis that most such references were added to the Johannine gospel by "Later John." I discuss this in detail in Chapter 9. But there is evidence that "Early John" used cover-up names in relation to some actions by family members, and that such a cover-up approach was developed further by canonical gospel writers. An example is described in the next section.

Who Wrote the "Early John" Gospel?

According to "Later John," the author of the Johannine gospel is the unnamed "disciple that Jesus loved" (John 21:24), who is also "the other disciple" (John 20:2). The reader infers that the author followed a common ancient practice of anonymity when referring to himself. The traditional interpretation has been that he must be the apostle John, son of Zebedee. After all, the style of the source used by "Later John" is clearly that of an eyewitness to a chain of events; therefore, "Early John" must have been an ongoing disciple of Jesus. On the other hand, the son of Zebedee's nickname, "son of thunder" (Mark 3:17), and his desire for glory (Mark 10:17) are rather inconsistent with someone who seeks anonymous authorship.

The true identity of "the other disciple" seems to hinge on the leadership question. "Later John" sets up a scenario to explain why Simon Peter was the true leader, and why Jesus had not promised to return to Earth before the death of "the disciple that Jesus loved." This takes the form of the special post-crucifixion appearance by Jesus to seven disciples at the Sea of Galilee. After confirming Peter's leadership role ("Feed my sheep"), the disciple whom Jesus loved appears and Peter asks "Lord, what about this man?" (John 21:22).

Jesus' reply is that Peter should not worry about it, even if Jesus should will "the beloved disciple" not to die until he returns. "The saying spread abroad among the brethren that this disciple was not to die; yet Jesus did not say to him (Peter) that he (beloved disciple) was not to die, but 'If it is my will that he remain until I come, what is that to you?' This is the disciple who is bearing witness to these things, and who has written these things; and we know that his testimony is true" (John 21:23).

"Later John" seems to be attempting to correct some repressed "Early John" statement (or perhaps a Thomas Gospel statement), that "the other disciple" (i.e. the disciple that Jesus loved) would be leader until Jesus returned. The correction was necessary because "the other disciple" had already died by the time of writing by "Later John." Jesus had not yet returned, and the idea of Peter as first leader had become politically correct. "Later John" admits explicitly that "the other disciple" is the author of his gospel "bearing witness to these things, and who has written these things" (John 21:22).

As expressed in the Thomas Gospel (Thomas 12), James the Just was chosen by Jesus as leader during his absence, which therefore equates him to the "other disciple," and "the disciple that Jesus loved." The idea that "the beloved disciple," referred to only in the Johannine gospel, is the brother of Jesus, seems consistent with John 19:25-27 where Jesus selects "the beloved disciple" to look after his mother. "When Jesus saw his mother and the disciple whom he loved standing near, he said to his mother, 'Woman, behold your son!' Then he said to the disciple, 'Behold your mother!' And from that hour the disciple took her to his own home" (John 19:26-27). Additionally, James is named "brother of the Lord" by Paul of Tarsus (Galatians 1:19), and "brother of Jesus" by Josephus (Jewish Antiquities 20.197.203).

As well, the Johannine gospel twice mentions the special love of Jesus for Lazarus, the man he raised from the dead. Is it possible that Lazarus could be the "other disciple," the "disciple that Jesus loves"? Mark's "Secret Gospel" describes the raising from the dead of an unnamed young man who is wealthy and has a close relationship with Jesus. This young man wears a linen cloth, which seems to equate him with the strange reference in canonical Mark (Mark 14:51) following the arrest of Jesus. "And a young man followed him, with nothing but a linen cloth about his body; and they seized him but he left the linen cloth and ran away naked." Apparently that is how Mark deals with the "other disciple" who otherwise, according to "Early John," is an eyewitness to the interrogation of Jesus by the high priest, in a version completely at variance with the story of a trial by the Sanhedrin in Mark's Gospel. Mark then presents the young man again to confirm a completely different story of the empty tomb than the one set out by "Early John." "And entering the tomb, they saw a young man sitting on the right side, dressed in a white robe, and they were amazed" (Mark 16:5).

The unnamed "young man" raised from the dead by Jesus in Mark's "Secret Gospel" is clearly the same person as Lazarus, raised from the dead by Jesus in the Johannine gospel. This "young man" is then used by Mark as a substitute for the Johannine "other disciple," thus becoming a Markan witness against the "Early John" version of the interrogation of Jesus and the Empty Tomb. The youthfulness of Mark's "young man" matches the youthfulness of John's "other disciple" as indicated by his ability to outrun Peter in the Empty Tomb scene (John 20:4). In other words, Lazarus is the same person as the "other disciple," who is the same person as "the disciple that Jesus loves," who seems to be the same person as James, brother of Jesus.

To further support my hypothesis that Lazarus and James are one and the same person, there is the inferred story of the Last Supper by "Early John," which, according to my argument, was separated into two parts by "Later John." The Johannine gospel states that Lazarus was present at the first supper, while "the disciple that Jesus loved" was present at the second supper. If there was, indeed, only one supper, it becomes possible that Lazarus equates with "the beloved disciple" and therefore with James.

The idea that James, brother of Jesus, was the author of the lost "Early John" Gospel helps to explain its nature, as will become clear in later chapters. Here, I will note only that James, as first post-crucifixion leader, was strongly motivated to rally all elements of the people of Israel around the notion that God the Father was about to restore his Kingdom in a new Israel encompassing the known world. In such a context, the aim was to soften ideological differences among Jews, while focusing on the personhood of the risen Jesus as the embodiment of God's will for the future.

Assessment of "Early John"

The concept of a lost "Early John" Gospel, embedded mainly in the canonical Gospel of John, is much more than the collection of miracle stories (the "Signs Gospel"), acknowledged as probable by many modern scholars. Rather it is a full-blown coherent narrative comprised of four discernible parts:

1. endorsements of Jesus by prominent citizens, particularly John the Baptist;
2. public self-explanation by Jesus (the "Signs Gospel");
3. the martyrdom of Jesus;
4. post-crucifixion appearances: vindication by God.

The argument for this interpretation rests on the interconnections between the various parts, clues in Mark and Luke concerning their sources, and the story that is revealed when the radical changes by "Later John" have been exposed. Chapters 5 to 8 and Appendix 2 offer the complete details.

Unlike the Thomas and Q1 gospels which find the significance of Jesus in his words, "Early John" focuses on the personhood of Jesus. In fact, there seems to be very little embedded text about his teachings, apart from the central message concerning the ongoing presence of the Holy Spirit or Kingdom of God. Instead, the teaching is presented by Jesus in the form of actions or "signs" that support his own special relationship with God and teaching authority. There is a relationship with scriptural tradition, not present in Thomas and Q1. Both message and messenger connect with messianic hope, thus validating traditional prophecies, and identifying Jesus as the traditionally expected Messiah of Israel. Jesus does not directly claim this title; rather he receives acclaim as such from his followers, and endorsements from prominent persons.

There is a notable focus on actions that bring people together rather than words that might tear people apart. The theme is expressed by the Pharisee Nicodemus when addressing the Sanhedrin or Council (John 8:51): "Does our law judge a man without first giving him a hearing and learning what he does?" Jesus reaches out to all the contending groups within Israel: Galileans, Samaritans, Judeans, Sadducees, Pharisees, Zealots and others. In so doing, he matches the egalitarian substance of the Thomas Gospel, with its openness of the Kingdom to all.

The relative absence of teaching words by Jesus in the "Early John" Gospel is consistent with the separate Q1 material, which seems to be a public instruction on how to live in the ideal Kingdom of God (see Chapter 2). Notably, the Q1 sayings exclude most of the material on the Gnostic belief system contained in the Thomas Gospel, that challenges the traditional precepts of Judaism. Generally the Q1 sayings can fit into Hebrew scriptural teachings about righteousness, and seem to parallel the "Early John" focus on reaching out to all groups.

In the inferred "Early John" scenario, Jesus moves into a political role, apparently because of John the Baptist's execution, but also apparently with some reluctance. He demonstrates the presence of God's divine Kingdom, primarily through "signs," but is betrayed not by Judas Iscariot (an invention of Mark as we shall see in Chapter 5), but by the militancy of some supporters, probably Zealot-type sympathizers inherited from John the Baptist. His death by Roman crucifixion on Passover day is explained as a sacrificial atonement for the people of Israel, sanctioned by God as a prelude to the imminent return of Jesus in glory to implement God's Plan. But in explaining the sacrificial death of Jesus, "Early John" departs radically from Jesus' own self-understanding as depicted in the Thomas Gospel, which regards death for Kingdom members as a joyful return to one's original spiritual self.

The contention of "Early John" seems to be that the question of God's intentions has been resolved in Jesus who is the Messiah of Israel. Jesus is defined as performing an act of self-sacrifice: "greater love has no man than this, that a man lay down his life for his friends" (John 15:13). The story is presented on two levels. At one end of the scale, it is as Josephus described the beliefs of the Sadducees—that each man is responsible for his own actions. Jesus freely chose to sacrifice himself to save the people of God. On the other hand, it is also as Josephus described the beliefs of the Essenes—the Fate of each one is pre-ordained by God, who decided that Jesus was to be the sacrificial Lamb of God.

It is noteworthy that "Early John" does not seem to demonize the authorities, the Romans or any of the conflicting groups in Israel. Events move along in a sort of pre-ordained way reflecting the will of God. But unlike later writings, God does not seem to be involved in a deadly cosmic duel with Satan. The priestly authorities and Pontius Pilate seem to be playing out their roles largely without malice, and the writer seems to be trying to defuse apocalyptic tensions. In this way he is consistent with the Gospel of Thomas in attempting a peaceful approach to proselytizing the population. He avoids direct challenges to traditional Jewish theology and Mosaic Law, while placating Roman authority.

As the earliest narrative account of the doings of Jesus, the inferred "Early John" Gospel merits serious attention. Partly this is because, in sharp contrast to the "Later John" revisions, Jesus seems to perform as an inspired human being responding to events and people as he attempts to spread his Kingdom of God message. But he is now more than a teacher of wisdom. He is in effect the specially adopted son of God, who turns out to be the long-promised traditional Messiah of Israel. The story focuses on endorsements and signs. The apparently tragic death of Jesus is the ultimate sign that God is about to rescue the people of Israel, and restore an idealized Kingdom for everyone who follows a new way of life. The time of writing seems to be the early years after Jesus' death.

---

[1]   Spong, John Shelby, *Resurrection: Myth or Reality*, Harper, San Francisco, 1994.

[2]   It is interesting that Matthew further amends the story into an instantaneous miracle: "And the fig tree withered at once" (Matthew 21:19).

[3]   Spong, op. cit., pp. 261-270.

[4]   Among the "Later John" trappings of the Cana incident are: the presence of the mother of Jesus, the quotation "My hour has not yet come" and the explanation to non-Jewish readers about the six stone jars "for the Jewish rites of purification." This borrowed Hellenistic myth about changing water into wine seems to have been added by "Later John" as an appropriate story for placing the "first of his signs" in Galilee.

[5]   Koester, Helmut, *Ancient Christian Gospels: Their History and Development*, SCM Press, London, 1990.

CHAPTER 4

THE EPISTLES OF PAUL

We come now to the earliest of the canonical writers, Paul of Tarsus. Although perhaps perceived as marginal by the other disciples during much of his own lifetime, the preaching and writings of Paul profoundly changed the whole direction of Christian development.

Like the author of "Early John," Paul of Tarsus began to focus on the personhood of Jesus, rather than his precise words. Moving away from the story and sayings of Jesus as a human being, Paul reinvented him as Lord of Heaven, Son of God and apocalyptic Judge of all persons at the imminent Last Days. And Paul brought his message to the world outside Palestine.

In Paul, we have an authenticated author, a convert through direct visionary experience of Jesus Christ, and an "outsider" who had never known Jesus "in the flesh." His writings are as much about himself as they are about the teachings of Jesus, although Paul did have a shared understanding with some of the original inner-group disciples about certain fundamentals.

The Epistles

The Epistles of Paul, dated by scholars as circa 50-55 C.E., are the earliest *canonical* body of material, written slightly later than my postulated dating for Thomas, Q1 and "Early John." They are not an exposition of the words of Jesus (as in Thomas and Q1), nor of the circumstances of his life and death (as in "Early John"), but provide instead what Paul believes to be a "revelation" by the resurrected Jesus Christ directly to Paul. "God had chosen me before I was born, called me through his grace, and chose to reveal his Son in me" (Galatians 1:15-16). Because Paul, too, "has seen Jesus our Lord" (1 Corinthians 9:1), his ongoing revelation gives him full teaching authority equivalent or superior to that of the others. Thus, his writings comprise his own idiosyncratic understanding of the risen Jesus and his message to the world.

The Pauline interpretation is a product not only of a strong conversion experience, but also of intense mystical and intellectual effort. This intensity of new discovery gives a sharper focus to the formulation of ideas than is apparent in the Thomas and "Early John" gospels.

Paul's mission ("received" from the risen Lord) was to preach the Gospel of Jesus Christ to the Gentiles. The purpose of the Letters was to provide support and instruction to communities already visited and converted by Paul after oral preaching of "the Gospel." Accordingly, Paul's presentation is often responsive to local problems and situations. But it is precisely these reactions and experiences that lead him to consider and express eloquently his emerging ideas.

The uniqueness of the Epistles is that they all originate with the author; they do not include fragments of other contemporary written material on Jesus. There is no evidence of direct access to Thomas, the Q Gospel, or the "Early John" script, although Paul did receive oral information from other apostles (particularly James and Peter).

Modern scholarship tends to accept as definitely authentic only about half of the 27 writings ascribed to Paul in the New Testament. These include 1 Thessalonians, 1 and 2 Corinthians, Philippians, Philemon, Galatians and Romans (in probable order of composition). Various other letters (in whole or in part) likely include contributions or amendments by unnamed writers beating their own drum. As with the much later Acts of the Apostles (written by Luke), this other material requires a great deal of caution. For present purposes, I stick to the authenticated writings of Paul.

Message and Teaching of Paul

The central message and teaching of Paul is the resurrection of Jesus by divine action, thus signifying his status as the Christ, Son of God, and Lord of Heaven. "If there is no resurrection of the dead" writes Paul, "our teaching is in vain" (1 Corinthians 15:13-14). The proof for Paul was that "Christ appeared also to me" (1 Corinthians 15:8), thus confirming what he had been told by some disciples that Jesus had been "raised on the third day in accordance with the scriptures and had appeared to them after his death by crucifixion" (1 Corinthians 15:3-7). Paul also reports that he was told "that Christ died for our sins in accordance with the scriptures" (1 Corinthians 15:3-4).

This central teaching on the resurrection is the only instance where Paul claims to have been instructed by disciples who had known Jesus during his earthly life. Otherwise, while acknowledging minimal contacts with some inner-group disciples, nowhere does Paul admit that any of his specific teachings were provided to him other than by direct revelation from Jesus Christ. "For I would have you know, brethren, that the gospel which was preached by me is not man's gospel. For I did not receive it from man, nor was I taught it, but it came through a revelation of Jesus Christ" (Galatians 1:11-12). God chose "to reveal his Son in me, in order that I might preach him among the Gentiles" (Galatians 1:16). And Paul was chosen despite his own unworthiness because "I persecuted the Church of God violently and tried to destroy it" (Galatians 1:13). Thus, Paul defends his unique teaching authority as a special grace from God to a repentant sinner. It might be described today as an ongoing special pipeline to the risen Christ.

In effect, Paul's whole approach is a radical elaboration of "Early John's" message that the personhood of Jesus (as well as his words) was still "alive." But Paul has raised the stakes. Jesus the Man is perceived more and more as the embodiment of divine Spirit. The personhood of Jesus has become fully situated in the divine cosmic realm, and the prospect of his return (envisioned in my hypothesized "Early John" script) means for Paul that the apocalyptic "end of days" is at hand for the entire world. Paul accepts the teaching that Jesus has directed his inner-group followers to actively convert the population in preparation for his return in the near future. He then proceeds to apply his own special knowledge and experience to develop a new synthesized theological structure that remoulds the original teachings of Jesus.

The basic original teachings of Jesus are reflected in the memorable sayings of the Thomas and Q1 Sayings Gospels. Clearly, Paul came to absorb them somehow, in a way that made a powerful impression on him. One example in his writings is perhaps the most beautiful inspirational poem about love ever written which begins, "If I speak in the tongue of men and of angels, but have not love" etc. (1 Corinthians 13:1-13). Significantly, Paul adds "faith" and "hope" to form the famous trilogy "So faith, hope and love abide, these three; but the greatest of these is love" (1 Corinthians 13:13).

By adopting these values, Paul goes beyond the Gnostic, "sapiential," ever-present Kingdom of God, to a future-oriented apocalyptic "end of days" scenario, designed to account for the death and resurrection of Jesus. Yes, Paul does accept a Gnostic dimension. He describes the pre-existent timeless universe of God, and its spark within each individual; mystical unification with it *is* the Kingdom of God. But instead of reaching the Kingdom through the inner-directed process of gnosis (knowledge), it is reached *by direct faith in Jesus*, who is titled Jesus Christ, Son of God, and incarnates God's spiritual universe. Therefore the mystical body of Christ *is* the Kingdom of God.

Paul brings a flair for drama to his interpretation. In the Gnostic Thomas Gospel, the pre-existent spiritual universe of God is available to all who seek it, but in Paul's world, God is actively intervening through his Son to bring about redemption of humankind. The evil cosmic powers that generated the Fall of Man

(Romans 5:12) are now being confronted by God's secret wisdom (1 Corinthians 2-8). Christ is God's special agent entering fallen creation in the "likeness of sinful flesh." His death by crucifixion is an expiation in blood for human sin, and those who believe in faith are released from bondage to Satan, "the god of this world" who blinds the minds of unbelievers. This release has been achieved by the power of the resurrection of Christ.[1]

The believer who has direct faith in Jesus participates in the dying and resurrection of Christ by receiving the Holy Spirit in baptism "dying to sin that he might be a slave to righteousness" (Romans 6:10-11). He shuns the "works of the flesh," while awaiting the Parousia, which is imminent. "The end of the ages has come" (1 Corinthians 10-11), and "the form of this cosmos is passing away" (1 Corinthians 7-31).

At this point, the apocalyptic world of certain Jewish traditions is joined with the Gnostic universe. As the glorified Christ returns to Earth, the faithful will rise to join Him in their spiritual bodies, because "flesh and blood cannot inherit the Kingdom" (1 Corinthians 15-50), and the forces of Satan will be destroyed in apocalyptic battle, along with all unrepentant sinners and enemies of Christ.

Verification According to Paul

The primary verification for Paul's teaching, as we have seen, is his ongoing revelation from the "Son in me." But as he also says, everything he teaches depends on the fact of the resurrection of Christ. "But if there is no resurrection of the dead, then Christ has not been raised" (1 Corinthians 15:13). For this one and only time, Paul does not rely solely on his own revelation in support of this point. As confirmation, Paul says that he was told that "Christ appeared to Cephas (i.e. Simon Peter) then to the twelve. Then he appeared to more than five hundred brethren at one time . . . Then he appeared to James, then to all the apostles. Last of all, as to one untimely born, he appeared also to me" (1 Corinthians 15:5-8). In explanation, Paul makes clear his opinion that the appearances are spiritual. "What is sown is perishable, what is raised is imperishable . . . It is sown a physical body, it is raised a spiritual body . . . flesh and blood cannot inherit the Kingdom of God, nor does the perishable inherit the imperishable" (1 Corinthians 15:42-50).

In regard to the physical Jesus before his death, Paul's only reference relates to action by Jesus at the Last Supper with his disciples. But this information comes as a revelation from the "Son in me."

> "For I received from the Lord what I also delivered to you, that the Lord Jesus on the night when he was betrayed took bread, and when he had given thanks, he broke it and said, 'This is my body which is for you. Do this in remembrance of me.' In the same way also the cup,

after supper, saying, 'This cup is the new covenant in my blood. Do this, as often as you drink it, in remembrance of me.' For as often as you eat this bread and drink this cup, you proclaim the Lord's death until he comes" (1 Corinthians 11:23-26).

There is no evidence that this information was provided to Paul by any disciples. He himself says that it came "from the Lord." There is no evidence in the Thomas, Q, or "Early John" gospels that the disciples experienced this "new covenant" event with Jesus. From available evidence the inference must be that this story originated with Paul, who was not present at the Last Supper.

For Paul, the New Covenant between God and all humankind at the Last Supper replaced the Mosaic Law and tradition, sanctioned by the Old Covenant between God and the people of Israel. The new Kingdom of God "in Christ" becomes the New Israel open to all humankind.

It is worth noticing that Paul locates the New Covenant event "on the night when Jesus was betrayed" (also translatable as "turned over"), the first mention of betrayal in the extant documents. There is no clarification as to whether this was betrayal by Judas Iscariot, by some or all of the disciples of Jesus, by the Chief Priest or Sanhedrin, by the whole Jewish people, or by Satan. There is no mention of a Passover meal, the absence of which is consistent with the inferred "Early John" text. Paul also refers to "Christ, our paschal lamb has been sacrificed" (1 Corinthians 5:7), thereby implying that the crucifixion occurred on the day of Passover. Apart from these hints there is little further reference to events in the earthly life of Jesus. Perhaps Paul avoided such discussion, not only because he was not a witness to Jesus' life on earth, but because the "Early John" understanding of the identity of Jesus was inconsistent with Paul's own revelations.

Disciples, Apostles and Family of Jesus

Since Paul was not involved with Jesus during his lifetime, he does not refer to the disciples of Jesus. Instead he writes about the brethren, the apostles, the elders or saints of Jerusalem, and the brothers of Jesus.

"The brethren" seems to be a term for accepted followers of Jesus. "The apostles" are the brethren commissioned by Jesus to preach the Gospel. As reported by Paul, the two leading apostles seem to be Peter and James, the brother of Jesus: each experienced private post-crucifixion appearances from Jesus, and following his conversion, according to his written account, Paul consulted only these two before commencing his own mission (Galatians: 1:18-19). Elsewhere, Paul refers ironically to the three "reputed pillars" of the Jerusalem Church: James, Peter and John (Galatians 2:9). He does not specify the total number of apostles, but refers once to "the twelve" as some sort of special group.

Assessment of Paul's Epistles

The author of the Epistles is Saul of Tarsus, a Diaspora Jew and Roman citizen who was converted to Christ through a mystical visionary process, reputed to be sudden and dramatic "on the road to Damascus."

The canonical Acts of the Apostles, written by Luke, tells the story of Saul (renamed Paul after his conversion), but contradicts certain details about Paul contained in his own Epistles. We do know that Paul studied traditional Judaism, and was initially hostile to the followers of Jesus. "I was circumcised on the eighth day, of the people of Israel, of the tribe of Benjamin, a Hebrew born of Hebrews, as to the law a Pharisee, as to zeal a persecutor of the church, as to righteousness under the law blameless" (Philippians 3:5-6). Through his conversion experience, Paul learned that Jesus Christ had selected him to spread the message of the Kingdom of God throughout the known world outside Israel.

Paul's mission was to fill the huge gap posed by the existence of the Gentiles. Thomas and Q1 had presented the teaching of Jesus, and "Early John" had described the works (or "signs") of Jesus—during his lifetime. But Paul who received the "revelation" from Jesus after his death and resurrection, focused on the needs of all "the other" people. It was a new amalgam of Hellenistic and Jewish ideas and values, centred on a divine saviour for all humankind.

There is an underlying Pharasaic legalism in Paul's thought, and continuity with tradition in the new covenant, which produces a "new Israel." The very idea of the new covenant embodied in the bread and wine Eucharist seems to connect with Essene rituals and ideas. His concepts of baptism and repentant sinners can be traced back to John the Baptist. Apocalyptic notions, the "end of days" and "the last judgment" are ideas of the Essenes and the traditional scriptures. His whole theory of inborn sinfulness and the ongoing battle between God and Satan emerges from Jewish scripture as well as pagan religion such as Zoroastrianism. In fact, his interpretation of the death and resurrection of Jesus Christ appears to be influenced by Hellenistic mystery cults. The solution of total faith in the personhood of Jesus Christ also has resonances of Greek Hellenism. As well, he models his ideas on the prevailing political reality of the universal Roman Empire, which he supported both before and after his conversion experience. At the same time, the Gnostic ideas of Jesus are present in his references to the timeless realm of the Spirit, and the Light of the Father. And within all this theology, the moral and lifestyle implications taught by Jesus also receive top billing and he does not hesitate to produce practical answers to everyday problems of living in the earthly world.

The Epistles of Paul were never used directly by the four canonical gospel writers in composing their texts, but the pervasive influence of his ideas is obvious. In fact, as will be shown in subsequent chapters, Paul's theology was a key factor in the mythologizing and rewriting of the events of the life and death of Jesus. While Paul himself evidently had little interest in the historical Jesus, these later writers looked back at Jesus in light of the Pauline understanding of Jesus Christ.

Perhaps more than anything else, the Epistles of Paul succeeded brilliantly in bringing the "open commensality" message of Jesus' Kingdom to the world at large. Paul's self-awareness was that of a Hellenistic "outsider" to the Jews, and a Jewish "outsider" to the Gentiles. Above all he conveyed the special worth of despised "outsiders" and lowly "sinners" in the eyes of God. His enormously creative amalgam of ideas was independent of other written texts.

---

[1]   See Frederickson, Paula, *From Jesus to Christ*, Yale University Press, 1988.

CHAPTER 5

THE GOSPEL OF MARK

The canonical gospels of Mark, Matthew, Luke and John, written from 40 to 80 years after the crucifixion of Jesus, were highly dependent upon earlier source materials. It is also important for modern readers to understand that the authors felt free to rewrite and reinterpret their sources, imagining what Jesus "would have said," or what "must have happened" in light of traditional scripture, oral transmission, and subsequent events. Mark was the first of these writers.

Mark's Gospel—Variant Versions

Most scholars date the Markan Gospel from circa 70 C.E., when the fledgling Christian Church was in crisis, and Paul, Peter, James and probably all the original disciples were dead. Jesus had not returned. And the disastrous Roman-Jewish War had placed the Jerusalem community in a situation of militant rebellion against Rome. Throughout the Empire, the scattered groups of Jesus people were being perceived widely as attempting to subvert Rome by foisting a Jewish God on unsuspecting Gentiles. A scribe named John Mark had lived in Jerusalem during the time of King Agrippa's persecution of the apostles (Acts 12:12); had been closely associated with Simon Peter (1 Peter 5:13 and Acts 12:12-17); and had travelled with Joseph Barnabas and Paul during their early missions (Acts 12:35). Whether or not the actual author of the Gospel of Mark was really John Mark we do not know.

Whoever it was who chose these turbulent times to reconstruct the story of Jesus wrote within a mixed framework of Jewish tradition and Paul's theological ideas. He was resistant to Gnostic understandings. Scholars agree that the intended readership for Mark was the Greek-speaking Jewish Diaspora and

Gentile population. It would seem likely that Mark had known both Paul and Peter, but had not been a disciple of Jesus during Jesus' lifetime. His gospel text indicates that he identified strongly with the "separation" of Paul and Peter from the "faithless" Jewish community, and supported the New Covenant preached by Paul, which focused on the Gentiles as the inheritors of the forthcoming Kingdom of God. But how to "bear witness" as a next-generation person would have been a problem. The evidence, as we shall see, is very strong that Mark was forced to rely mainly on the Gospel of Thomas and the Gospel of "Early John." Bishop Clement of Alexandria (circa 150 C.E.) mentions that Mark used some notes written by Peter but apparently these were fragmentary. The limitations of these sources from Mark's perspective would have necessitated changes that "he thought most useful for increasing the faith of those who were being instructed."[1]

The canonical version of Mark's Gospel involves certain problems of authentication. Most scholars agree that the last paragraphs (Mark 16:9-19) were added much later by another writer, who was attempting to bring Mark's resurrection story into line with the Gospels of Matthew and Luke. Whether these passages (which deal with post-crucifixion appearances by Jesus to Mary of Magdala, two disciples walking in the country, and eleven inner-group disciples) replace deleted words, or are an add-on is not known. However, the idea that some details of Mark's text were deleted (by himself or others), is supported by the purported twentieth-century discovery of some fragments of a "secret" gospel by Mark.[2] While these fragments (if authentic) support the possibility of at least two editions of Mark, the canonical version (excluding Mark 16:9-19) seems close to the text available to Matthew and Luke. There is no evidence that "Secret Mark" was known to them.

Re-structuring the Story of Jesus[3]

The primary problem faced by Mark was how to produce a credible story of the man Jesus (i.e. "bear witness") in a way that would reinforce the Pauline understanding of his identity as the divine Saviour of all humankind. Paul had received revelation from a resurrected Jesus Christ, but apparently had written virtually nothing about the earthly life of Jesus. The need was for a story of Jesus' life that would fit the teachings of Paul. In a sense, Paul's teachings had to be retrojected backwards to provide a thematic framework for the story of Jesus.

Mark believed (along with Paul) that Jesus was the fully divine Son of God, resurrected from death as Lord of Heaven, and destined to return in glory to implement God's Plan for humankind. Sharing Paul's understanding of history as a cosmic battle between the Forces of Light (God), and the forces of darkness (Satan), Mark's Jesus is a type of primordial hero of divine essence, assigned by God to bring about a resolution of the conflict.

As the *secretly* divine Son of God, Jesus is responsible for the announcement of a new covenant between God and his people to replace the old Mosaic arrangement. The notion of secrecy seems to derive from Thomas, who describes secret knowledge about a hidden spiritual Kingdom of God. Mark transforms the secret Kingdom into the secret that Jesus is the hidden Son of God. Miracles performed by Jesus provide evidence of his divine identity, but only faith brings true understanding. Jesus explains these matters during his lifetime, and prophesies his own death and resurrection to uncomprehending disciples.

In so doing, Mark's Jesus renders redundant any need for gnostic-type post-crucifixion appearances and revelations to the disciples to validate his resurrection. A messenger at the Empty Tomb simply reminds the first visitors what Jesus had told them. All of "Early John's" reported appearances (confirmed in Paul's First Epistle to the Corinthians) are omitted from Mark's story. But not actually, because what Mark did was to retroject these events to the lifetime of Jesus, using them in revised form as a narrative base for his new description of Jesus' mission in Galilee.

Mark creates his narrative by rearranging the five appearances and seven signs from "Early John," with altered roles for John the Baptist, members of Jesus' family, the disciples of Jesus, God, Satan, and Jesus himself.

Endorsement of Jesus comes from God directly rather than from prominent citizens as in "Early John." John the Baptist is a precursor messenger. Jesus launches his mission in Galilee instead of Judea. Four post-crucifixion appearance stories from "Early John" are transformed into the narrative base of the Galilean story: recruitment of disciples, commissioning of apostles, the transfiguration, and an extra feeding of the multitude. Several "sign" stories become "miracles" and are performed in Galilee—not Jerusalem. Two of them are transferred from the Feast of Tabernacles to Passover: the entry into Jerusalem and the cleansing of the Temple. The Lazarus story is deleted. A single journey to Jerusalem for Passover encompasses the destiny of Jesus. The insurrection at the Feast of Tabernacles is deleted. The Passion Story is about betrayal and abandonment of the Son of God by family, disciples and the Jewish people.

The Identity and Mission of Jesus

Mark's story begins with John the Baptist in the desert just as specified by "Early John." And immediately we note some parallels with the Johannine text. John is the Isaiahan prophet, "the voice of one crying in the wilderness" (John 1:23); the people seeking baptism come from Judea and Jerusalem, paralleling "the priests and Levites from Jerusalem" (John 1:19); Jesus is mighty, "the thong of whose sandal I am not worthy to untie" (John 1:27); and Jesus will "baptize with the Holy Spirit" (John 1:33).

But whereas "Early John" presents John the Baptist as endorsing Jesus because of a vision of the Spirit descending upon him as a dove from heaven, Mark turns it into a miraculous intervention by God, accompanying John's water baptism of Jesus. Thus, the earthly holy man through baptism provides certification of God's decision to send the divine hero on a mission, intended to bring about the overthrow of the forces of darkness in the world. Endorsement of Jesus comes directly from God rather than from a variety of important citizens as in "Early John": "And a voice came from Heaven 'Thou art my beloved Son: with thee, I am well pleased'" (Mark 1:11). Thus, God's direct endorsement of Jesus has been moved forward by Mark to the beginning of the story, and is expressed in words; in contrast to "Early John's" endorsement of Jesus by God which occurs at the end of his life story and is expressed by events (death and resurrection).

Mark adds a further classical mythical element (consistent with Paul's approach) requiring Jesus to be tested and tempted by Satan before commencing his mission: "The Spirit immediately drove him out into the wilderness. And he was in the wilderness forty days, tempted by Satan; and he was with the wild beasts; and the angels ministered to him" (Mark 1:12-13).

Mark does not feel the same need to downgrade John the Baptist as did "Early John." Instead, John the Baptist becomes a precursor "messenger" who baptizes Jesus with water, in the same way that he baptized "everyone from the countryside of Judea, and all the people of Jerusalem" (Mark 1:3). In fact, Mark equates John the Baptist with the prophet Elijah returned to earth (Mark 9:10-13), in direct opposition to the "Early John" text, where John states unequivocally that the he is not Elijah (John 1:21). Mark's Jesus teaches that "Elijah does come first to restore all things" (Mark: 9:13). Until the moment of Jesus' baptism with water, John is superior to the earthly Jesus, but with the descent of the Holy Spirit, Jesus becomes "mightier than I . . . he will baptize you with the Holy Spirit" (Mark 1:7-8).

It is interesting to note that Mark omits any reference to baptisms by Jesus himself in his subsequent text, which is consistent with Paul's idea that Christian baptism is a participation in the dying and resurrection of Christ. Thus, Mark makes no mention of the baptismal mission of Jesus in Judea, which according to "Early John" was undertaken by Jesus before the arrest of John the Baptist (John 3:22-30). Mark also omits the visit of the priests and Levites from Jerusalem to John the Baptist, where "Early John" appears to identify Jesus as "standing among you" (John 1:26). Instead, Mark says that Jesus came up from Galilee to be baptized by John. He confirms later that Jesus is a humble carpenter from Nazareth (Mark 6:3) rather than an apparent member of the priestly class, as hinted by "Early John" (John 1:26).

It is noteworthy also that Mark tends to perceive the earthly Jesus in the image of John the Baptist; he seems to have discovered that John's message, of a future Kingdom of God following apocalyptic events, is a close match of the ideas of Paul. Mark therefore rejects the Thomas Gospel version of Jesus teaching the ongoing timeless presence in the world of the Kingdom of God and the Holy Spirit. Instead, when Jesus begins his mission, "after John was arrested," he comes into Galilee saying: "The time is fulfilled, and the Kingdom of God is closing in; repent and believe in the Gospel" (Mark 1:15). Thus Mark suggests that the messages of Jesus and John the Baptist were almost identical. Both were bringing the same good news. When Jesus says the Kingdom is already here, (as reported by Thomas), it means the same thing as John's preaching that the Kingdom is closing in. When Jesus says that people should "change their ways" (as reported by Thomas), it means the same thing as John's instruction to people to "repent their sins."

In carrying out his mission of spreading the word about the Kingdom of God, Jesus recruits disciples. The "Early John" scenario for the first recruitment is about Andrew and Simon, former disciples of John the Baptist in the Judean wilderness before his arrest, as well as other recruits named Philip and Nathaniel. Their recruitment precedes the baptismal mission of Jesus in Judea.

Mark ignores this story but produces a remarkably parallel "happening": the recruitment of four disciples in Galilee, his first retrojected "happening." He describes two fishing scenes in Lake Galilee where Jesus recruits Simon and brother Andrew and (separately) James and brother John (sons of Zebedee) with the words: "Follow me and I will make you become fishers of men" (Mark 1:17). The parallel twin stories, and the "follow me" words in Mark seem strangely suggestive of inspiration from "Early John" (John 1:35-44). In particular, the call to the fishermen implies that they already know the teaching of Jesus. An even more significant aspect is the way in which Luke's later gospel changes the scene while ostensibly using Mark as his source. Luke does several things: he combines the two scenes into one; he mentions an indeterminate number of fishermen; he describes a miraculous harvest of fish so large that the boats begin to sink; and Simon Peter says "Depart from me, for I am a sinful man, O Lord" (Luke 5:1-11). Luke's embellishments of the story seem clearly derivative from the Johannine Gospel post-crucifixion story of Jesus' appearance to seven disciples fishing in Lake Galilee, inclusive of Simon Peter, James and John (John 21:1-8). That "Later John's" story was an elaboration of an "Early John" source will be proposed in Chapter 9. Luke's story is a somewhat parallel elaboration, which suggests that Luke had access to the "Early John" text, as will be discussed in Chapter 8. And Luke's radical changes to Mark's text indicate that Luke perceived the "Early John" text to be directly connected to Mark's version. Hence, my conclusion that Mark borrowed basic elements of an "Early John" post-crucifixion appearance story to provide an alternative to "Early John's" recruitment of disciples story. This retrojection of events by Mark to the lifetime of Jesus sets up a new storyline focused on Galilee. I infer that Mark's account of an instruction by Jesus to his disciples to become "fishers of men" represents a Markan transfer from an "Early John" text partially embedded in the Johannine gospel, that would have ascribed such a message to a post-crucifixion appearance of Jesus to seven disciples (John 21:1-2), *parallel to that mentioned by Paul to twelve disciples (apparently in Galilee)*.

Mark's second major "happening" of the Galilean mission (with two parts) is the appointment of twelve disciples, named apostles, with authority to "preach and cast out demons" (Mark 3:13-18); later he sends them forth "two by two" to carry out these functions (Mark 6:7-11). Luke repeats the Markan delegation of authority by Jesus during his lifetime (Luke 6:12-17 and 9:1-6), but also adds another delegation of authority to 72 others (Luke 10:1). Unlike Mark, however, Luke reports two post-crucifixion appearances by Jesus where he converses first with two traveling apostles (on the road to Emmaus), and secondly to eleven apostles and "all who were with them" in Jerusalem (Luke 24:13-53). My hypothesis is that in his second post-crucifixion event, Luke is describing the appearance by Jesus "to all the apostles" mentioned by Paul (1 Corinthians 15:7). Luke's post-crucifixion appearance story, greatly elaborated for his own purposes (see Chapter 8) is derivative from "Early John" as evidenced by the question from the apostles: "Lord, will you at this time restore the Kingdom to Israel?" (Acts 1:6) And then comes the delegation of authority when Jesus says "You shall receive power when the Holy Spirit has come upon you; and you shall be my witnesses in Jerusalem and in all Judea and Samaria and to the end of the earth" (Acts 1:8).

I infer that Luke had access to an "Early John" appearance story, where "Early John" reports an instruction from Jesus delegating authority to all the apostles to spread his teaching message, going out two by two. But since Luke was also using Mark as a source, he accepted that Jesus had already delegated his authority to twelve apostles during his lifetime, and to account for other additional apostles after his death, Luke added another retrojected delegation of authority to seventy-two apostles while Jesus was alive (Luke 10:1). Thus, having followed Mark in retrojecting the "Early John" story of the appointment of apostles to the lifetime of Jesus, Luke was free to redesign "Early John's" post-crucifixion appearance story to fit a new Lukan interpretation (See Chapter 8). My conclusion is that Mark's second major "happening" of the Galilean mission of Jesus, the appointment of apostles and delegation of authority to them, is a retrojection of a post-crucifixion appearance event recorded by "Early John" and by Paul.

The third "happening" in Mark is the strange "second feeding of the multitude" (Mark 8:1-21). Scholars have had a difficult time explaining why Mark described a second feeding of the multitude, together with his puzzling comparative numbers of twelve and seven for the baskets of scraps picked up afterward by the disciples, and his warnings about the leaven of the Pharisees and the leaven of Herod. My solution to this puzzle is the post-crucifixion appearance by Jesus "to more than 500 brethren at one time" reported by Paul (1 Corinthians 15:6); associated with Peter, the event presumably occurred in Galilee. It was perhaps an assembly of followers of Jesus in Galilee after his death, attempting to repeat their earlier experience of the presence of the Spirit when Jesus fed the multitude of 5000 men. While it is difficult to show that this event was recorded in "Early John," Mark's mysterious questions and warnings may signify precisely that it was. Mark seems to have a yen for odd clues. The baskets of bread scraps may refer to spiritual bread dispensed by Jesus; the leaven may refer to bad spiritual bread dispensed by Pharisees and Herodians.

The twelve baskets of Jesus' bread were picked up by twelve inner group disciples at the first feeding of the multitude, and seven baskets were picked up by seven inner-group disciples the second time. Coincidentally, seven inner-group disciples were in Galilee for the post-crucifixion appearance of Jesus there, if we accept "Later John's" version (John 21:1-2) on the number of disciples as derivative from the "Early John" text. Paul may not have been aware that only seven (rather than twelve) disciples were in Galilee at the time of the appearances. At this critical post-crucifixion time, the danger from "the leaven" of the Pharisees and Herodians might have been particularly acute for the disciples. Further evidence that Mark retrojected this "Early John" appearance story is the fact that Luke omitted it. He couldn't include a post-crucifixion scenario because of his new post-crucifixion storyline confined geographically to Jerusalem. And he must have rejected Mark's retrojection of a second feeding of the multitude to the lifetime of Jesus as not credible.

The fourth retrojection is the Transfiguration story (Mark 9:1-8), transferred by Mark from "Early John." It represents the first post-crucifixion appearance mentioned by Paul, which was privately to Peter. In Mark's story, Peter experiences a vision of Jesus in dazzling white garments talking to Elijah and Moses, after Jesus takes him up a high mountain in Galilee. Mark throws us off the track by including James and John with Peter, but only Peter actually converses with the transfigured Jesus, who is also talking to Moses and Elijah. Also, Luke brings realism into the story by mentioning that the three disciples fell asleep. In Mark's version, God's voice from a cloud reiterates that Jesus is His beloved Son. According to Mark: "Jesus charged them to tell no one what they had seen, until the Son of Man should have risen from the dead" (Mark 9:9); an apparent rebuttal of any "Early John" claim that it was a post-crucifixion event.

The fifth relevant "happening" described by Mark is a replacement rather than a retrojection from "Early John." It relates to the private appearance of Jesus to James mentioned by Paul (1 Corinthians 15:7). Evidence from "Later John's" Gospel (to be discussed in Chapter 9) indicates that the Parousia message came from this appearance event, because the message reported by James (termed "the beloved disciple" by "Later John") was that Jesus would return in glory before his (i.e. James') own death (John 21:21-23). But Mark knows that James is dead, and therefore wrong. So Mark alters the Parousia message from the risen Jesus to "this generation will not pass away before all those things take place" as part of a direct prophecy by Jesus to four disciples during his lifetime (Mark 13). The original story of an appearance to James (repressed by Mark) is contained in the Road to Emmaus story adapted by Luke from the "Early John" text (see Chapter 8). The odd thing is (and this is a clue to the "Early John" source) that Mark's version in Mark 13 has some parallel features to Luke's story; (i) it is *private*, except that it is to four disciples—Peter, Andrew, James and John; (ii) it includes *James* as a recipient, except that this is James, son of Zebedee; and (iii) it is delivered by Jesus near *Jerusalem*, except that it is two days before his death instead of afterwards. Here Mark brings out the full panoply of apocalyptic theology, bolstered by the evident fact of the disastrous Roman-Jewish War. Mark can, therefore, present a dramatic prophecy of the destruction of the Temple and Jerusalem as divine punishment, and apocalyptic warnings of further trials and horrible disasters as signs of the "end of days," to be finally accomplished by "the Son of Man coming in clouds with great power and glory," "for the sake of the elect whom he chose to save." "Truly I say to you, this generation will not pass away before all these things take place" (Mark 13).

The Teachings of Jesus

One of the most extraordinary quotations in Mark's Gospel occurs when Jesus explains his teaching system to his inner-group disciples as follows:

"To you has been given the secret of the Kingdom of God, but for those outside everything is in parables; so that they may indeed see but not perceive, and may indeed hear but not understand lest they should turn again and be forgiven" (Mark 4:11-12).

In other words, the outsiders (whoever they may be) are denied any knowledge of the secret Kingdom, and even the possibility of having their sins forgiven; "but privately, to his own disciples Jesus explained everything" (Mark 4:34).

The notion of secret wisdom in Mark promulgated by Jesus to his disciples seems highly derivative from the Thomas Gospel description of "hidden sayings." The words of Jesus do not speak for themselves. Frequently they may seem puzzling, enigmatic, paradoxical or ambiguous, but a secret meaning is embedded in them. In Thomas, access to the secret of the Kingdom of God comes through gnosis, a process of inward self-discovery, becoming like a child (i.e. non-entity) and casting off worldly concerns; it is available to everyone. In Mark, the secret is accessed through Pauline faith in the divine personhood of Jesus, who explains everything to insiders. This has special importance for Mark's readers, because they too will be able to understand the special meaning of Jesus' words. Faith in Jesus pre-empts gnosis.

The dichotomy between insiders and outsiders appears first in the Thomas Gospel, where the sayings of Jesus function as a warning or explanation why certain groups are "standing outside" or have no preferred status within the Kingdom. Thomas mentions "dogs" (i.e. some non-Jews), Pharisees and scribes, merchants and Jesus' own family (Thomas 39, 64, 93, 99). His reference "do not give what is holy to dogs" seems to support the importance of missionizing the Jews. Mark accepts the obvious fact that the mission of Jesus was to the Jews, but expresses their rejection of him in the form of confrontational debate between Jesus and scribes (occasionally Pharisees and the general public). Somehow the Jews have succumbed to the wiles of Satan and have become outsiders, so that while the teachings of Jesus are public, the true understanding remains secret or private. Mark takes his cues from Thomas on specific groups of outsiders, but with more explicit rejections or condemnations by Jesus. For example, Thomas 64, "Businessmen and merchants will not enter the places of my father," becomes Mark 10:23, "It is easier for a camel to go through the eye of a needle than for a rich man to enter the Kingdom of God." And in another instance, Mark takes Thomas 31, "no prophet is accepted in his own village; no physician heals those who know him," and restates it as "A prophet is not without honor, except in his own country, and among his own kin and in his own house" (Mark 6:4).

Mark's presentation of the teachings of Jesus is selected carefully from his sources. That the primary source was the Thomas Gospel is verified by the fact that *at least 80 percent* of the sayings of Jesus used by Mark (excluding "signs and prophesies") can be traced to that gospel. The Q1 Sayings Gospel was not available to Mark; this is verified by the fact that the only Q1 sayings found in Mark are those that are also in the Thomas Gospel.[4]

The dependence of Mark on Thomas has been overlooked by most scholars, who point out that the majority of Jesus' sayings in the Thomas Gospel are ignored by Mark. These omitted sayings include the gnostic-oriented material, the timeless presence of the Spiritual Kingdom, and some precepts about radical lifestyle ethics, found also in Q1.

My response is that Mark excluded enigmatic or gnostic-type source material that seemed to contradict his own perception of Jesus and might confuse his readers. He relegated such matters to the realm of secret mysteries according to Bishop Clement of Alexandria (circa 150 C.E.). "He did not divulge the things not to be uttered, nor did he write down the hierophantic teaching of the Lord" (see endnote 1).

In regard to his minimal use of lifestyle sayings, Mark makes up for this when Jesus and "a scribe" (perhaps a stand-in for Paul) concur in the primacy of love of

God and neighbour as the greatest of God's commandments, "much more than all whole burnt offerings and sacrifices" (Mark 12:28-34).

Also, Mark includes the Pauline teaching on divorce and marriage (Mark 10:5-10 versus 1 Corinthians 7), which may be inferred as paralleling Thomas' sayings about the primordial wholeness of male and female becoming one (Thomas 11, 22 and 106).

Most of the Thomas sayings selected by Mark deal with entry into the Kingdom of God, its growth, the separation of insiders from outsiders and the obsolescence of Jewish dietary laws and fasting. In Thomas, one enters the Kingdom through a mystical process of gnosis or self-knowledge, which is equated with becoming like a child or infant (Thomas 3, 22 and 46). Mark supports child-like entry (ignoring gnosis), and uses the theme to show that those who seek greatness must be "servant of all." But he seems worried about oppression of child-like disciples, and has Jesus invoke dire warnings of hellfire for "whoever causes one of these little ones (followers) to sin" (Mark 9:33-37 and 42-50). For Mark, the key to entry into the Kingdom becomes the Pauline concept of innocent faith in the personhood of Jesus.

Growth of the Kingdom for Mark seems to parallel the Pauline idea of hope, which he finds in the Thomas parables of the seeds (Mark 4 and Thomas 9, 20 and 21). Mark seems particularly entranced by the mysterious quality of the seed which grows secretly, paralleling the mysterious growth of the secret Kingdom until harvest time (Mark 4:26-29).

In regard to the Mosaic purification rituals and dietary laws, Mark uses what little he can find in Thomas (Thomas 14, 47 and 104), to fortify the attitude of Jesus against them (Mark 2:18-22 and 7:1-23). For example, "And he said, 'What comes out of a man is what defiles a man. For from within, out of the heart of man, come evil thoughts, fornication, theft, murder, adultery, coveting, wickedness, deceit, licentiousness, envy, slander, pride, foolishness. All these evil things come from within, and they defile a man'" (Mark 7:20-22).

In acknowledging the demonic evil forces within men, Mark's Jesus gives priority to battling against them. Hence, the reaching out to sinners such as Paul, tax collectors, drunkards, collaborators with Rome, and Gentiles. "Early John's" Jesus reached out to all Jews (see Chapter 3), but Mark's Jesus reaches out to all sinning Jews and Gentiles that have faith in Him.

The Acts of Jesus

The public teaching mission of Jesus required actions as well as words. Spreading of the message, as with Old Testament prophets, implied deeds or wonders that provided credentials for the messenger. In "Early John," there were perhaps seven wonders or "signs," public demonstrations initiated by Jesus of the presence of the Kingdom or Holy Spirit of God.

Mark had a problem. He knew that Jesus was engaged in a battle against Satan, which was destined to end in his own suffering and death, followed by the triumph of resurrection. Deeds must have been performed by Jesus to demonstrate divine power in support of the teaching message. Such deeds would normally be considered as "signs." Why then did people not recognize and accept Jesus during his lifetime? Mark's weak answer is that Jesus told everyone who did recognize him (including demons) not to tell anyone else. According to Mark, Jesus said: "Why does this generation seek a sign? Truly I say to you, no sign shall be given to this generation" (Mark 8:12). Mark has Jesus enjoin healed persons to "say nothing to anyone" (Mark 1:44). But we can see that Mark's idea of privacy contradicts the notion of "signs" which are intended to teach and foster spreading of the message.

"Early John" included two healing events, the paralytic and the blind man, among his public signs. Mark transforms these into "miracles," moves them from Jerusalem to a Galilean setting, and adds a considerable number of additional "miracle" healing events, in which Jesus uses a wide gamut of healing techniques. Many of these additional stories seem to be sourced from Simon Peter, apparently from his written notes.

When Jesus heals in the "Early John" Gospel, the recipients are surprised at his action, as they did not expect anything (John 5:2-9 and John 9:1-12); healing is an expression or demonstration of the timeless presence of the Spirit which reaches the eternal light within. Such a transfer of Spirit opens the possibility of entry into the Kingdom of God through self-understanding, achievable regardless of past sins, which removes the traditional need for forgiveness of sins, and the issue of where authority to forgive sins resides. This is a Gnostic perception.

The Pauline interpretation, expressed in Mark, re-asserts the ancient brokerage system. Sins and disease are the works of Satan, and have to be exorcised through forgiveness. An intimate person-to-person flow of energy between the healer and the recipient expels the demonic within. Those who express unconditional faith in Jesus may receive complete forgiveness of their sins, along with healing of disease or disability. In so doing, Jesus drives out evil spirits and demons by direct miracles, which are generated by the faith of the person concerned. By exercising such faith, the recipient participates in responsibility for the outcome. When faith is lacking, as "among his own kin" (Mark 6:4), the healing and forgiveness does not take place.

Just as Mark incorporated the five post-crucifixion appearances of Jesus into altered narrative contexts, he also adapted seven signs by Jesus described by "Early John" to his own narrative purpose. Note that Mark apparently omitted as not credible the two Cana "signs" reported by "Early John" (Cana wedding events and healing at a distance). Presumably "Later John" elaborated the stories to improve their credibility (see Chapter 3).

The first two signs from "Early John" accepted by the author of Mark are the "feeding of the 5000 men" and the "walking on water" story. Mark's stories match the source stories in major details, but are slanted in the direction of pure miracle as opposed to "theatrical happening." It is notable that "Early John's" wording retains a certain degree of ambiguity that permits the possibility of a non-supernatural explanation. For example, in the "walking on water" story, the disciples in their boat at night perceive Jesus walking on water, and when they are about to take him aboard "immediately the boat was at the land" (John 6:16-21). In Mark, Jesus on land sees the disciples' boat in difficulty, walks out to them on the water, climbs aboard and calms the waters (Mark 6:45-51).

Mark's "feeding of the 5000" story is immediately preceded by a description of John the Baptist's execution by King Herod Antipas, which assigns blame to the King's wife and daughter. Significantly, Luke reduces the same story to a one-line sentence: "Herod said, John I beheaded" (Luke 9:8), while the Johannine gospel omits it entirely. Which leads to an inference that "Later John" deleted all mention of this in order to remove any hint of connection between the execution of John, and the feeding of the multitude event. Luke and Mark retain the sequence of the two stories, but leave indeterminate the time of John's execution. Luke's exclusion of Mark's elaborated execution story suggests that the detailed story was not sourced in the "Early John" text, but rather imagined by Mark as a means of whitewashing the role of King Herod. The sequencing of the two events (beheading John and feeding the multitude) by both Luke and Mark suggests that they were linked in their "Early John" source. A further reference by Mark that the crowd in the latter story were "like sheep without a shepherd" (Mark 6:34) is also suggestive. A very important change by Mark to the feeding of the multitude story is his omission of the crowd's response, wanting to take Jesus by force and make him King (John 6:15). Instead of Jesus going up to the Feast of Tabernacles in Jerusalem, Mark sends him in the opposite direction to the Gentile region of Tyre and Sidon. Later, the entire Feast of Tabernacles scenario is omitted by Mark, and replaced by one sentence: "And he left there and went to the region of Judea and beyond the Jordan" (Mark 10:1), which confirms the sequence, but omits the Feast.

As discussed in Chapter 3, my explanation for the omission of the Feast of Tabernacles is the "insurrection," referred to obliquely by Mark in the story of Barabbas. It seems that complete disassociation of Jesus from Zealot violence was considered fundamental to the credibility of Mark's Gospel among the Gentiles.

The next two signs inferred from the "Early John" text, the entry into Jerusalem and the cleansing of the Temple, had to be moved by Mark to the

Passover Feast, and fitted into an alternative scenario for the final days of Jesus. Similarly, the two healing signs of "Early John" performed by Jesus at the feast in Jerusalem (on the paralytic and the blind man), are transferred by Mark to Galilee, with some change of detail to include Markan themes of faith, forgiveness of sin and secrecy. Mark deletes entirely the climactic "raising of Lazarus" sign as unable to fit, but apparently feels compelled to place it in his "Secret Gospel."

The Passion Story

Mark's Passion Story was shaped by his Pauline understanding of Jesus as God-Man, who died in expiation for human sin, and was resurrected as Lord of Heaven to return at the imminent "end of days," bringing about Satan's final defeat, and saving all faithful believers. "Early John" and many disciples, on the other hand, believed that Jesus was resurrected to bring about the restoration of the Kingdom of Israel in glory in conjunction with a new way of life on earth. For Mark, the proof that they were wrong and Paul was right was the disaster of the Roman-Jewish War. Other disciples had misunderstood the "secret wisdom" of God embodied in the message and personhood of Jesus Christ. This being so, the source materials emanating from them reflected their misunderstanding, and therefore had to be re-written to match the Pauline interpretation.

Very early in Mark's story the Pharisees and authorities start plotting to destroy Jesus (Mark 3:6), and the conflict with evil powers continues throughout the narrative. From time to time Jesus prophesies to his disciples the outcome of the struggle in words reminiscent of Paul's rhetoric (1 Corinthians 15:3-4, Mark 8:31-33, 9:31, 10:32-34) and explains what it is all about to uncomprehending listeners. This conveys the impression to readers that the various details have been pre-ordained by God as part of a cosmic drama. Within this context, however, human pain and suffering by Jesus is vividly portrayed, together with primordial sadness that human sin requires such a scenario.

My inferred "Early John" narrative (Chapter 3) explains the arrest of Jesus in terms of an insurrection in Jerusalem by some of his followers at the Feast of Tabernacles. After fleeing to the wilderness, as reported in the Johannine gospel, Jesus returns to surrender to Roman authorities to avoid retaliatory crucifixion of one (or more) insurrectionists, and "that the whole nation should not perish" (John 11:50). For Mark, such an association between Jesus and rebellion against Rome was impossible. To him, "Early John's" cleansing of the Temple story was about Jesus expressing God's anger at the Jewish people for the wickedness and corruption of the Temple system, and their inability to accept the new Kingdom of God. Activated by Satan, the authorities arrested Jesus and persuaded Pontius Pilate to crucify him, with support from the fickle people of Jerusalem.

Mark begins the Passion Story with the triumphant but peaceful entry into Jerusalem. He has no qualms about transferring the event from the Feast of Tabernacles to the Spring Passover Feast, nor of confirming that Jesus was accompanied by a crowd of Galileans who cheered him as the traditional Messiah of Israel. The crowd cries: "Blessed is he who comes in the name of the Lord! Blessed is the Kingdom of our father David that is coming" (Mark 11:9-10). Mark does leave out, however, the Johannine reference to "King of Israel."

A major difficulty for Mark is why Jesus would initiate such a provocative entry into Jerusalem at a time when Pontius Pilate was in town, as compared with the "Early John" entry story which fitted unprovocatively into a Thanksgiving Harvest Festival scenario. Mark therefore refocuses attention (and raises the stakes) on the Temple with the "withered fig tree" symbolism, the reference to "a den of robbers" (compared to "Early John's" "house of trade") and the hostile reaction of the Temple authorities. In particular, Jesus' arrest is by "a crowd with swords and clubs, from the chief priests and the scribes and the elders" (Mark 14:43); no Roman soldiers are mentioned. Mark sets the stage by having Jesus take direct aim at the Temple authorities using scripture: "My house shall be called a house of prayer for all nations." By accusing them of being "a den of robbers," Mark provides motivation for spiteful action against Jesus by the authorities (and for God's later action in allowing the destruction of the corrupt Temple by the Romans).

Evidence that Mark borrowed from "Early John" includes Jesus teaching in the Temple, and that "they tried to arrest him but feared the multitude" (Mark 12:12 and John 7:32). "Early John" notes that "no man ever spoke like this man" (John 7:46), and Mark sets out to illustrate this with a series of choice parables and sayings by Jesus in the Temple. In particular, the reference to John's baptism and the teaching authority of Jesus shows a connection to the "Early John" text when Mark writes about the chief priests: "they were afraid of the people, for all held that John was a real prophet" (Mark 11:32). And Mark lets slip a mention of the insurrection in explaining the incarceration of Barabbas by Pontius Pilate (Mark 15:6).

An important change for Mark was to separate the supper at Bethany from the Last Supper, which had to occur as the ritual Passover meal in order to fit Paul's doctrine of the New Covenant. In my inferred "Early John" write-up, the supper at Bethany and the Last Supper were the same meal, occurring before Passover. Mark feels compelled to contradict explicitly John's version that Jesus was crucified on Passover day as the Lamb of God. Mark writes: "And the chief priests and the scribes were seeking how to arrest him by stealth and kill him; for they said '*Not during the feast lest there be a tumult of the people*'" (Mark 14:2, emphasis added). Mark thus separates the supper at Bethany from the Last Supper two days later at Passover, and emphasizes the separation by generating a story about the preparation of a special "upper room" in Jerusalem. (Details of the story seem modeled on the earlier story emanating from Peter about the colt in Bethany). Mark then excludes the two "washing of the feet" stories (Mary of Bethany washing Jesus' feet, and Jesus washing the disciples' feet). In the case of Mary of Bethany, he substitutes an unnamed woman who pours costly ointment over Jesus' head; "she has anointed my body beforehand for burying . . . what she has done will be told in memory of her" (Mark 14:8-9).

According to Mark, at Passover two days later, Jesus held the Eucharistic bread and wine meal signifying the New Covenant to replace the Passover meal. There is nothing in the Johannine gospel about the Last Supper Covenant. This was Paul's idea of a new contract between God and humankind to replace the old Mosaic arrangement; Paul writes that it took place on "the night that he was betrayed (turned over)" (1 Corinthians 11:23-26).

Mark writes that Jesus was betrayed by Judas Iscariot. Who was Judas Iscariot? Most scholars now agree that the word Iscariot is an epithet meaning Sicariot or Zealot extremist; according to the Jewish writer Josephus the Sicarios or "Zealot Assassins" were Jewish Zealot extremists engaged in terrorist activities. "Later John" writes that Judas Iscariot was the brother (or son) of Simon Iscariot (John 13:26), the information coming presumably from his "Early John" source. Consequently, my inferred "Early John" list of apostles (see Chapter 3) shows Judas brother of Simon as the twelfth apostle, and Simon the Iscariot as the eleventh apostle. Mark's list of apostles shows Judas Iscariot as the twelfth apostle, and Simon of Cana as the eleventh apostle (Mark 3:16-18). Mark's source for his list of apostles was the "Early John" Gospel. "Later John's" source for the relationship between Judas and Simon was also the "Early John" Gospel.

My conclusion is that Mark transferred the Iscariot designation from Simon to Judas, changed Simon's nickname to "Cananaean" (Simon of Cana), and suppressed the brother relationship of Simon and Judas. Why did Mark do this? The answer is that he needed an alternative explanation for the arrest of Jesus to replace the story contained in the "Early John" Gospel. Perhaps Mark's concern about suppressing the insurrection story is reflected unconsciously in his description of the situation "And the chief priests and the scribes were seeking how to arrest him by stealth and kill him; for they said, 'Not during the feast, lest there be a tumult of the people'" (Mark 14:1-2). And for Mark, an alternative Judas betrayal story may have been a way of symbolizing the betrayal of Jesus by followers who had used violence in the insurrection at the Feast of Tabernacles. Also, he may have noticed in his "Early John" source that a disciple named Judas was the emissary sent by Jesus to the Roman and Jewish officials, and could therefore be made the scapegoat for subsequent events. Mark could then compose a mythic story in which the despicable Judas, who had plotted earlier with the chief priests in return for money, would guide them to Gethsemane and identify Jesus by a kiss. Mark naturally omitted "Early John's" mention that Jesus had sent

Judas to fetch the Roman soldiers (John 13:26-30), as there were no Romans in the Markan account. Later writers, including "Later John," took up this betrayal story with enthusiasm, and embellished it in various ways.

Mark's well-known story of the trial and crucifixion of Jesus continues to contrast in almost every respect with the inferred version by "Early John." In John's Gospel, Jesus saves his disciples from arrest and condemns violence; Peter's presence at the court of the high priest seems courageous, and his denial of Jesus seems a reasonable tactic in light of his own violent response in cutting off the ear of the high priest's slave. But for Mark, Jesus is shamefully abandoned by everyone: the disciples run away; Peter denies Jesus without any mention by Mark that he is the disciple that cut off the slave's ear. There is also the shame of the "young man" who runs away naked from the arresting officials.

Mark reports an immediate meeting of the Sanhedrin that same evening to try Jesus, in direct contradiction to the Johannine text which says only that Jesus was interrogated by the High Priest Annas, followed by his transfer to the house of Caiaphas, "high priest that year" (John 18:13). The Markan version seems unlikely in terms of the time available that night. Mark's picture of Jesus, who proclaims himself the Son of God and is condemned as deserving death for blasphemy, seems totally at odds with "Early John's" temporizing Jesus who does not answer questions directly. One may conclude that Mark introduced the Sanhedrin trial scene at this point to replace the earlier Sanhedrin meeting in "Early John," where the High Priest stated that "one man should die for the people" (John 11:51). Since this meeting in "Early John" related directly to the failed insurrection at the Jerusalem Temple (see Chapter 3), Mark invented a totally different version that dramatically depicts Jewish opposition to the Pauline interpretation of Jesus as the only Son of God, a "blasphemous" notion to them. And Mark's references to false testimony about Jesus' actions and words in the Temple also seem like a replacement for earlier source material associating him with the failed insurrection.

And so, the demonic activity on the part of the priests and a crowd of Judeans continues the next day in front of Pontius Pilate, who is sympathetic to Jesus, but crucifies him anyway at the request of the priests and the crowd. In the end only the Roman centurion seems to understand: "Truly this man was the Son of God" (Mark 15:39).

In the inferred "Early John" story, Pilate proposes that Jesus be flogged and crucified as a warning, but that his life is to be spared (as in Luke's Gospel). According to my interpretation of "Early John," the Jewish priests and officers respond that Barabbas should receive the punishment and be released, while Jesus presumably would remain a prisoner (see Chapter 3). Mark's revised story introduces a crowd of ordinary Judean people, friendly to Pilate and hostile to Jesus. The "crowd," presented by Mark as representative of the Jewish people as a whole, agitates for the crucifixion and death of Jesus. The priests want Jesus to be punished, and Barabbas to be released. Pontius Pilate perceives Jesus' innocence, but bows to the will of the crowd. Barabbas is released, and Jesus dies in torment on the cross uttering the resonant immortal words "My God, my God, why has thou forsaken me?" (Mark 15:24 taken from Ps 22:1). According to Mark, even Jesus was unable to comprehend God's purpose at the final moment of agony. He reacted like King David in Psalm 22:1.

Mark's Empty Tomb story seems, on the face of it, to display a curious confusion about how to end the narrative. When three women visit the tomb "when the Sabbath was past," a young man inside "dressed in a white robe," explains that Jesus "has risen," and requests the women to "tell his disciples and Peter that he is going before you to Galilee; there you will see him as he told you" (Mark 16:6-7). And the fearful women run away and say nothing to anybody; their reaction of "trembling astonishment and fear" to the message (Mark 16:8) seems drawn from an earlier source reporting a vision of Jesus. There ends the gospel. Presumably the disciples return home unaware of the resurrection of Jesus.

Perhaps this lame ending can best be understood as a refutation of the whole "Early John" interpretation. Linkage with the "Early John" Empty Tomb story seems apparent (see Chapter 3). Mark's women include Mary of Magdala, as in "Early John"; Mark's unnamed young man who reports that Jesus has risen corresponds to the "other disciple" (i.e. James) who "saw and believed" (John 20:8); the awe and fear of the women fits an earlier story of Mary's vision of Jesus; Peter is singled out by Mark as returning home not knowing about the resurrection of Jesus. The disciples (i.e. all the other disciples) return to their homes (in "Early John"), and to Galilee (in Mark) without knowing that Jesus has risen from the dead.

But Mark's whole thesis is based on a secret mission from God, destined never to be properly understood by the Jewish disciples and followers of Jesus. The three foolish women are too stupid and fearful to tell anyone about the message from the "young man" in the tomb. There is no appearance or vision of Jesus by Mary, and no other later appearances to other disciples, because they never received the message. By contrast, the upshot of the appearances in "Early John's" inferred gospel had been that Jesus would return in glory to Jerusalem "in the present generation" (or lifetime of James) to install a traditionalist version of the Kingdom of God equated with the Kingdom of Israel. This message came to James (the "other disciple"). Mark reinvents the "other disciple" as the "young man" who states that Jesus will reappear in Galilee, making him a witness against the previous "Early John" interpretation which turned out to be wrong since Jesus had not returned to Jerusalem during the lifetime of James. For Mark, Jesus has already explained everything during his lifetime, including "after I am raised up, I will go before you to Galilee" (Mark 14:28). And the word "Galilee" symbolizes the whole world outside Judea, which will inherit the new Kingdom of God. Jesus prophesies it all in Mark 13.

Disciples, Apostles and Family of Jesus

According to Mark, Jesus commissioned twelve named disciples as apostles during his lifetime, to preach the message of the Kingdom of God. I have hypothesized that this event is a retrojection of a post-crucifixion appearance described in the "Early John" Gospel. The retrojected text includes a list of twelve names, reproduced from "Early John" with amendments by Mark. My further hypothesis is that the main purpose of the amendments was to conceal the presence of brothers of Jesus as members of the inner group of twelve apostles.

Mark does not deny the existence of the brothers of Jesus, who are mentioned in his Thomas source as "standing outside" (see Chapter 1). In fact, he elaborates on the Thomas theme of no special status for the earthly family of Jesus (Thomas 99 and Mark 3:32-35), by identifying his family as uncomprehending (Mark 6:4), and associating them with Jesus' inability to perform healing miracles in Nazareth (Mark 6:5-6). In particular, by mentioning the names of Jesus' brothers (James, Judas, Simon and Joses) in association with faithless Nazareth, Mark is emphasizing that they were not followers of Jesus. He seems to have been aware, however, that "Early John's" post-crucifixion list of twelve apostles included brothers of Jesus (see Chapter 3), even though the list might not have identified them as such. In the following comparison of the inferred "Early John" list with Mark's list of apostles, I offer detailed name by name evidence that Mark made changes focused on suppression of clues to the identity of the brothers; I begin at the bottom of the list.

Inferred "Early John" List of Apostles	Mark's List of Apostles (Mark 3:16-19)
1) Simon Peter	1) Simon, whom he called Peter
2) John	2) James, the son of Zebedee
3) James	3) John, the brother of James
4) Andrew	4) Andrew
5) Philip	5) Philip
6) Judas Thomas	6) Bartholomew
7) Nathaniel	7) Matthew
8) Matthew	8) Thomas
9) James, Justus (the Just)	9) James, the son of Alphaeus
10) Joseph, of James Justus	10) Thaddaeus
11) Simon Iscariot	11) Simon, the Cananaean (of Cana)
12) Judas, of Simon Iscariot	12) Judas Iscariot

12. **Judas, of Simon Iscariot** is a name in the Johannine gospel text (see Chapter 9). Mark shortened it to Judas Iscariot. For "Early John," the nickname Iscariot may have simply meant Zealot. But for Mark, years later, the word is a term of opprobrium meaning Zealot extremist or assassin. Judas Iscariot is portrayed as the betrayer of Jesus, his name reminiscent of Judas of Galilee, Zealot rebel leader against Rome in 6 C.E.

11. **Simon Iscariot,** also inferred from the Johannine text, becomes Simon the Cananaean (of Cana) according to Mark, thus losing his identification as brother of Judas, and losing his nickname showing him to be a Zealot. Also, Mark's specification of his geographic origin in Cana of Galilee seems to ensure that he will not be mistaken for Simon the Leper, resident of Bethany in Judea, or for Simon of Cyrene who carries the cross of Jesus to the place of execution. Residence in Cana has been reassigned from Nathaniel (mentioned as being "of Cana," John 21:2).

10. **Joseph, of James Justus,** inferred from Luke (see Chapter 8), is replaced by Thaddeaus. Mark seems particularly worried about Joseph, perhaps because his name "Joseph *Barsabbas* Justus" according to Luke (Acts 1:23) seems to imply that Joseph is the son of Joseph, and brother of James. For Mark, the name Joseph may have been perceived as a clue pointing to a brother of Jesus in the "Early John" List of Apostles. So in addition to suppressing mention of Joseph as father of Jesus, Mark renames Joseph, brother of Jesus, as Joses (Mark 6:3); he replaces him by the name Thaddaeus in the List of Apostles.

9. **James Justus,** inferred from Thomas and Luke (see Chapters 1 and 8), becomes James, son of Alphaeus, which could be a concealed way of conceding that he is the brother of Joseph, who has been renamed Levi, son of Alphaeus, and placed outside the List of Apostles. But as sons of Alphaeus (first letter of the Greek alphabet) James and Levi are assigned a Greek identity, which enables Mark to distance them from any status as brothers of Jesus.

8. **Matthew** remains unchanged.

7. **Nathaniel,** inferred from the Johannine gospel (see Chapter 9), apparently becomes Bartholomew or son of Tholomew.

6. **Judas Thomas,** inferred from Thomas and "Later John" (see Chapters 1 and 9), becomes Thomas, thus concealing his name Judas.

5. **Philip** and 4. **Andrew** remain unchanged.

3. **James** is re-designated as James, son of Zebedee, and elevated to second position next to Peter.

2. **John** is confirmed as brother of James, son of Zebedee, and moved to third position. Both John and James are nicknamed Boanerges, meaning "thunder brothers."

1. **Simon Peter** remains unchanged.

Mark's narrative differs from his sources in giving top billing to a triumvirate of named apostles: Simon Peter, James and John, the sons of Zebedee. These are the main actors during the lifetime of Jesus. It may not be coincidence that when Paul of Tarsus comments on the post-crucifixion leadership, he refers to Peter, James and John as the "reputed pillars" (Galatians 2:9). But the James described by Paul is James, brother of Jesus. According to Acts 12:2, "Herod killed James the brother of John with the sword," some years before Paul began to write his epistles. My inference is that Mark deliberately emphasizes James, the brother of John, in order to ignore James Justus (renamed son of Alphaeus).

And what about the two apostles Matthew and Thomas, part of an insider triumvirate according to the Thomas Sayings Gospel? Thomas 13 states that the three followers invited by Jesus to define his identity were: Simon Peter, Matthew and Thomas. The latter two are the probable scribal authors of the Q1 and Thomas sayings gospels. But for Mark, they are only names on a list; they play no role in his narrative.

And what about the three apostles: Andrew, Philip and Nathaniel? They receive special attention in "Early John," as the first to discover the status of Jesus as traditional Messiah and King of Israel:

Andrew: "We have found the Messiah" (John 1:41).
Philip: "We have found him of whom Moses in the law and also the prophets
   wrote, Jesus of Nazareth, the son of Joseph" (John 1:45).
Nathaniel: "Rabbi . . . You are the King of Israel" (John 1:49).

In Mark's Gospel, these three are only names. Indeed, Mark carefully omits the specific roles of Andrew and Philip in the feeding of the multitude as described by "Early John." He renders Nathaniel nameless by listing him only as Bartholomew, or son of Tholomew.

Within the List of Apostles, brotherly identities are suppressed and changed. In the case of the Zealot-oriented brothers Simon and Judas, one is transformed into the scapegoat villain of the crucifixion of Jesus, while the other is transformed into a quiet Galilean from Cana (previously the role of Nathaniel). The other two brothers, Joseph and James, are transformed into Greek Hellenists (i.e. sons of Alphaeus), and Joseph (with a name change) is removed from the list of twelve apostles.

And Mark locates them explicitly in Galilee, apparently to keep them out of the Jerusalem Passion story.

Assessment of Mark's Gospel

Mark's Gospel was a turning point, a direct result of the collision of Paul's earlier vision with the brutal horrors of the Roman-Jewish War.

Paul envisaged a cosmic struggle between God and Satan that was soon to reach an apocalyptic climax in an "end of days" scenario. He had preached about a divine Saviour, the resurrected Son of God and Lord of Heaven, filled with love and compassion for all human beings, sent by God to rescue the sinful population of the whole world from its own folly.

Mark apparently perceived the War as confirmation of the Pauline interpretation. God's action disproved Thomas' view about the evolution of God's Kingdom through Gnostic connection to the Spirit within. And it demonstrated that God no longer accepted the Temple cult and traditional practices of Mosaic Law. Jesus was not the Davidic Messiah of Israel as portrayed by the author of "Early John." He was the God-Man, simultaneously Son of God and Son of Man, the divine Messiah or Christ.

Jesus had come from God in the form of the Son of Man to explain God's Plan, to suffer, die and be resurrected, and to return again as apocalyptic Son of Man (according to the scriptures) "to gather his elect . . . from the ends of the earth to the ends of heaven" (Mark 13:27). God announced the divine identity of Jesus when he was baptized by John the Baptist. And Jesus brought the new message of salvation through repentance and faith in Jesus Christ. He explained everything during his lifetime, and carried out the will of God, his Father. But the people of Israel and even his chosen disciples were predestined to not understand.

The role of Mark was to bear witness to the true revealing message by "selecting those (doings of the Lord) he thought most useful for increasing the faith."[1] In effect, this involved careful selection, rearrangement, and revision of his written source materials deriving from "Early John," Thomas, and Simon Peter. The historical facts could be adjusted to match the divine secret truth underlying them.

The most important part of the "secret" truth was the imminence of the apocalyptic arrival of the Kingdom of God. And the good news was that God's Son had come to share the sufferings and humiliation of his new "chosen people," to redeem them from sin. The spreading of the message was all that mattered now. Credibility required omission of the Feast of Tabernacles events, especially the insurrection. It also required the transfer of the post-crucifixion stories to the lifetime of Jesus, the transfer of Jerusalem stories to the Passover Feast, and suppression of the roles of Jesus' family members in Jerusalem.

The new story used many elements written by disciples of Jesus, while simultaneously rebutting traditionalist and Gnostic themes. Mark was an excellent storyteller, well grounded in ancient scriptures, with a powerful imagination. The result, perhaps, was like a well-crafted movie—exciting and dramatic—but with a screenplay bearing a somewhat superficial resemblance to the original story.

---

1   In 1958, Professor Morton Smith of Columbia University discovered, in a monastery near Jerusalem, a copy of part of a letter from Bishop Clement of Alexandria (circa 150 C.E.) to a certain Theodore concerning disputes with "Carpocrations" over interpretation of Mark's Gospel. A relevant quotation from this letter reads as follows:

"(As for) Mark, then, during Peter's stay in Rome he wrote (an account of) the Lord's doings; not, however, declaring all (of them), nor yet hinting at the secret (ones), but *selecting those he thought most useful for increasing the faith* of those who were being instructed. But when Peter died as a martyr (circa 62 C.E.), Mark came over to Alexandria, bringing both his own notes and those of Peter, from which he transferred to his former book the things suitable to whatever makes for progress towards knowledge (gnosis). (Thus) he composed a more spiritual gospel for the use of those who were being perfected. Nevertheless, he yet did not divulge the things not to be uttered, nor did he write down the hierophantic teaching of the Lord, but to the stories already written he added yet others and, moreover, brought in certain sayings of which he knew the interpretation would, as a mystagogue, lead the hearers into the innermost sanctuary of that truth hidden by seven (veils). Thus, in sum, *he prearranged matters*, neither grudgingly nor incautiously, in my opinion, and dying, he left his composition to the church in Alexandria, where it even yet is most carefully guarded, being read only to those who are being initiated into the great mysteries" (emphasis added).

See Smith, Morton, *The Secret Gospel, the Discovery and Interpretation of the Secret Gospel According to Mark*, Harper and Row, New York, 1973.

2   This ancient reference to a non-canonical "secret" gospel composed by Mark is regarded by some modern scholars as part of an elaborate hoax. See for example, Akenson, Donald Harman, *Surpassing Wonder, The Invention of the Bible and the Talmuds*, McGill-Queen's University Press, Montreal, 1998, pp. 595-597.

3   For further details on my interpretation of inferred sources for Mark's re-structuring of the story and sayings of Jesus, see APPENDIX 1.

4   In a couple of instances where apparent Q1 sayings in Mark are not found in Thomas, I argue that the saying belongs to Q2 rather than Q1. Some Q2 sayings may be derivative from Mark. For example, Mark's elaborated version of Thomas' instructions for the road (Thomas 14) is duplicated in Q. This seems to imply Q1 as Mark's source, whereas instead it should be assigned to Q2 as derivative from Mark.

CHAPTER 6

THE LOST SAYINGS GOSPEL
OF Q—LAYER 2[1]

We return now to the hypothetical and mysterious lost Gospel of Q, proposed by many scholars as a common source of sayings of Jesus used by both the Gospels of Matthew and Luke (see Chapter 2). The mystery relates to the so-called second layer, Q2, which presents a sharp change of tone and direction from the first layer. Interspersed with optimistic Q1 maxims for living an ideal way of life in God's Kingdom, are darker statements about conflict, sinful behaviour, shortcomings of others, prophetic judgments and apocalyptic pronouncements. And so the reader thinks: Jesus must be talking about the dire fate awaiting immoral outsiders such as Roman oppressors and pagan Greeks. But not so: the mentioned sinners are all Jews, or various groups within Israel that have rejected or failed to understand Jesus' message.

The Contents of Q2[2]

Q2 begins with a dark message of doom from John the Baptist in the role of "fire and brimstone" prophet, a message directed squarely at the people of Israel who are seeking baptism. He berates them as "offspring of vipers," and warns them of the fury of a coming apocalyptic judgment. "Every tree that does not bear fruit is cut down and thrown into the fire" . . . "the wheat will go into the granary, while the chaff will burn in an eternal fire" (Matthew 3:3-12 and Luke 3:7-17).

Then Q2 elaborates Mark's story of Jesus in the wilderness, accompanied by the Holy Spirit, where he overcomes temptations by Satan. Here Jesus is tested as the Son of God, and confirms himself as the receiver of revelation.

Next, Jesus performs as a healer (the first such mention in a sayings gospel), which connects him with Elijah and Isaiah's prediction of healing miracles. "Go and tell John what you hear and see; the blind recover their sight, the lame walk, lepers are cleansed, the deaf hear, the dead are raised, and the poor are given good news. And fortunate is the one who is not disturbed about me." John had asked "Are you he who is to come, or shall we look for another?" There is no indication here that John knew and understood the mission of Jesus. In fact, to emphasize John's lack of understanding, Q2 presents the contrasting story of the Roman centurion's servant and his confidence in Jesus. "Sir, I am not worthy to have you enter my home. Just say the word and my servant will be healed" (Matthew 8 and 11, and Luke 7).

However, Jesus lines himself up with John, in describing both himself and John as "children of wisdom," and attention turns to those who have not responded properly to either of them. "We played the pipes for you and you did not dance. We sang a dirge and you did not wail." "Whoever is not with me is against me, and the one who does not gather with me scatters" (Matthew 11:16-19 and Luke 7:29-35).

Among groups condemned for "not changing their ways" are residents of the Galilean towns of Chorazin, Bethsaida and Capernaum. Very bitter pronouncements are reserved for the Pharisees and scribes who are chastised as hypocrites, oppressors, full of greed, and responsible for murdering prophets. "This generation will be held accountable for the blood of all the prophets shed from the foundation of the world" (Matthew 23:36 and Luke 11:50).

Noticeable is a particular concern about those who have joined the Kingdom, and then lapsed in their resolve. Emphasis is placed on the need for constant vigilance. Jesus is quoted as saying that even when an unclean spirit (demon) leaves a person, the expelled spirit may return with "seven other spirits more wicked than itself, and the last state of that person is worse than the first" (Matthew 12:43-45 and Luke 11:24-26).

Another unexpected feature of Q2 is the emphasis on Mosaic Law. "It is easier for heaven and earth to pass away, than for one dot of the law to become void" (Luke 16:17). "Till heaven and earth pass away, not an iota, not a dot, will pass from law until all is accomplished" (Matthew 5:18).

Q2 denies that Jesus taught through signs. "Some said to him 'Teacher, we wish to see a sign from you.' He answered them 'A wicked generation looks for a sign, but no sign will be shown to it, except the sign of Jonah. For as Jonah became a sign to the Ninevites, so will the Son of Man be to this generation'"

(Matthew 12:38-40 and Luke 11:29-32). So Jesus himself acquires a title and becomes the Sign, which is a radical change from self-endorsement through signs (or actions) in the "Early John" Gospel.

Q2 (as reconstructed by scholars) skips over the crucifixion and resurrection of Jesus, but includes a lament over Jerusalem: "Look your house is left desolate" (Matthew 23:37-39 and Luke 13:34-35). Much is said about the final judgment at the "end of days," when the good "sheep" will be separated from the evil "goats," and when "you who have followed me will sit on thrones, judging the twelve tribes of Israel" (Matthew 19:28 and Luke 22:28-30).

Interpretation of Q2

The essential novelty of Q2 is a new double pairing of Jesus and John the Baptist as "children of wisdom," and as apocalyptic prophets. The Q1 Jesus, of course, is already a Teacher of Wisdom, and he identifies John as a fellow messenger who is "much more than a prophet" (Matthew 11:7-11 and Luke 7:24-28). For the author of Q2, both are rejected by "this generation"; John's "repentance of past sins" is simply the same message as Jesus' "changing of ways." Similarly, according to Q2, for those who reject the Kingdom of God, Jesus shares the prophetic apocalyptic teaching of John about the dire fate that awaits them.

Perhaps the key to understanding Q2 is the references to "violent men" in both Luke and Matthew. Scholars have long been puzzled by the texts. In Luke 16:16 Jesus says: "The law and the prophets were until John; since then the good news of the Kingdom of God is preached, *and every one enters it violently*" (emphasis added). And in Matthew 11:12 Jesus says: "From the days of John the Baptist until now the Kingdom of Heaven has been coming violently, and men of violence are taking it by force." If my interpretation of the "Early John" Gospel is correct, the references here could be to some former followers of John the Baptist who accompanied Jesus to Jerusalem and provoked an insurrection (see Chapter 3). Or alternatively, it could refer to the activities of post-crucifixion followers of Jesus in Jerusalem up to and including the Roman-Jewish War. Note the time period implied by the phrase "from the days of John the Baptist until now."

The parable of the weeds (Thomas 59) is especially important as an expression of Jesus' view that human violence against sinners is wrong, and that the matter should be left in the hands of God. Q2 follows up this hint by identifying Jesus with John the Baptist's apocalyptic idea that God will act in the future to punish sinners.

It is noteworthy that Q2 is the first of the Sayings Gospel collection to mention Jesus' role as healer, thus connecting him with the prophet Elijah, and Isaiah's prediction of healing miracles. Also, Jesus is quoted as condemning the "present generation" for the supposed sins of their ancestors in persecuting and murdering prophets. Clearly, Jesus is being identified with the persecuted prophets of the past and their battle against sin.

It is not much of a stretch to move from Jesus and John as persecuted prophets, to Jesus and John as apocalyptic prophets warning of forthcoming action by God against those who oppose their particular teachings. In this respect, Q2 closely resembles the tone of writings found among the Dead Sea Scrolls. No longer is it the intrinsic beauty and value of the message that counts, but rather the terrible consequences of failure to accept God's offer of his Kingdom. The writing resonates with wholesale condemnations of the children of Abraham, the Pharisees, and the people of certain Galilean cities.

In a way it might be argued that Q2 is simply adding an apocalyptic interpretative framework to Q1 to explain the difference between insiders who accept the Q1 message, and outsiders who reject it. Previously, the Q1 writer had ignored the Gnostic interpretative framework of the Thomas Gospel; Q2 provides a new alternative framework of understanding, focused on what happens to outsiders.

When Was Q2 Written and Who Wrote It?

The sayings of Q2 display many indications of dependence on the Gospel of Mark, despite the relative absence of direct quotes. Examples of echoes of the Markan approach are the parallel images of Jesus and John the Baptist, the presentation of Jesus as a healer, the denial of signs by Jesus, and the rejection of Jesus' message by the "children of Abraham." In some instances, Q2 relates more directly to Mark, such as with the elaboration of Jesus' temptations in the wilderness, and with its apparent knowledge of the Roman-Jewish War (in the Lament over Jerusalem). In general, the narrative structure of Q seems to imply a reading of Mark.

Contrariwise, some scholars contend that Mark was using the combined Q1-Q2 document as a source. If so, Mark managed to ignore Q1, except for the Q1 sayings also contained in Thomas; he also used various sayings from Thomas not in Q1. My conclusion is that Mark was unaware of both Q1 and Q2, and that the author of Q2 was inspired to add additional sayings to Q1 after reading Mark's Gospel.

The evidence is strong that Q2 was written later than Q1, which had been written much earlier by the disciple Matthew. Could Matthew also be the author of Q2? This seems unlikely since this material is dated after the Gospel of Mark, and therefore after the Roman-Jewish War. A more probable hypothesis is that another later writer decided to update the Q1 document to reflect the presumed punishment of the Jewish people by the Romans, authorized by God as a consequence of their failure to "change their ways" and enter the Kingdom of God. Revised Q became available to Luke as a source in constructing Luke's own gospel. Later, the same author of Q2 decided to rewrite Mark's narrative gospel, but this latter document (which became known as the Gospel of Matthew) was never seen by Luke. Such a hypothesis seems the best solution to the Q Gospel problem.

---

1   For the purposes of my hypothesis, I have combined Q2 (apocalyptic layer) and Q3 (later additions) which I believe to be the work of the same author.

2   For a full review of the contents of Q2 and Q3, see Kloppenberg, John, *The Formation of Q: Trajectories in Ancient Wisdom Collections*, Philadelphia, Fortress Press, 1987; and Mack, Burton L., *The Lost Gospel of Q*, Harper, San Francisco, 1993.

CHAPTER 7

THE GOSPEL OF MATTHEW

The canonical Gospel of Matthew was written circa 80-90 C.E., perhaps ten or fifteen years after the Gospel of Mark. Broadly speaking, it enfolds together the Sayings Gospel Q and the Gospel of Mark in a new synthesis, located in a traditional prophetic framework derived from searching Old Testament scriptures.

The presentation of the Q1-based teachings of Jesus reaches new heights of poetic brilliance, expressed especially in the famous Sermon on the Mount. These teachings are resituated in a theological structure of Mosaic Law, thus diverging sharply from the Thomas Gospel's Gnostic framework of understanding. In addition it elaborates the Q2 text, which was probably written earlier by the same author. The Matthewan gospel relies closely on Mark's account for narrative structure and description of events, while expanding the story forward and backward to birth and death. Its aggressive pre-emption of interpretation of Hebrew scriptures becomes increasingly an anti-Jewish polemic with strong apocalyptic overtones.

His Method

Matthew (the anonymous Jewish scribe successor to the disciple Matthew) relied on Mark, but was obviously dissatisfied with the Markan approach. Jesus' humanness was accepted, but God's endorsement did not begin at the time of presumed baptism by John the Baptist. For Matthew, God's action began with Jesus' conception, when the Holy Spirit descended on his mother Mary.

This was not the true beginning, however, because God had spoken previously through prophecies contained in the scriptures. Accordingly, Matthew searched diligently through the ancient scriptures, quoting directly from the Old Testament over 60 times in the course of his gospel. The purpose of his search was to find support for the notion that the scriptures foretold what was to come, and that the story and sayings of Jesus matched these prophecies. In so doing, he finds many quotations to show how various features of the Markan narrative and the Q sayings "fulfil the scriptures." But he goes much farther than this, modifying and reinterpreting his sources, adding new details, and essentially creating new narrative to match his selected ancient texts. In this way, it is ultimately the scriptures that reveal God's Plan to Matthew in contrast to Paul's direct revelation from Jesus Christ.

The Pedigree of Jesus

Mark had already merged the concept of Jesus as Messiah of Israel with the more universalist titles of Son of God and Son of Man. But Matthew feels the need to strengthen this identification with reference to history. Hence, on the one hand there's a traditional messianic lineage going back to Abraham, and on the other hand the "virgin" birth of Jesus (who is conceived through the Holy Spirit), supposedly prophesied in Isaiah 7:14.

Matthew's new birth narrative shows a father Joseph, a birth in Bethlehem, Magi journeying from the East who innocently tell Herod the Great of the birth of the King of the Jews, the family's flight into Egypt before Herod's slaughter of the male babies in Bethlehem, and after Herod's death, the family's return from Egypt to settle in Galilee. Virtually the whole story in all its details contains the possibility of inferences from scripture that create story events. Whether Matthew had any independent access to facts about the birth of Jesus we do not know. One possibility is that Joseph was a "carpenter" who had a major role in building Herod's Temple in Jerusalem, then turned against him and was forced to flee to Egypt, later returning to Galilee after Herod's death.

The Teachings of Jesus

Matthew does a marvellous job of re-assembling and expanding the Q Gospel teachings of Jesus, in poetic format. There is a creative mix of Q sayings and selected scriptural passages to produce a sort of new Torah. In fact, Matthew's structure, which presents the teachings in five separate teaching blocks, matches the five basic books of the Torah in the Old Testament. The teachings themselves, in contrast to both Thomas and Paul, are placed in a context of Mosaic Law: "Think not that I have come to abolish the law and the prophets; I have come not to abolish them but to fulfil them. For truly, I say to you, till heaven and earth pass away, not an iota, not a dot, will pass from the law until all is accomplished"

(Matthew 5:17-18). The moral demands made upon the followers of Jesus have become more exacting, combining as they do Mosaic Law and the radical requirements of Q. The words of Jesus are important, but positive action based on Jesus' words is even more important.

In its aggressive pre-emption of Jewish scriptures, Matthew's Gospel engages in strong polemic against alternative scriptural interpretation, particularly that of the Pharisees, but also against "false insiders." It follows Q2 in taking a strong position against violence by human beings, combined with prophecy of dire consequences for those who fail to "change their ways." The severe apocalyptic tone is unmistakable, and the statement on the "last judgment" moves well beyond both Q2 and Mark. Not only is Jesus now fully identified with the returning Son of Man figure, but he will preside over a horrendous last judgment that will "separate the sheep from the goats." The extraordinarily eloquent and vivid Matthewan prophecy of the last judgment (Matthew 25) is perhaps the most spell-binding and powerful statement ever written about the contrasting everlasting fates of insiders and sinful outsiders.

The Narrative Story

Matthew's Gospel follows the Markan narrative structure very closely, after separating out the Q-based teaching messages of Jesus. There are a number of corrections and improvements of Mark based on the Q perspective, scriptural prophecy, and perceived outsider objections. It is clear that the Matthewan writer, unlike Mark and Luke, had no direct access to the "Early John" text, nor to eyewitness accounts of events. But there are some indications that he may have been dimly aware, from Q or oral transmission, of some aspects of the Markan cover-up.

The Matthewan author is somewhat dubious about Jesus' baptism by John the Baptist, since Q ignores it (see Matthew 3:13-15), but he elaborates with gusto on the temptation by Satan scenario. After Jesus goes down into Galilee "when he heard that John had been arrested" (Matthew 4:12), the Matthew Gospel text repeats Mark's narrative structure with very little change of detail, and with verbatim use of many Markan descriptions of healing and teaching encounters in Galilee. Matthew's text is strongly supportive of the Pauline-type authority of Jesus to forgive sins (e.g. Matthew 9:1-8); on the other hand Matthew's strong emphasis on Mosaic Law places him in opposition to parts of Pauline theology.

In regard to the journey to Jerusalem and the Passion Story, Matthew seems somewhat of an accomplice to Mark in covering up the Feast of Tabernacles insurrection event. For instance, he explicitly adds "women and children" to the feeding of the 5000 event (Matthew 14:21), thus further concealing its "Early

John" Gospel presentation as a gathering of men. Another example of change is the withering of the fig tree in Bethany, which takes place as an instantaneous miracle. And Matthew makes sure that only twelve disciples are explicitly present at the Last Supper. Mark's "young man in a linen cloth" disappears from the scene, and his "young man in a white robe" at the Empty Tomb is replaced by "an angel of the Lord."

In regard to the Passion Story, Matthew's Gospel focuses vividly on the anti-violence position of Jesus. When "one of those who were with Jesus" cut off the ear of the high priest's slave, Jesus said to him "Put your sword back into its place: for all who take the sword will perish by the sword" (Matthew 26:52). In the Barabbas story, Matthew omits Mark's reference that he "had committed murder in the insurrection" (Mark 15:7), and enigmatically supplies the information that his proper name is Jesus, son of the father (Matthew 27:16).

By far Matthew's most notorious change to Mark's text is the infamous line during the trial of Jesus before Pilate, when "All the people answered, 'His blood be on us and on our children'" (Matthew 27:25). With this single devastating phrase, Matthew condemned the entire people of Israel and their descendants to responsibility for killing the divine Son of God. Thus, while castigating human violence, the Matthew Gospel revels simultaneously in the divine punishment and retribution that awaits all unrepentant sinners.

The Appearances

By the time the Gospel of Matthew was written, the resurrection may have become more of a problem. Mark's Gospel had contained a promise from Jesus, given during his lifetime, that he would return in glory as the mythical Son of Man: "Truly, I say to you, this generation will not pass away before all these things take place" (Mark 13:30). Matthew's Gospel repeats this promise (Matthew 24:34). But "this generation" had passed away, and the absence of any new appearance was perhaps leading to scepticism. Mark had described promises, but had failed to present any concrete evidence to support a resurrection; in fact he had suppressed the story of Lazarus, and the six stories of post-crucifixion appearances to disciples of Jesus. Given Mark's description, sceptics could easily suggest that the disciples had stolen the body of Jesus as a basis for fabricating his "rise from the dead."

The Matthew author, being unaware of the five appearances mentioned by Paul (and written up in the inferred "Early John" Gospel) was forced to rely on Mark's text as source. He imagined, first, that the "chief priests and Pharisees" would have sealed the entrance and set up guards at the tomb to prevent the disciples from stealing the body of Jesus. Next he changed Mark's "young man" into an "angel of the Lord" who terrified the guards into paralysis, "rolled back the stone," and delivered the message that Jesus "had risen from the dead" to the women who came to the tomb. But his master stroke was an immediate appearance of the resurrected Jesus to Mary of Magdala and the "other Mary," who "took hold of his feet and worshipped him" (Matthew 28:1-10). Thus, instead of separate visionary appearances to various disciples and followers, here was a single appearance in the flesh (confirmed by touching) to two women, illustrating clearly both the physical resurrection of Jesus, and that "the last shall be first." The follow-up was a visionary appearance to inner-group disciples on a mountain in Galilee which "some doubted" (Matthew 28:17). But the writer of the Matthew Gospel had revolutionized the story.

Matthew's report on the subsequent appearance of Jesus on a mountain, somewhat like the five appearances mentioned by Paul, and reported in the inferred "Early John" Gospel, was explicitly open to doubt. Certainly, Mark had doubted these appearance stories, since he retrojected them back into the lifetime of Jesus. Matthew's Galilean appearance story is perhaps intended as a composite of all of them. But his new story of bodily touching by the two Mary's had changed the whole picture. In the Thomas Gospel, where Mary is shown as a disciple of Jesus, the resurrection is a non-event; now, however, Mary has become a witness of Jesus' bodily resurrection. Mark had not gone this far; he had reported only that the women at the tomb were witnesses to a young man's statement that Jesus had risen, and would see his disciples in Galilee, and "said nothing to anyone for they were afraid" (Mark 16:8). But now the author of the Matthew Gospel has lined up Mary (a Gnostic of the Thomas viewpoint according to the Gospel of Thomas) as a witness of the bodily resurrection of Jesus "on the third day." Moreover, the disciple Matthew himself (the attributed author of this new gospel), becomes a witness by virtue of his supposed authorship.

Disciples, Apostles and Family of Jesus

In regard to disciples, list of apostles and family members of Jesus, the Matthew author makes some corrections to Mark, but in general follows him quite closely. These corrections seem to be logical changes emanating from what the author knew about the Q Gospel, and from his reinterpretation of what Mark was trying to say. There is no hard evidence that the Matthew author derived any information from the "Early John" Gospel or from eyewitnesses.

Two changes in the list of apostles seem to derive from the author's awareness that the Matthew who wrote the Q1 Gospel was a former tax collector. Accordingly, Levi, Son of Alphaeus, who appears in Mark's recruitment story about the tax collector, is replaced by Matthew, and Matthew is re-designated as "Matthew the tax collector" in the apostles list. But in apparent consideration of Mark's description of James and Levi as brothers, Levi is reinserted back into the list of apostles as Lebbaeus by combining the name Levi with the name Thaddaeus, two names invented by Mark.

It is intriguing that the name changes by Matthew are focused on some of Mark's presumed cover-up adjustments to the identities of members of Jesus' earthly family. Thus, the tenth apostle Lebbaeus is a replacement for Thaddaeus, Mark's substitute for Joseph, the brother of Jesus. At the same time, Matthew's Gospel finds a replacement for Mark's other version of the same brother of Jesus (i.e. Joses). Matthew's Gospel states that this brother is named Joseph, and that the brother of James the Lesser, named Joses by Mark, is also named Joseph. Mark's apparently fictitious name Joses for a brother of Jesus seems suspiciously close to the name Jesus, which Matthew's Gospel asserts was in fact the proper name of the prisoner Barabbas in the Passion Story. Is it possible that Mark might have transferred the name Jesus from Barabbas (son of the father) to the fourth brother of Jesus and changed his name to Joses? In the Markan text, the absence of the name Jesus attached to Barabbas is matched by the absence of the name Joseph for a brother of Jesus, and for the father of Jesus. All this seems to imply that Mark felt compelled to conceal any evidence that Jesus had a son or an earthly father, since his gospel had defined Jesus explicitly as the Son of God. For the Matthew writer, on the other hand, his new mythological birth story had defined a role for an earthly father named Joseph, who could logically have a son named Joseph.

The Matthew Gospel repeats the Markan denigration of Jesus' family, and the cover-up of his brothers and sisters' participation in his mission. It goes further than Mark in enhancing the role of authority of Simon Peter in the famous "keys of the Kingdom" prophecy (Matthew 16:15-20).

Assessment

The Matthewan gospel takes a long step forward in consolidating the contradictions of the "sapiential" understanding of Jesus expressed in the Sayings Gospels of Thomas and Q, and the more apocalyptic interpretation emanating via Mark from Paul of Tarsus. He connects Jesus as Teacher of Wisdom with John the Baptist, the traditional prophets of Israel, ancient scriptural writings, and fulfilment of God's Plan.

The absence of any Gnostic interpretive framework in the Matthewan gospel may be a consequence of the omission of it in the Q1 Sayings Gospel by the original Matthew. This opens the door to an alternative framework located in ancient prophecy and scripture that could account for the failure of the Jewish people to embrace the new version of the Kingdom of God proposed by Jesus.

Among its contradictions the Matthew Gospel accepts the Markan version of the New Covenant preached by Paul, but also insists on continuation of the old

Mosaic covenant between God and his people. It presents a beautiful idealized version of the teachings of Jesus, while simultaneously associating him with John the Baptist's apocalyptic preaching, and turning him into a divine judge administering punishment to all unrepentant sinners after the second coming of Christ.

Many of the changes from Mark serve to strengthen the distinction between Kingdom of God insiders and everyone else. Peter's authority is strengthened; the blame of the Jewish people is sharpened; dramatic elements are enhanced; Judas Iscariot kills himself.

The teaching of Jesus is presented as a fulfilment of the Law of Moses, rather than a replacement of it. The augmented anti-Semitic tone may reflect the expulsion of Jewish Christians from Diaspora synagogues in 85 C.E., the culmination of the controversies initiated by Paul.

The Matthewan gospel reaches backwards. It goes back to the "pure" teachings of Jesus in the Q1 Gospel. It goes back to the birth of Jesus for the appearance of the Holy Spirit. It goes back to Old Testament scriptures, prophecies and Mosaic Law. Here it differs radically from Paul of Tarsus. But at the same time it goes forward with Paul. It rejects violence by human beings. It accepts the mission to the Gentiles. It looks forward to the second coming of Jesus. And it prophesies future apocalyptic doom and the last judgment.

CHAPTER 8

THE GOSPEL OF LUKE

The Gospel of Luke parallels the Gospel of Matthew as an innovative synthesis of the Markan and Q gospels, but incorporates a broader range of sources, the most significant of which (according to my hypothesis) is the Gospel of "Early John." Additionally, Luke seems to have had access to some Essene writings, some direct exposure to the ideas of Paul of Tarsus, and perhaps a special Lukan source (beyond his own wide-ranging imagination) that could be a more extensive Q document than that which is recognized by most scholars.

In contrast with Matthew, Luke was a Gentile writing for a Gentile audience. Like Mark he seems weak on the geography of Palestine, but nevertheless demonstrates a quite extraordinary understanding of Jewish traditions. His purpose is to present a unified story in two parts: the life and death of Jesus, and the growth of the Church of the Risen Christ. He writes like an historian, even though he participates with Mark in the cover-up of some events recorded by "Early John," and is at times contradictory and inaccurate. He professes good intentions, however, that "you may know the truth concerning the things of which you have been informed" (Luke 1:1-4). He is writing "an orderly account—a story of salvation," of how the Holy Spirit came into human history definitively through Jesus, and then passed from the Risen Christ to the largely Gentile Church.[1]

Writing some 50 to 60 years after the death of Jesus, and 15 to 20 years after the Roman-Jewish War, Luke is responding to some of the same imperatives as Mark and Matthew. The fundamental need is to disassociate the struggling Christian Church from any connection with the Jewish rebellion against Rome. Fortunately, Paul's theology and Mark's revised narrative provide a framework, while Q offers a richly textured link with the historical Jesus. Luke's task is to bring it all together, with an expanded mythology and birth narrative, liberal interpretation of what Jesus would have said and done to fill in gaps in source material, and imaginative reconstruction to deal with latter-day objections.

The Nativity Story

Luke is a superb storyteller: more relaxed than Mark (who hurries), and less angry than Matthew.

His birth narrative responds to the same imperative as the Matthew Gospel story—the messianic need to move the action of the Holy Spirit backwards from John's presumed baptism of Jesus (as in Mark), to Jesus' conception. The procreation of the Son of God requires a divine myth appropriate to his role in God's Plan, as envisaged by Paul and transmitted by Mark. Luke matches the Matthewan response of conception by the Holy Spirit, birth to a virgin named Mary, and putative fatherhood to a man called Joseph. Both scenarios include the places of Nazareth in Galilee and Bethlehem in Judea; and both take place when King Herod the Great ruled Israel. Otherwise, Luke's story is completely different.

Features of the Lukan story include kinship with the priestly family of John the Baptist, highly poetic messianic prophecy, ordinary human parents, a Roman census compelling birth under humble circumstances in Bethlehem instead of Nazareth, and pious links to the Jerusalem Temple as Jesus grows up. Also, Luke provides Jesus with a traditional messianic lineage going all the way back to Adam, the first man (Matthew's Gospel only goes back as far as Abraham), a more appropriate beginning for a Gentile audience. Although Luke provides some "accoutrements" of historical accuracy, this fails with the Roman census "when Quirinius was governor of Syria"(Luke 2:2). Historically, the census occurred in 6 C.E., and could not have occurred "In the days of Herod, King of Judea" (Luke 1:5), since he died in 4 B.C.E.

The joyously traditional John the Baptist birth poetry (which may have included "the Magnificat" borrowed for Mary, the mother of Jesus) suggests that Luke had special access to Essene-like Baptist writings, which he linked with his own imagined story about Mary and Jesus. While his sources convinced him that Jesus came from Nazareth, scriptural prophecy mandated his birth in Bethlehem, and his Markan-inspired connection to all struggling humans required a very humble birth.

Teachings and Images of Jesus

Luke stands at a distance in time and space from the traumatic events and disputes associated with the story of Jesus and Israel. As a researcher using many sources he is drawn above all to the Q1 words and sayings of Jesus, and apparently even to the Thomas Gospel source. For Luke goes beyond Q and Mark, back to the central message from Thomas' gospel that the Kingdom of God is timeless, spiritual, always present and already here.

> "He answered them, 'The Kingdom of God is not coming with signs
> to be observed; nor will they say 'Lo, here it is!' or 'There!' for behold,
> the Kingdom of God is in the midst of you'" (Luke 17:20-21).

Luke is virtually in love with the Q1 sayings of Jesus. He has Jesus expounding them in all their beauty and uniqueness, and he adds much more. The parables of the Good Samaritan and the Prodigal Son are examples of extraordinary stories found only in the Gospel of Luke, and nowhere else. Whether they were actually in the Q source, or composed directly by Luke is a moot question. They are not to be found in the Matthew Gospel. But in terms of authenticity, they capture the very special qualities of the many parables emanating directly from Jesus. Luke's perception of Jesus as being especially close to the sick, the despised, and the powerless people of this world seems to spur his own creative idealization of his sayings and parables.

When it comes to the harsher Q2 sayings of Jesus, Luke tends to soften their impact as compared to Matthew, although he remains very hard on the wealthy and powerful. Jesus remains a traditionally pious Jew, but the focus is on openness to everyone, including his various opponents, and, of course, Gentiles. Luke fully endorses the personhood of Jesus as Son of God (as with Paul and Mark), and the apocalyptic scenario of John the Baptist (Q2) which leaves violence up to God. But he seems to envisage a future Kingdom of God on earth, in this case apparently choosing from both Thomas and "Early John" rather than Paul and Mark.

Separated as he is from the internecine quarrels of the Jews, Luke seems to reach out to an idealized Jesus reflected in the Q1 Sayings Gospel. He also follows Mark quite closely in the settings for other teachings of Jesus that are derived mainly from Thomas' Gospel.

Narrative Events

In dealing with the storyline, we need to realize that Luke had access to both the Gospel of Mark and the Gospel of "Early John," as indicated by frequent use of details that imply an "Early John" source. This means that Luke was aware of the major changes made by Mark, and accepted them—Jesus had to be disassociated from Jewish rebellion against Rome. He therefore followed Mark's narrative approach, while making changes, additions and deletions here and there, some of which derived from information in "Early John." The evidence for this is simultaneously further evidence for the "Early John" hypothesis.

Beginning with the mission of John the Baptist, Luke notes that he began preaching "in the high-priesthood of Annas and Caiphas" (Luke 3:2); the Johannine gospel is the only other written source that mentions Annas (John 18:13). Luke also deals explicitly with the issue of whether John is the Messiah, touched upon by "Early John," but ignored by Mark (Luke 3:15).

A special aspect of Luke is that he presents Jesus as a scribal literate man reading ancient scriptures when he visits Nazareth (Luke 4:16-20), in contrast to the other canonical gospels. Luke's scene about Jesus at the age of twelve learning from teachers at the Jerusalem Temple (Luke 2:41-52), supports this interpretation. Although these stories sound suspiciously fictitious, they could reflect lost indications in the "Early John" Gospel that Jesus was an educated literate person. Special efforts by "Later John" to deny Jesus' literacy as evidence of his divinity (e.g. John 7:15-18), may indicate that "Later John" suppressed any indications to the contrary in his "Early John" source.

Luke accepts Mark's retrojection to the lifetime of Jesus of various post-crucifixion appearances, sourced from the inferred "Early John" Gospel, this being confirmed by the changes Luke made to Mark's versions, using an alternative source that had placed the events in a post-crucifixion context.

In the "transfiguration" story for example, Luke adds the following information: Peter and his companions were asleep on the mountain, they awoke and saw the transfigured Jesus with Moses and Elijah, Peter spoke to Jesus ("not knowing what he said") and a cloud overshadowed them. This version is consistent with the possibility of a "waking vision" and confused speech by Peter, lack of corroboration by his companions and derivation from "Early John."

In the "recruitment of disciples" story, Luke makes changes to Mark that provide clues to derivation from an "Early John" account of a post-crucifixion appearance to seven disciples fishing in the Sea of Galilee. Luke's version (Luke 5:1-12) matches the Johannine gospel post-crucifixion story (John 21:1-8) by describing a miraculous haul of fish, and including James and John, and "all who were with him (Simon Peter)" in the incident. The most telling clue, however, comes when Peter falls on his knees saying "Depart from me for I am a sinful man, O Lord," probably referring to his "denial" of Jesus after his arrest in Jerusalem. This statement fits a post-crucifixion scenario, rather than an event in the lifetime of Jesus as reported by Luke.

The second "feeding of the multitude" story in Mark (my inferred appearance to 500 brethren from Paul's epistle), is conspicuous by its absence in Luke. His decision to exclude it may have reflected a feeling that it didn't make much sense to locate this second feeding story during the lifetime of Jesus.

In regard to the two other post-crucifixion appearances (to James, and to "all the apostles"), Luke includes Mark's replacement material retrojected to the lifetime of Jesus, while simultaneously going back to the "Early John" source to develop his own idiosyncratic understanding of what actually happened after the death of Jesus (as we shall see in the next section).

In the first feeding of the multitude story during the lifetime of Jesus, Luke sticks mainly with Mark, but for the journey to Jerusalem, he uses some items from another source that could be "Early John" (suppressed by "Later John"). In Galilee, "some Pharisees came and said to him, 'Get away from here for Herod wants to kill you'" (Luke 13:31). And when going to Jerusalem he travels through Samaria (Luke 17:11) as in the Johannine gospel.

Next we come to the insurrection at the Feast of Tabernacles, concealed by Mark, but described in the inferred "Early John" text. While Luke follows Mark's suppression of this event, he seems unable to avoid using it as a morality tale against violence.

"There were some present at that very time who told him of the Galileans whose blood Pilate had mingled with their sacrifices. And he answered them, 'Do you think that these Galileans were worse sinners then all the other Galileans because they suffered thus? I tell you, no; but unless you repent you will likewise perish'" (Luke 13:1-3).

This is very revealing: in the context of the later Roman-Jewish War, Luke's Jesus is indicating that the insurrectionists should not be demonized as worse sinners than others who did not revolt. Luke has read "Early John," and perceives Jesus' sympathy with the Zealot rebels, even while agreeing with Mark in his suppression of Jesus' relationship with them.

Further evidence of Luke's access to "Early John" comes from the Lazarus story, which Luke draws upon to compose his own special stories, while following canonical Mark in suppressing the "Early John" account. Luke's unique "widow of Nain" story (Luke 7:11-16), concerns the physical resurrection by Jesus of a young dead man, bearing resemblances to the Lazarus story. Similarly, Luke's unique story about "Mary and Martha" (Luke 10:38-41)—which focuses on Mary's merit as an attentive disciple of Jesus (as in the Thomas Gospel)—reflects the characters of the two sisters presented by "Early John" in two anecdotes (John 11:19-32 and John 12:2-3). Next, Luke's parable of "the rich man and Lazarus" refers to a dead Lazarus who is comforted "in Abraham's bosom," while a dead rich man who had lived "sumptuously" suffers endless torments. When the rich man proposes resurrection of Lazarus to warn his family to change their ways, Abraham says "If they do not hear Moses and the prophets, neither will they be convinced if some one should rise from the dead" (Luke 16:19-31). This is the only parable throughout the canonical gospels in which Jesus names a protagonist; it is obviously composed by Luke, harking back to an "Early John" version of the Lazarus story. And finally, as he did with the second feeding of the multitude story, Luke omits the supper at Bethany story described in Mark, perhaps from concern about the credibility of Mark's separation of this story from the rest of the Last Supper account. But in moving elements of the Markan story to a meal in Galilee with Pharisees, Luke inadvertently uses some "Early John" elements, implying full knowledge of that story; he refers to a sinner who anoints Jesus' feet with ointment and wipes them with her hair as in "Early John," but not in Mark.

Various other changes by Luke seem connected to the "Early John" text. For example, Luke omits the Markan story of the withering of the fig tree, which symbolizes destruction of the Temple (Mark 11:12-14 and 20-24), and omits Mark's charge by a false witness that Jesus planned to destroy the Temple; neither of these are confirmed in "Early John." Also, Luke's statement by Jesus "I am among you as one who serves" (Luke 22:27) is placed in the Johannine context of the Last Supper rather than Mark's context of being on the road up to Jerusalem. Similarly, Luke follows the Johannine version of Jesus predicting Peter's later denial at the Last Supper (Luke 22:33-34) rather than Mark's setting of the Mount of Olives for this story; the absence of any similar prediction by Jesus for Judas Iscariot in Luke, supports the view that this was not in "Early John" but was added by "Later John." And finally, Luke reports the cutting off of the *right* ear of the slave of the High Priest (Luke 22:50) as mentioned in "Early John" but not in Mark.

Luke adds an extra day to the trial and crucifixion of Jesus, in contradiction to both Mark and the Johannine gospel. Although the extra day is not explicit, it is the only way to account for all the events that Luke includes: a trial by the Sanhedrin in the morning, an appearance before Pontius Pilate, referral of the matter to King Herod, return of Jesus to Pontius Pilate, condemnation and crucifixion, and death of Jesus at noon hour. Mark's version of the trial focuses on false witnesses, abuse of Jesus by the High Priest, and condemnation for blasphemy. Luke tones this down, and emphasizes accusations before Pilate that sound highly consistent with the "Early John" approach: Jesus stirs up the people throughout *all Judea*, perverts the nation, forbids tribute to Caesar, and says he is the Messiah King (Luke 23:2-5).

In regard to the story of Barabbas, Luke enlarges on Mark by describing him as "a man who had been thrown into prison for an insurrection started in the city, and for murder" (Luke 23:18). Since Mark had not specified the location of the insurrection, Luke's modification implies an alternative source (i.e. "Early John").

All the above examples are additional evidence for my hypothesis of a narrative account by "Early John" that was significantly altered by both Mark and "Later John." Luke followed Mark's major changes to "Early John," but frequently used "Early John" in his own modifications and improvements to what Mark had written. The most important of all Luke's changes to Mark and "Early John" relate to the resurrection of Jesus.

The Resurrection of Jesus

Luke must have been deeply dissatisfied with accounts in both Mark and "Early John" of what happened after the death of Jesus. He therefore resolved to write two histories: the life of Jesus beginning in Nazareth and ending in Jerusalem, and the Acts of the Apostles beginning in Jerusalem and ending in Rome. Following the Pauline interpretation, the key point of the story would be the unique resurrection of Jesus, and its meaning for all humankind.

Scouring his sources, Luke searched for a means of reconciling Paul's resurrected Christ with "Early John's" appearance stories, the words of Jesus, and Mark's retrojection of these messages and events to the lifetime of Jesus.

According to Mark, Jesus had promised his disciples that "after I am raised up, I will go before you to Galilee" (Mark 14:28), and this was confirmed by the young man in the Empty Tomb "there you will see him, as he told you" (Mark 16:7). "Early John's" gospel had described three visionary experiences to disciples in Galilee: to Peter, to seven disciples, and to 500 brethren. But Mark had retrojected these stories to the lifetime of Jesus, apparently not accepting their credibility as resurrection events. Mark believed that Jesus would return in the near future as the Son of Man, presumably in Galilee as he had promised.

Luke agreed with Mark that the three post-crucifixion appearance events in Galilee actually occurred during the lifetime of Jesus, but denied that Jesus had promised to see his disciples in Galilee after his resurrection. The key point for Luke was that the bodily resurrection of Jesus took place "on the third day" after his death "according to the scriptures." The historical manifestation of the physical resurrection of Jesus could only be related to events in Judea—not Galilee. As Paul had written: "If there is no resurrection of the dead our teaching is in vain" (1 Corinthians 15:13-14). The Empty Tomb story was meaningless without concrete confirmation that Jesus had risen "on the third day" and appeared to his disciples, before ascending to God. Accordingly, Luke retrojected the fourth and fifth "Early John" appearances of Jesus in Judea (to James and all the apostles) to the actual day of Jesus' resurrection in Jerusalem, rather than some time after the first three appearances.

The first task was to reconcile "Early John's" Empty Tomb story with the version written by Mark. Luke proposed an early morning visit to the tomb by an unnumbered company of women, which included among others Mary of Magdala, Mary, the mother of James, and another woman, Joanna. They see a rolled-away stone and no body (as in "Early John"), and two men in shining garments (instead of one as in Mark). The extra women and the extra man seem to be there as witnesses. Instead of being terrified and telling no one of the message that Jesus has risen (as in Mark), the women report to the disciples (as in "Early John"). The disciples do not believe them (perhaps from "Early John").

Peter runs to the tomb (as in "Early John"), but without mention of the "other disciple." Peter stoops, looks in, sees the linen cloths with no body, wonders what happened, and returns home (as in "Early John").

Luke's second task was to record the private appearance to James (as mentioned by Paul and presumably by "Early John"), in a revised scenario consistent with Mark's suppression both of the role of James, and of the Galilean appearances. It had to happen "on the third day" instead of some time after three appearances of Jesus in Galilee. In this version, an unnamed other disciple (as in "Early John"), instead of accompanying Peter to the tomb, is walking to Emmaeus with a named disciple Cleopas. They encounter a stranger who discusses scripture and the events of the day, and eats with them at their invitation; as the stranger vanishes (despite not having looked or sounded like Jesus), one or both of them "recognize" him (reminiscent of the "other disciple" who first recognized the resurrection of Jesus when he entered the Empty Tomb in the "Early John" version). The oddest part of the story is that when these two return to Jerusalem, according to the Revised Standard Version of the Bible, the other disciples say "The Lord has risen indeed, and has appeared to Simon," which seems to contradict both "Early John's" Empty Tomb story, and Luke's own Empty Tomb story. Other translators have rectified this by attributing this statement to the two Emmaeus disciples (addressing the other assembled disciples). This therefore identifies the other Emmaeus disciple as Simon. In this way, Luke manages to reverse "Early John" by making Simon rather than James the first to experience the reality of the resurrected Jesus in bodily form, with another person Cleopas as witness. In view of the way the story is structured, with Peter apparently at the Tomb instead of at Emmaeus, it seems that Luke may originally have named James as the Emmaeus disciple rather than Simon (in accordance with his "Early John" source), followed by a change to Simon in order to keep James out of it. Here we have real signs of confusion. Could this be Simon the Zealot? Or does it refer to Simon Peter as the first disciple to see the risen Jesus, as reported also by Paul in his first letter to the Corinthians?

And then, suddenly, in Luke's third scenario (Paul's appearance of Jesus to all the apostles) doubt and confusion fall away as Jesus stands among the assembled apostles. Gone are the confusion of the frightened women, the confusion about the appearances in Galilee, the confusion between "Early John" and Mark, even the confusion of the translators about who is who. In the timeless realm of the Kingdom of God, Luke returns the scene to Jerusalem and produces a retrojected resurrected Jesus in the flesh. Yet at first, the apostles still "supposed that they saw a spirit" (Luke 24:37), but Jesus quickly proves his physical presence by eating "a piece of broiled fish" (Luke 24:42-43). And after delivering his messages Jesus walks out to Bethany with them "and was carried up into heaven" (Luke 24:51). The Gospel of Luke ends with the rejoicing apostles, in parallel to the rejoicing shepherds at the beginning of Jesus' story.

The subsequent Acts of the Apostles carries forward Luke's understanding of how the apostles took up the challenge to bring the new Christian message to the Gentile world. In setting the stage, Luke's "orderly account" (Luke 1:3) completes the division of "Early John's" fifth appearance story (to all the apostles) into two separate parts.

Jesus had taught (according to inferences from the Gospel of Thomas) that the Kingdom of God equated with the ongoing presence of the Holy Spirit. When, however, Jesus began "to baptize with the Spirit," he was perceived by some disciples as possessing and bestowing the Holy Spirit. As he manifested the presence on Earth of the Spirit through signs, Jesus' own personhood could be identified with the Spirit. Consequently, when the physical Jesus died, his physical and spiritual personhood, together with the Holy Spirit, returned to God.

As implied by Paul (see Chapter 4), and presumably also by "Early John," the appearances by Jesus to his disciples were in spiritual form (excepting the Emmaeus event), reflected in the Lukan account of a Jesus who could walk through walls, disappear suddenly, and rise up spontaneously to Heaven. But Luke's sources also implied that the ongoing spiritual Jesus could occupy a physical body when visiting Earth, either his own or another. Indeed, how else could Jesus be distinguished from the Holy Spirit, except by some element of physical identity? So for Luke, the valid appearances had to be manifested by a physically resurrected Jesus, accompanied by his spiritual self, but not accompanied by the Holy Spirit. Using Mark's concept of the Holy Spirit as a separate entity descending on Jesus at the commencement of his mission, Luke could envisage a separation of the resurrected Jesus from the Holy Spirit, and separate ascents and descents from Heaven. The physically resurrected Jesus could visit his followers for initial explanations and instructions, and later the Holy Spirit could descend on them as an ongoing support until the eventual return of the resurrected Jesus for the establishment of the Kingdom of God on earth.

In the Acts of the Apostles, Luke outlined the grand drama. Just as Jesus had spent 40 days in the wilderness testing and preparing for his mission on earth, so the apostles spent 40 days with the resurrected Jesus before beginning their mission (a revision of the preceding ending of Luke's Gospel). Then came the descent of the Holy Spirit at Pentecost with tongues of fire, and the apostles speaking in tongues, as a reversal of the Old Testament Tower of Babel story.

Disciples, Apostles and Family of Jesus

In writing about the disciples and apostles of Jesus, Luke followed the Markan story where Jesus selects twelve apostles in Galilee during his lifetime (Luke 6:12-16). Luke embellishes the story with a reference to seventy other apostles (Luke 10:1) not mentioned by Mark. Accompanying the selection of the twelve is a list of twelve names, based primarily on Mark, but with a few differences derived apparently from an alternative source.

Unlike Mark, Luke also describes an immediate post-crucifixion appearance in Jerusalem to "the eleven and all who were with them" (Luke 24:33), where Jesus re-commissions them to preach "in his name to all nations, beginning from Jerusalem" (Luke 24:47). In his introduction to the Acts of the Apostles, Luke extends the period of instruction by the resurrected Jesus to forty days, and provides a second list of eleven apostles, which of course excludes Judas Iscariot. While this second list includes the same eleven individuals as the first list, there are differences in presentation that suggest that Luke was using an alternative source.

Writing explicitly for the Gentile community, Luke was probably under even greater pressure than the other synoptic scribes to conceal any association of Jesus with the anti-Roman rebellious Jewish Zealots, particularly since Luke was writing a history of the early days of the Acts of the Apostles preceding the Roman-Jewish War. In writing the Acts, Luke felt compelled to avoid all references to the War, the events leading up to it, and anything that would associate the Palestine Christian community with anti-Roman activities. One aspect of this was to suppress any mention that James, leader of the community, was the brother of Jesus. Luke follows through on this in his gospel by deleting the names of Jesus' brothers as listed by Mark (Mark 6:3); the brothers are both unnumbered and unnamed by Luke (Luke 8:19).

Luke's exclusion of the specific names of Jesus' brothers made it easier for him to disguise their presence among the apostles. He knew, however, from his research for the Acts of the Apostles that James had become leader and that Judas, his brother, was active (letters attributed to James and his brother Judas are part of the New Testament canon). But nowhere does Luke mention that James is the brother of Jesus. Instead, he follows Mark in listing him as James, the son of Alphaeus. Luke then removes Mark's reference to Levi as another son of Alphaeus, while continuing Levi's role as tax collector and disciple of Jesus. Instead of Levi, another Judas is added as a brother of James. He enters the charmed circle of the twelve apostles, even though he is already there in the form of Judas Iscariot, according to Mark, and in the form of Judas, of Simon Iscariot according to "Early John." To make way for Judas, of James, Luke is forced to rid himself of Mark's fictitious Thaddeaus, a replacement by Mark for Joseph, of James (see Chapter 5). In effect, Luke has replaced Joseph, of James (i.e. Thaddeaus) by Judas, of James. As well, Luke apparently noted that Mark replaced Simon Iscariot (from his "Early John" source) by a fictitious Simon the Cananaean (of Cana); by substituting the less pejorative Simon the Zealot for Simon Iscariot (which means Zealot Assassin), Luke weakens the connection with Judas Iscariot, distances Simon's name to the tenth position, and gets rid of the fictitious Simon of Cana.

List of Apostles

Mark's List (Mark 3:16-19)	Luke's First List (Luke 6:14-17)
1) Simon whom he called Peter	1) Simon whom he called Peter
2) James, the son of Zebedee	2) Andrew, brother of Peter
3) John, the brother of James	3) James
4) Andrew	4) John
5) Philip	5) Philip
6) Bartholomew	6) Bartholomew
7) Matthew	7) Matthew
8) Thomas	8) Thomas
9) James, the son of Alphaeus	9) James, the son of Alphaeus
10) Thaddaeus	10) Simon, the Zealot
11) Simon, the Cananaean (of Cana)	11) Judas, of James
12) Judas Iscariot	12) Judas Iscariot
Inferred "Early John" List	**Luke's Second List (Acts 1:13)**
1) Simon Peter	1) Peter
2) John	2) John
3) James	3) James
4) Andrew	4) Andrew
5) Philip	5) Philip
6) Judas Thomas	6) Thomas
7) Nathaniel	7) Bartholomew
8) Matthew	8) Matthew
9) James Justus (the Just)	9) James the son of Alphaeus
10) Joseph, of James Justus	10) Simon the Zealot
11) Simon Iscariot	11) Judas, of James
12) Judas, of Simon Iscariot	

Assessment

Somehow, working at considerable distance in time from the actual events, Luke acquired a fuller range of source documents than any other gospel writer. These included Thomas, Q1 and Q2, "Early John," Mark and other unknown writings. The only missing source for Luke was the Gospel of Matthew. The common narrative framework for both Matthew and Luke came from Mark. Whereas Matthew sticks closely to Mark, intensifying the darker apocalyptic elements of his story, Luke does not hesitate to modify and soften Mark's approach in order to bring out Luke's own gentler version. Luke is a consummate storyteller and poet.

The writings of Luke come as a kind of surprise confirmation of the reality of the Gospel of "Early John." Many of the modifications that Luke makes to Mark's account can be perceived as adjustments in light of information from "Early John." Thus, Luke is aware of the insurrection story in "Early John," but is even more determined than Mark to suppress any impression that Jesus was connected with anti-Roman activities.

Along with the author of Matthew (although apparently unaware of his gospel), Luke was concerned about the gaps in Mark's story of Jesus; particularly his origins and birth, and his destiny after death. Moreover, Luke wanted to write about the spread of the Kingdom of God after the death of Jesus, and was faced with the problem of bridging the transition from Mark's Galilean tradition to the Judean tradition centred in Jerusalem. The upshot was a new approach to the resurrection story and appearances by Jesus to his disciples. Luke ensures that the complete bodily resurrection of Jesus in Jerusalem is confirmed by many witnesses on the third day after his death. This supersedes the various earlier understandings of the spiritual resurrection of Jesus after death.

Luke follows a familiar path. In utilizing his sources, he selects and amends the stories to refute earlier interpretations. In particular, he melds together the concepts of physical and spiritual resurrection, and manages to combine the notion of an ongoing spiritual Kingdom in this world with continuing expectations of a future apocalypse to end it.

---

[1]   See Frederickson, Paula, *From Jesus to Christ*, p. 27, Yale University Press, 1988.

CHAPTER 9

THE GOSPEL OF "LATER JOHN"

The Gospel of John, the last of the four narrative canonical gospels, was written circa 100 C.E. It encompasses substantial embedded material from another earlier text, which I have designated as "Early John" (see Chapter 3). I refer to the later material as the Gospel of "Later John." Appendix 2 provides an analysis of the Gospel of John by chapter and verse.

The purpose of "Later John" was to "bear witness" and proclaim that Jesus is the divine Redeemer descended from Heaven—God made flesh—co-existent with God from the Beginning of creation. Here is the culmination of a divinization process that evolved from Jesus' own teaching of spiritual survival after death, combined with his followers' focus on his personhood. Mark situated his divinization during the lifetime of Jesus. Matthew and Luke had it begin at the time of his conception as a human being. "Later John" went back to the creation of the world.

In so doing "Later John" transforms the teachings of Jesus, which had been presented by the Thomas Gospel as explanations of the "real" meaning of the divine realm of light. For "Later John" the words of Jesus become the Word, which equates with God and with Jesus himself who is "the Word made flesh." "Later John" then proceeds to imagine what Jesus would have said in this context, and uses the historical setting written by "Early John" as the narrative framework for his version of the words of Jesus. Not only did this master stroke provide us with the extraordinary ideas of "Later John" concerning Jesus, it also preserved "Early John's" written materials that throw much light on the actual events and motivation of Jesus (see Part II).

Hence also the famous "double context" of the Johannine gospel. The "true" context is the divine realm of the light beyond, whence Jesus came; but this is accompanied by the historical setting of this world where people are blinded to "real" meanings.[1] This Gnostic comprehension of "Later John" parallels that of the teachings of Jesus in the Thomas Gospel.

In creating his poetic masterpiece, "Later John" brought about his own idiosyncratic resolution of the conflicts between the original Gnostic teachings of Jesus, the traditional messianic message of "Early John," and the Pauline interpretation embodied in the three synoptic gospels. Paul had focused on the need for total commitment and belief in Jesus Christ, which for "Later John" simply meant belief that access to God the Father is exclusively through Jesus the Son.

Both Paul and "Later John" show strong evidence that they depended on Gnostic sources for their ideas about the divine context of Jesus' life and death. A basic difference was that Paul was a crusading missionary; he received his beliefs through "revelation," and did not hesitate to propagate their implications for a "way of life" for his converts. His Kingdom of God was a "new Israel" composed mainly of Gentiles. "Later John" seems to have been closer to his Gnostic sources and more oriented to the Gnostic structure of reality, while less interested in behavioural and lifestyle implications on this earth. Paradoxically, Paul simply ignored the life of Jesus on earth, receiving his inspiration from the risen Jesus Christ, while "Later John" ignored the Gnostic lifestyle teachings of Jesus in favour of re-inventing a Jesus on earth who focused on explaining his own personhood. "Later John" describes a totally divine Redeemer who descends to Earth—God made flesh—to empower all "who believe in Him" to become children of God.

Like the synoptic gospel writers, "Later John" was writing for an audience outside Israel, but by now it consisted mainly of Hellenized Gentiles (evidenced by his frequent explanations of Jewish practices for non-Jewish readers). There is no evidence of direct textual dependence on the Gnostic Thomas Gospel, or the Epistles of Paul. Moreover, there is nothing in it from Q, Matthew or Luke. If the author had access to these texts, he almost totally ignored them. His narrative framework is borrowed from "Early John," which in turn accounts for significant similarities between Mark and the Johannine gospel, since both were using a common source. This source encompasses a "Judean" tradition, as opposed to the "Galilean" tradition contained in the three synoptic gospels.

The Narrative Framework

It is important to comprehend that "Later John's" special vision meant that "facts" about Jesus reported by other writers were relatively unimportant. Since all that really mattered was the revealed truth, it was perfectly acceptable to amend or ignore previous written materials in order to fit John's idealized portrait of a divine God-Man.

Unlike Mark and Luke, "Later John" used "Early John" as his basic framework to express his own vision. Mark fitted bits and pieces of "Early John" into his own radical restructuring of the story of Jesus. Luke used "Early John" information as an occasional alternative source.

As argued in Chapter 3, "Later John's" objectives necessitated that he make major structural changes to the narrative of his source text.

One purpose (as in Mark) was to separate Jesus from his apparent connections with Jewish rebels against Rome. In suppressing "Early John's" insurrection story, Mark had chosen to move the "entry into Jerusalem" and "the cleansing of the Temple" from the Feast of Tabernacles to the later Passover Feast. "Later John" did it differently by moving the entry into Jerusalem to the later Passover Feast, while moving the cleansing of the Temple to an earlier Passover Feast. This latter change facilitated a *second purpose*, which was to enlarge and refocus the signs performed by Jesus in the "Early John" text, to support Jesus as The Sign. Thus, the cleansing of the Temple incident becomes simultaneously the launching pad for the public teaching mission of Jesus, and the prophetic sign of his future death and resurrection. Further signs such as "changing water into wine" and teaching dialogues such as "Jesus as the bread of life" are added by "Later John" to enhance the symbolic identification of Jesus as the Word that "became flesh and dwelt among us." The location of these additional signs in Galilee, and of other signs at various feasts in Jerusalem fitted a *third purpose*, which was to rebalance the Galilean and Judean elements of the narrative. A *fourth purpose* was to redesign "Early John's" Passion and post-crucifixion appearance stories to fit "Later John's" interpretation.

The Divine Context

Like the synoptic gospel writers, "Early John" drew inspiration from the gnostic-oriented teachings of Jesus. The synoptic writers, however, focused on the lifestyle implications for this world: Mark drawing from Thomas, and Matthew and Luke using Q. Their divine framework derived from the Pauline interpretation which focused on divinely ordained events following the crucifixion of Jesus. The synoptic gospels were tuned into the Hebrew scriptures (as reinterpreted by Paul and others) as explanatory bases for the resurrection of Jesus.

But Jesus himself, according to the Thomas Gospel, had described a timeless spiritual universe reaching beyond the created material world, and accessible to every human through a process of self-discovery. Gnostic timelessness was essentially a revision of Genesis, placing all who "discovered" the Kingdom of God both "at the beginning and at the end." For example, "Jesus said, 'Where the beginning is, the end will be. Fortunate is the one who stands at the beginning: That one will know the end and will not taste death'" (Thomas 18). For Jesus, then, there was no special distinction between himself and other human beings who shared the divine spark located within each person. What Jesus had discovered could be shared holistically: "Jesus said, 'Whoever drinks from my mouth will become like me; I myself shall become that person, and the hidden things will be revealed to that person'" (Thomas 108).

"Later John," while evidently attached to the Gnostic picture of God's universe as expressed in the Thomas Gospel, must have been strongly influenced by the post-crucifixion trend to elevate the personhood of Jesus to a divine level, beyond all other human beings. Much progress in this direction was made by Paul and the synoptic gospels. But the full Gnostic understanding provided the ultimate possibility. If all human beings could participate in the divine Kingdom, one special human being might be totally identified with the totality of divine power. Accordingly, Jesus could simply be God descended to Earth, and therefore be equated with God, with Him from the beginning. The progression becomes complete. For "Early John," God bestowed special status on Jesus at the time of his death. For Mark, the special status of Jesus began in adulthood when he was baptized by John the Baptist. For Matthew and Luke, the special status was bestowed on Jesus at the time of his conception, when the Holy Spirit descended on his mother Mary. And finally, for "Later John," his special status went back to the beginning of everything, when "He was in the beginning with God; through him were all things made" (John 1:2-3).

The Mission of Jesus

For "Later John" the mission of Jesus was pre-ordained, and Jesus himself is the message. Similarly pre-ordained are those who hear the message and believe. "He who is of God hears the words of God; the reason you do not hear them is that you are not of God" (John 8:47). Such believers perceive the true image of Jesus as the divine Son of God, whereas those "not of God," including the Jews in general who know only the "ruler of this world" Satan, are condemned to non-understanding.

The broad outlines of "Later John's" revised Gnostic universe are contained in the introductory paragraphs of the Johannine gospel, grafted on to the inferred "Early John" text. John the Baptist's endorsement of Jesus thus becomes an expression of John's role as "a man sent from God . . . to bear witness to the light" (John 1:6-7). But John the Baptist's immediate denial of his own messiahship, and confession of his own unworthiness seem to lower his status, a probable indication of sentences written by "Early John." Because by the time "Later John" was writing circa 100 C.E. for a Gentile audience, there would have been no need to cook up such a put-down of John the Baptist. So "Later John" simply puts in some amended wording such as a second Lamb of God statement (John 1:29-34) which precedes the first (John 1:35-36). The duplication is intended to explain that Jesus is the timeless Redeemer who "takes away the sins of the world," rather than "Early John's" humanly rooted Messiah King.

The main innovations by "Later John" to launch the mission of Jesus were the story of the wedding feast in Cana, and the transfer of the cleansing of the Temple scenario from the Feast of Tabernacles to top billing at an earlier Passover Feast. Among the "Later John" trappings of the Cana incident are: the presence of the mother of Jesus, the quotation "My hour has not yet come" and the explanation to non-Jewish readers about the six stone jars "for the Jewish rites of purification." Apparently, "Later John" thought that this borrowed Hellenistic myth about changing water into wine was a good metaphor for the "new age" of God's Kingdom, symbolized by the good wine. Additionally, this sign in Galilee could be linked with a second later sign at Cana (healing of the official's son at a distance—John 4:46-54) that helps to restore a balance between actions in Galilee and Judea that was absent from the inferred "Early John" text. Conscious awareness of this motivation is implied by the "Later John" sentence: "This was now the second sign that Jesus did when he had come from Judea to Galilee" (John 4:54).

The cleansing of the Temple incident seems to have been perceived by "Later John" as an ideal way to begin the public mission of Jesus. The author apparently noted that in his source material, Jesus had referred to destroying the Temple made of stones (see also Thomas 71), and building another "not made with hands" (see also Mark 14:58) in three days (presumably a Temple of people). Thus, the "Early John" text may have contained an implied threat by Jesus to destroy the Temple. "Later John" reinterpreted this as a prophecy by Jesus of his own resurrection: "But he spoke of the temple of his body" (John 2:21). And so "Later John" changed the wording to: "Destroy this temple, and in three days I will raise it up" (John 2:19), thus neatly having Jesus blame "the Jews" for his own later murder by crucifixion, while metaphorically replacing the Temple by his own resurrected personhood. From such a launching pad, Jesus begins his mission in Judea, as described by "Early John."

The Signs of Jesus

In the inferred "Early John" Gospel, there were seven signs by Jesus: the feeding of the multitude, walking on water, the entry into Jerusalem, the cleansing of the Temple, the healing of the paralytic, the healing of the blind man, and the resurrection of Lazarus. The action of feeding the multitude in Galilee became a stimulus to all the others, because of its symbolic significance as a re-creation of the Old Testament story about manna in the wilderness, which had stimulated the despairing Jews in the desert to survive and occupy the promised land of Israel. According to the inferred "Early John" text, this event led the crowd to try "to take him (Jesus) by force and make him King" (John 6:15).

"Later John" retained all seven sign stories, and added a few more such as water into wine (apparently a Hellenistic myth), and the woman caught in adultery ("let him who is without sin throw the first stone"—John 8:7). Also, "Later John" rearranged the order of the stories. The evidence for such a re-arrangement is set out in Chapter 3.

The story re-arrangement was facilitated by the role assigned by "Later John" to the brothers of Jesus. According to "Later John," these brothers "did not believe in him" (John 7:5), but nevertheless urged him to "go to Judea, that your disciples may see the works you are doing" (John 7:3). "If you do these things, show yourself to the world" (John 7:4). They were referring to the Feast of Tabernacles in Jerusalem. Evidently, these brothers of Jesus had a similar point of view to the members of the multitude who wanted "to make him King." So Jesus lied to his brothers, "I am not going up to this feast" (John 7:8), but then went up privately, conveniently avoiding a public entry into Jerusalem and the public cleansing of the Temple. This allowed "Later John" to change the text so as to move the cleansing of the Temple to an earlier Passover Feast, and transfer the public entry into Jerusalem to a later Passover Feast. But "Later John" wanted to disassociate all signs of Jesus from the Feast of Tabernacles, so the healing of the paralytic was moved to an earlier unnamed Feast, and the healing of the blind man transferred to days after the Feast.

According to "Later John," only a "chosen few" disciples, and a few others directly affected were predestined "to know" Jesus; "knowing Jesus" (as a way to enter the Kingdom of God), was apparently much more difficult than learning to discover God within oneself as in the Thomas Gospel. Nevertheless, "Later John" does seem to go along with "Early John's" contention that many people were impressed by Jesus' signs and wonders. In particular, the final sign of the raising of Lazarus was of great importance to "Later John." The Sanhedrin (council) said: "What are we to do? For this man performs many signs. If we let him go on thus, every one will believe in him" (John 11:47-48). And the Pharisees said: "You see that you can do nothing; look, the world has gone after him" (John 12:19). How then to explain all the hostility that "Later John" attributed to the Jews? His answer was the "words of Jesus." Not the words of the original Gnostic sayings of Jesus, but the words that "Later John" had Jesus say about himself as divine Redeemer and eternal Son of God. Thus, the people accepted the "signs" of Jesus, but rejected his "words."

The Words of Jesus

The beautiful and troubling words of Jesus formulated by "Later John" are vastly different from most of the sayings in the other gospels. "Later John" is concerned with his vision of Jesus as God, and his Jesus does not hesitate to speak out about the reality and meaning of this vision. The language of "Later John" is high poetry, appropriate to a Jesus considered to be God. The question is about Jesus' true identity. And the answer is repeated again and again.

All access to God is mediated through Jesus; this is the fundamental message. It contrasts strikingly with the original Gnostic message of Jesus that those who discover the Kingdom of God within achieve unmediated access to God the Father. "Later John" transforms the earlier Thomas Gospel message, not through direct action by Jesus at the Last Supper as envisaged by Paul, but through his prophetic words delivered publicly to the whole population (John 6:27-58). His "I am the bread of life" speech expresses the same Eucharistic message as Paul, but in a much more detailed replacement of the contrary teaching of Jesus set out in the Thomas Gospel. However, the Gnostic emphasis on the importance of Jesus' words remains fundamental to "Later John." And although he tries to associate Passover (John 6:4) and "the feeding of the five thousand" (John 6:5-14) with Jesus' words about the bread and wine Eucharist, his later narrative structure for the Passion Story (derived from "Early John") does not allow the Last Supper to include the bread and wine covenant as presented in the synoptic gospels (see below).

Another aspect of the concept of Jesus as God made flesh is the anti-gnostic position that pushes the presence of the Spirit (or Kingdom of God) into the future after Jesus has been raised to Heaven. In the Thomas text, the Holy Spirit is ever-present in the world, and in "Early John," Jesus baptizes on earth with the Holy Spirit. "Later John" is forced into corrections of his source text such as: "although Jesus himself did not baptize but only his disciples" (John 4:2), and "Now this he said about the Spirit, which those who believed in him were to receive; for as yet the Spirit had not been given, because Jesus was not yet glorified" (John 7:39).

The Passion Story

From early on in the Johannine gospel, "the Judeans" are trying to kill Jesus (e.g. John 5:18), but nothing happens because "his time has not yet come." The hostility arises from the explicit claims by Jesus that not only has he been sent by God, but he is the Son of God incarnate in human flesh. When Jesus performs signs, the people respond with acclaim ("Early John"), but when Jesus explains who he is, hostility is rampant ("Later John").

And so it is, after "the feeding of the multitude." In squelching "Early John's" journey of Jesus and the multitude of followers to Jerusalem, "Later John" has Jesus touting himself in public discourse as the divine Bread of Life. Predictably, his supporters and most disciples melt away, and he is left entirely alone. He ends up going privately to Jerusalem for the Feast of Tabernacles even though "He decided not to go into Judea, because the Judeans were looking for a chance to kill him" (John 7:1). At the Feast, he continues to speak publicly; his enemies try to arrest him but nothing happens because "his time has not yet come." In continuing to do signs such as restoring the sight of a blind man, some respond to him while others reject him as "out of his mind," because of his claims of divinity. Jesus flees to the desert with some disciples. Despite the turmoil and attempts to arrest Jesus, "Later John" has successfully evaded mention of an insurrection, and indeed totally avoids any back references to it anywhere else in his text; most clues to the cover-up of the insurrection are in the Markan and Lukan gospels.

However, given the insurrection story, it becomes clear what "Later John" was compelled to write to get around it. He needed Jesus to publicly enter Jerusalem at Passover time, with a "welcoming crowd." This he achieved by turning "Early John's" rescue of Lazarus story into a public resurrection event. As word spreads about it, it becomes the stimulus for an enthusiastic welcome by crowds of Judeans at Festival time. Simultaneously, it becomes the stimulus for action by the Sanhedrin to order the arrest of Jesus, on the mysterious grounds "that one man should die for the people, and that the whole nation should not perish" (John 11:50). "Later John" is having difficulties. The Lazarus story seems an unlikely threat to the Roman Empire. He tries to write it up as a climactic miracle event. But "Later John's" credibility is weakened by having the Sanhedrin respond prior to Jesus' dramatic entry into Jerusalem. In the context of Pilate's presence in the city, such an entry by Jesus, with crowds greeting him as "King of Israel," is a dramatic challenge to Roman authority. And if the Sanhedrin had already decreed his death, without any trial, Jesus would seem to be deliberately provoking a confrontation with dolorous consequences.

In the "Later John" scenario, nothing happens—not a whiff of violence. Presumably because of "fear of the people" the authorities initiate no action; they wait for Jesus to do something. So Jesus at the time of his own choosing arranges for them to come for him, through the contact person, Judas Iscariot. Roman soldiers arrest him, but he is brought before Annas the High Priest. There is no trial by the Sanhedrin. When Jesus is brought before Pontius Pilate the next morning, they cannot even specify an accusation. "So Pilate . . . said 'What accusation do you bring against this man?' They answered 'If this man were not an evildoer we would not have handed him over'" (John 18:30). Later they say "he ought to die, because he has made himself Son of God" (John 19:7). Pilate himself raises the question of Jesus as King of the Jews, apparently treating it as sick comedy. He turns Jesus over to "the Judeans" for crucifixion. Somehow, all the enthusiastic supporters of Jesus have vanished.

There is little need to go into detail on the fairly lengthy "Later John" text, which includes various elements intended to ensure that the story is "according to the scriptures." His use of the term "Judeans" seems intended to imply that the "chief priests and officers" represented all Jewish people. There is no explicit mention of a "crowd." The story has simply been edited to fit a climactic scene in the divine drama, where the Jewish people complete their rejection of God and his Kingdom. The slate is now clear for the New Dispensation.

The Resurrection of Jesus

"Later John" seems to be addressing a Gentile audience that is confused about the resurrection of Jesus.

According to all versions of the Empty Tomb story, the disappearance of the physical body of Jesus meant that it had been "raised up" by God. For Thomas Gospel Gnostics, this was presumably irrelevant, since the spiritual Jesus was returning to the spiritual world of God the Father, in the same way as would all persons belonging to the Kingdom of God. The inferred "Early John" Gospel reports the Empty Tomb, the later spiritual appearances of Jesus, and his anticipated return to Earth as Messiah of Israel, presumably in bodily form. Paul explains this differently as the transformation of the physical body of Jesus into the holistic Mystical Body of Christ that will bring about the "end of days" upon return to Earth, presumably in spiritual form; there is no explicit mention of an Empty Tomb. Mark agrees with Paul, but feels compelled to include an Empty Tomb story (different from that of "Early John") to verify the "raising up." For Mark it would seem that post-crucifixion appearance stories lack credibility as a form of "bearing witness"; all that matters is faith in the words that Jesus spoke when alive. Matthew and Luke attempt to rectify the confusion through appearance stories that show Jesus resurrected in bodily form in Jerusalem, on the third day after his death.

"Later John's" direct knowledge of other texts was limited probably to the "Early John" Gospel that would have contained descriptions of six spiritual appearances of Jesus after his death (see Chapter 3). Just as these stories lacked credibility for Mark as resurrection appearances, it appears they also lacked credibility for "Later John," who required nothing less than a living physical body. He therefore reduces all the spiritual appearances into one appearance to Mary of Magdala on the third day, which is a doubtful ghost of Jesus rather than a genuine physical body. When Jesus says: "Do not hold me for I have not yet ascended to the Father" (John 20:17), the lack of verification by touching is confirmed. Mary has faith (like the other disciple at the Empty Tomb), but evidence of a truly physical resurrection will also be necessary. This evidence is quickly forthcoming that same evening when Jesus comes through a closed door to meet his disciples and shows them "his hands and his side." Jesus has ascended to the Father and descended again. Confirmation of the presence of his physical body comes eight days later at another appearance, when doubting Thomas touches the prints of the nails, and says "My Lord and my God." This is the ultimate triumph of "Later John's" interpretation; Thomas, the Gnostic who does not believe in physical resurrection, has become a witness against himself.

"Later John" believes that God may "descend and ascend" in the form of Jesus, whenever he wishes. So he adds a postscript to the story (perhaps written by someone else) to make the point that Jesus had not promised to come "in glory" before the death of "the beloved disciple" (i.e. James, the brother of Jesus). This disciple had died by the time "Later John" was writing his gospel, so Jesus makes an appearance to the disciples while fishing on Lake Galilee to correct the rumour about "the beloved disciple," and confirm Peter's leadership instead. "Later John" then claims that "the beloved disciple" is the author of the Johannine gospel with the words "This is the disciple who is bearing witness to these things, and who has written these things; and we know that his testimony is true" (John 21:24). In this way, "Later John" acknowledges a sort of joint authorship with "Early John."

It is important to note how "Later John's" resurrection stories demonstrate dependence on his "Early John" source, and support the hypothesis that the earlier text described the various appearances mentioned by the apostle Paul. "Later John's" Lake of Galilee fishing story seems to encompass elements from the three "Early John" post-crucifixion appearances in Galilee: 1) the private Transfiguration appearance to Peter is transformed into a private "feed my sheep" discussion about Peter's repentance and leadership designation; 2) the inner circle fishing appearance on Lake Galilee becomes a shared eating experience demonstrating physical resurrection; 3) the appearance at the feeding of the multitude of 500 brethren is reflected in the specified seven disciples (corresponding to the seven baskets of food fragments), and the distribution of bread and fish by Jesus ("Jesus came and took the bread and gave it to them, and so with the fish"—John 21:13). The three "Early John" stories probably described spiritual visions or appearances of a shadowy non-physical nature; "Later John" ties them all together in an unmistakable physical resurrection of Jesus.

Similarly, "Later John" deals with the private appearance to James, and its message that Jesus would return before James died. He integrates it into the Galilean story by postulating the presence of "the disciple whom Jesus loved," and explaining a previous misunderstanding of what Jesus had said. Finally, "Later John" repeats the commissioning of the apostles appearance story with highly significant differences: it occurs on the third day after the crucifixion; Jesus appears in his physical body and bestows the Holy Spirit; and the commissioned persons are "disciples" instead of specially chosen apostles.

Disciples and Family of Jesus

In the double context world of "Later John," the disciples and family of Jesus belong to "this world" where people are blinded to the "real" meanings of God's divine realm of light. Although Jesus explains in full that his own personhood equates with God, it is predetermined that most people will not understand, since the devil is in charge of "this world." Accordingly, "many of his disciples drew back and no longer went about with him" (John 6:66), and "even his brothers did not believe in him" (John 7:5).

Unlike the synoptic gospel writers, "Later John" does not use the term "apostles," even though "Early John" had almost certainly described a list of twelve apostles, with names, in the context of a post-crucifixion appearance story where Jesus commissions them. By avoiding this list of named apostles, "Later John" could fudge the question of who they were. Interestingly, "Later John" does make reference to "the twelve" (John 6:67 and 71, and 20:24), without explicitly identifying them either as disciples or apostles. Elsewhere, he refers to "his brothers and his disciples" (John 2:12), which seems to leave open the possibility that "the twelve" includes both brothers and disciples.

In any event, the absence of a reference list of names permits "Later John" to shift names around in support of his revised storyline.

Thomas plays a special role. As a sceptical witness of Jesus' bodily resurrection, he recovers his faith by touching the bodily wounds of Jesus. With the words "My Lord and my God" (John 20:28), he becomes a witness against himself. The Gnostic Thomas, spiritual twin of Jesus, represents the Gnostic interpretation of the teachings of Jesus, which excludes both bodily resurrection and privileged access to God only through Jesus. His conversion, therefore, parallels that of "Later John" himself, who seems to have moved from a Thomistic Gnostic tradition to a modified Pauline interpretation of the resurrection.

My hypothesis is that "Later John" made idiosyncratic name changes to his source names in support of his story changes. In the case of Judas Thomas he removed the name "Judas," which he associated with the devil: "one of you is a devil" (John 6:70); and then added the Greek word Didymos (meaning twin) as a nickname, thus indicating that Thomas was the disciple's proper name. The removal of the "devil" name and its replacement with the "spiritual twin" nickname correspond with "Later John's" story of the conversion experience of the sceptical Thomas.

"Later John" knew that two disciples of Jesus had the name "Judas" (John 14:22); evidence that one of them was the brother of Jesus emerges from the dialogue at the Last Supper (John 14:22), in which "Judas (not Iscariot)" expresses the same idea as "the brothers" of Jesus much earlier (John 7:14) in almost identical words. Judas asks: "Lord, how is it that you will manifest yourself to us, and not to the world"? The brothers of Jesus say: "For no man works in secret if he seeks to be known openly. If you do these things, show yourself to the world." This points to the possibility that the "Early John" author may have referred to Thomas as "Judas," and to the brother of Jesus as "Judas, of Simon Iscariot"; "Early John" seems to have preferred proper names without nicknames, except where necessary to distinguish two different persons with the same name. My hypothesis is that he used the name Judas when referring to Thomas in two particular scenarios (which were in fact the same), the supper at Bethany and the Last Supper. Thus, according to "Early John," it would have been "Judas" (i.e. Judas Thomas) who protested the use of expensive ointment by Mary to anoint Jesus' feet (John 12:1-8); and it would have been the same "Judas" who went out to get the Roman soldiers at Jesus' request (John 13:27-30). Such a hypothesis fits the picture of a Gnostic Thomas, spiritual twin of Jesus, who believes in the practical consequences of Jesus' teachings, and especially that anyone who follows the teachings, including Jesus, "will not taste death" (Thomas 1). "Later John," however, with an entirely different outlook, perceives a cosmic plot by Satan "who enters into Judas" (John 13:27), to bring about the arrest and crucifixion of Jesus. He concludes that this Judas must be Judas, of Simon Iscariot, probably listed by "Early John" as one of the twelve apostles. When "Early John" wrote (long before the Roman-Jewish War), the nickname "Iscariot" perhaps meant an especially zealous upholder of the Mosaic Law; by the time "Later John" was writing it was probably an epithet meaning Zealot Assassin (Sicarios). It was therefore quite a simple step for both "Later John" and Mark to equate the holder of such a name with Satan.

Judas Iscariot is referred to several times by "Later John" as Judas, of Simon Iscariot (John 6:71, 13:2, and 13:26), which is the ambiguous Greek way of writing either "son of" or "brother of." Whichever was intended by "Later John," it seems likely that his "Early John" source was referring to Judas as the brother of Simon Iscariot, or alternatively of Simon, the Zealot, one of the twelve apostles. Evidence from Mark's Gospel that the Bethany supper took place at the house of Simon, the Leper, supports the idea that "Early John" had located the Bethany supper (which also included the Last Supper) at Simon's house. The hypothesis is that Mark modified the name to Simon, the Leper, while "Later John" deleted the reference entirely as a simple way to avoid the name. Luke transferred the story to the house of Simon the Pharisee in Galilee.

While references to the **brothers of Jesus** seem conspicuous by their absence from "Early John" (see Chapter 3), it is interesting that "Later John" decided to invoke them (without names) in his revision and suppression of the insurrection story. According to "Later John," the brothers of Jesus went up to the Feast of Tabernacles in Jerusalem, after failing to convince Jesus to attend. Jesus does go up later privately, and speaks in public to the people. "Later John" may be trying to say that if there was an insurrection (as his "Early John" source claimed), his brothers might have been involved, but Jesus himself had nothing to do with it. "Later John" wrote nothing about an insurrection, and nothing further about the brothers of Jesus as such.

James, the brother of Jesus could not be avoided, however, because the "Early John" text was "Later John's" basic source for the life story of Jesus. In the inferred "Early John" material it was probably made clear that an unnamed "other disciple" was a link between the Empty Tomb story, and the occupied tomb in the resurrection of Lazarus story. This disciple had a special love for Jesus arising from his rescue from the tomb, which informed his own insight into the meaning of the later Empty Tomb. He was the first to understand the truth: "he saw and believed" (John 20:8). For "Later John" this person was therefore "the disciple whom Jesus loved"; his rescue from the tomb was the culminating sign of the forthcoming resurrection of Jesus as the divine Redeemer of all humankind. "Later John" would have identified closely with this man as a sort of joint author of the story of Jesus. And "Later John" noticed that the author had given himself the cover-up name of Lazarus, and referred to himself later only as "the other disciple." So perhaps "Later John" saw the earthly family of Jesus as divided by Satan with Judas Iscariot on one side and James the "beloved disciple" on the other. Maybe God's intention was that their earthly identities as brothers of Jesus should remain secret, which "Later John" accomplishes in his edited text.

Assessment

The Gospel of John combines authorship of "Early John" and "Later John." But "Early John," long since dead, would have been shocked to read what later writers had done to his narrative. The same can be said for Thomas; he would no doubt have been shocked by the dialogue attributed to Jesus, where he equates himself with God.

Paul had focused on the need for total commitment and belief in Jesus Christ, which for "Later John" meant the belief that access to God the Father is exclusively through Jesus the Son. "Later John" reduced attention to Jesus' return to earth, focusing more completely on the message that "God so loved the world that he gave his only Son, that whoever believes in him should not perish but have eternal life" (John 3:16).

"Later John's" Gospel was the death knell for the Gnostic outlook in the new Christian Church, which was not as congenial to the Roman-Greek mentality as the story of a God descended to earth in human form. And the Johannine concept of personal survival after death linked to physical resurrection had more direct emotional appeal.

In terms of the actual life of Jesus, "Later John" is useful insofar as his gospel helps to provide evidence about what "Early John" had written. Fortunately, the "Later John" writer accepted considerable amounts of "Early John" material without major amendment. In combination with other uses of "Early John" by Mark and Luke, it becomes possible to have a fairly accurate idea of what was written about Jesus by this early writer. Careful analysis of the Johannine gospel facilitates the hypothesis that "Early John" was actually James, the brother of Jesus. Through all of these writings, it becomes possible to develop a reconstruction of the life of Jesus, which is the subject of the next part of this book.

---

[1]   See Frederickson, Paula, *From Jesus to Christ*, p. 20, Yale University Press, 1988.

PART II

RECONSTRUCTION OF
THE LIFE OF JESUS

CHAPTER 10

THE CONTEXT
(A BRIEF SUMMARY)

Jesus was born in either Judea or Galilee during the final years of the reign of King Herod the Great (circa 6 to 7 B.C.E.) Modern science seems to have confirmed unusual astral phenomena at this time,[1] which may have stimulated speculation by some religious thinkers concerning the birth of a Messiah who would herald the restoration of the Kingdom of Israel, and/or the coming of the last days and the Kingdom of God.

In common with other cultures, the basic thought structure within Israel at this time was three-fold:

1. The sky (or heaven above)—occupied by God and related divine beings
2. The world below inhabited by devils, demons, etc.
3. The world in-between composed of living beings

In Israel, the focus was on a single God, and the historically grounded relationship between God above and his "chosen people" in the in-between world. All history in this latter world unfolded in accordance with God's directions as expressed in written chronicles such as the books of the Torah and related writings.

This unique accumulation of scriptures about the myths and history of the Jewish people provided a dramatic story of ups and downs, interpreted in terms of God's response to the behaviour of His people. Because of their worthiness, God had saved them from the Egyptians, supplied Moses to lead them to the promised land, bestowed the Law as a criterion for worthiness, and enabled Israel to become a great power under King David, among others. Because of their unworthiness, however, God allowed such disasters as the Babylonian exile, the Hellenic and Seleucid conquests, and the recent Roman domination. But always there remained hope that by thorough adherence to God's Law, the worthy people at least would be restored to freedom and glory under a new Moses and a new Kingdom of God. The search for signs of when this time would come became a preoccupation for some scribes and prophets during the last millennium before the Common Era.

But as the centuries went by, the encircling presence of Hellenistic culture exerted increasingly destructive pressure. Many Jews were forced to move abroad into the swirling Greco-Roman melting pot to live as a Diaspora. Within Palestine, foreign domination became increasingly onerous, recalling the ancient days of enslavement in Egypt. Although the imprint of written tradition provided a strong shield, the threat of pagan culture was constant, and in time contributed to ever-sharper divisions of opinion within the Jewish polity.

The Mosaic Law, the central focus of the relationship between Jews and their God, served to measure both individual worthiness and the collective worthiness of the whole community. Ritual practice, derived from this arrangement or "covenant," was intended to achieve "purification" from pollution and sin by following "ways" that would be pleasing to God, as prescribed in ancient scriptures. As in other surrounding societies, a Temple culture had evolved which focused the relationship between the divine and human realms. But in Israel this culture was anchored by its scriptural base—the Torah.

By the time of the Roman Empire, the predominantly Jewish territory of Palestine was composed geographically of four entities: Judea, Samaria, Galilee, and Perea. But a broader Jewish presence stretched out in all directions from Jerusalem, particularly northward to the cities of Syria and Asia Minor, and southward to Alexandria in Egypt. The outer residents in the major cities of the Greco-Roman world, known as Diaspora Jews, were heavily exposed to Greek influences, especially the language, even while clinging to their Jewish cultural identities; increasingly some of them were perceived by other Jews as "Hellenists." Further inward in northern Palestine and Syria, Greek influence was also pervasive in the Decapolis and some cities of Galilee and Samaria; while many "Hebrews" and "Samaritans" maintained their distinctiveness, particularly the rural Aramaic-speaking peasants, others in larger towns were infiltrated by Greekness. The more southern Judeans, in and around Jerusalem, were more thoroughly "Hebrews," although linked with diaspora Greekness in Egypt and the west, and with administrative "Hellenism" deriving from the occupying Romans.

After the direct conquest of Palestine by the Romans (circa 60 B.C.E.), a client King, Herod the Great from Idumea, south of Judea, was installed by the

Romans. He ruled Judea, Samaria, Galilee and other territories from 35 to 4 B.C.E. Although a cruel despotic ruler, King Herod attempted "to gather into one the children of God" (John 11:52) by building the wondrous Second Temple in Jerusalem. After he died, there were years of disturbance, which included the brutal crushing by Roman forces of a revolt led by a certain Judas of Galilee (circa 8 C.E.). The outcome was the establishment of Herod Antipas (son of Herod the Great) as client King of Galilee and Perea, while Judea and Samaria became a Roman province, administered directly by a governor (procurator). Within this political setting, the magnificent new Temple in Jerusalem became increasingly the focal point around which swirled the complex controversies of Jewish religion and identity in a pagan world.

In fact, the renewal of the Jewish Temple cult through architecture was somewhat of a last ditch attempt to maintain a traditional model of Israel and Jewish culture within the framework of the all-powerful Roman Empire. When the client King structure began to crumble, a series of compromises were negotiated, allowing an uneasy continuation of Jewish religious authority to co-exist with Roman and client King authorities. The Sanhedrin (or Council of Elders), headed by a High Priest and appointed by the Roman Governor in Judea (with input from the client King), was responsible for the administration of both the Temple and the Law of Moses, within a confusing overall structure of executive powers exercised by the Roman Governor, client Kings, and the Roman Emperor.

Much ink has been spilled by scholars attempting to come to grips with the diverse information available on the complicated range of politico-religious opinion in the Jewish polity of first century C.E.; the primary sources are the writings of Flavius Josephus, the canonical and apocryphal scriptures, and the 20th-century manuscript discoveries at Qumram and Nag Hammadi.

Clearly, the main defenders of the Temple cult system were members of an establishment, a sort of sacerdotal aristocracy claiming the allegiance of persons denoted varyingly by such terms as "Herodians," "High Priests," "Sadducees," some "Pharisees" and "Scribes," as well as officials and tax collectors. In collaboration with the Roman overlords, they managed a Temple system based on rituals and laws derived mainly from literal interpretation of ancient scriptures and Mosaic Law. Their flexibility toward working with the Romans, and the corruption and oppression that accompanied it, were rationalized by the rather unusual degree of religious freedom accorded to the Jews by the Romans. The Sadducees seem to have been the teaching expression of conservative traditional values, and exploitive Temple practices. Of particular interest is that both Josephus and the synoptic gospels report that the Sadducees rejected the relatively new "Hellenist" idea of the survival or resurrection of the individual soul after death. Nevertheless, for practical purposes, outside a minimalist literal interpretation of Mosaic Law, the establishment groups presumably were somewhat "Hellenized" in their outlook and practice of daily life.

The Pharisees, on the other hand, focused on a greater expression of ritual law in the home (especially dietary regulations), representing a more flexible interpretation of Mosaic Law as a defensive reaction to corroding Hellenistic influences. Tradition has suggested that they produced many famous teachers, such as Gamaliel and Hillel, and we know that both Josephus and Paul of Tarsus claimed to be Pharisees; there is no parallel record of any famous Sadducee teacher. It seems that a widespread connection of the Pharisees with ordinary people motivated the Temple establishment to include some Pharisees in their ranks. Note that the Pharisees believed with "Hellenists" in the eventual spiritual or bodily resurrection of the dead. As their range of views widened, it seems that there were many divisions among them as related to Temple practice and collaboration with the Romans. Their deep-seated aim of protecting and preserving Mosaic Law and Jewish identity was probably in conflict with the survival need for peaceful relationships with Roman authorities.

Josephus also describes a Fourth Philosophy founded by the rebel Judas of Galilee, which most scholars have identified with the Zealots, strongly anti-Roman defenders of traditional Jewish values. In contrast with Sadducees and Pharisees, located primarily in Jerusalem, the Zealots appear to have been mainly hinterland people, particularly Galileans. According to Josephus "this school agrees in all other respects with the opinions of the Pharisees, except that they have a passion for liberty that is almost unconquerable" (Josephus, Antiquities 18:23). Perhaps some of these Zealots moved into Jerusalem to become known as the Sicarri, whom Josephus denotes as being assassins of venal officials and priests. They tended towards apocalyptic thinking, which predicted cataclysmic events to destroy the evil forces responsible for the oppression of the Jews.

The Zealots and Pharisees may have been equivocal about the Jerusalem Temple, but there had always been another way in Palestine of reacting to a centralizing Temple cult. Separation was the path followed by the Samaritans (presumably remnants of the ten northern tribes of Israel deported by Assyria circa 800 B.C.E.). Very little information is available, except that they maintained their own scriptural records and Mosaic tradition, refused to worship at the Temple in Jerusalem, and built their own Temple on Mount Gerizim in Samaria. Here was a model of a separate form of Temple Judaism, which could provide a precedent for coping with conflict through geographic separation.

The Essenes, another separatist group, apparently evolved from a break-away group of hereditary Temple priests, who settled in the desert at Qumram in the second century B.C.E. As self-styled Keepers of the Covenant (the original agreement with God arranged by Moses), they followed an ascetic existence of strict ritual observance, including celibacy, while awaiting apocalyptic intervention by God in the form of cataclysmic events, and the last judgment. The writings of Josephus reveal that the separatist vision of the Essenes encompassed contradictory elements. On the one hand, their physical separation from other Jews promoted intense ritual observance, obsessive study of traditional scripture, messianic prophecy, and hostility towards other Jews and Gentiles. But in their retreat from Temple culture they embraced, perhaps unconsciously, some rather non-Jewish ideas of monastic-type community living, sharing of goods, ascetic celibate life and survival of the soul after death. They, too, could not escape Hellenistic influences.

To maintain their central community near the shores of the Dead Sea, the celibate Essenes needed broader connections. And so, according to Josephus, other Essene groups who were married with children, emerged in many towns and villages. They had a less strict ritual observance, but lived apart from their neighbours. Apartness from other Jews may well have contributed to alternative contacts with Greek-speaking persons. Here perhaps, in the hinterland towns and villages, at the margins of Judaism, was the incubator that produced the Kingdom of God movements led by John the Baptist and Jesus of Nazareth.

But we must not overlook the largest group of all in Israel, the people of the land. This term may be used to encompass the peasants, unskilled workers, dispossessed wanderers, the sick and poor in general, oppressed women and children, and other marginal groups. Perhaps they were 90 percent or more of the total population. Their primary problem was how to eke out a miserable existence and find their daily bread.

---

[1]   Various astronomers have calculated that a conjunction of the planets Saturn and Jupiter, giving the appearance of a new bright star, probably occurred in 7-6 B.C.E. See Funk, Robert and the Jesus Seminar, *The Acts of Jesus*, p. 508, Harper Collins, 1998.

CHAPTER 11

JOHN THE BAPTIST

John the Baptist was a charismatic prophet who lived in the wilderness near Qumram, close to the Dead Sea, circa 25-35 C.E. Mentioned in all canonical gospels, as well as the pre-canonical gospels of Thomas, Q, and "Early John," his importance is acknowledged also in the writings of the outsider historian Josephus. Many scholars today suspect that he had links with the desert community of Qumram.

The 20th-century discovery of the Dead Sea Scrolls has provided some fascinating insights into the thinking of the community at Qumram, believed by most scholars to have been Essenes.[1] According to the Qumram Manual of Discipline, community members practised a life of strict observance of ritual purity of body and soul, "combining the prophetic and the priestly ideals in a holy life, characterized by repentance and the expectancy of the final judgment . . . The Qumram Essenes separated themselves from the Jerusalem Temple and its sacrificial cult. The Temple's offerings of animals were replaced by offerings of the lips (that is prayers) and by works of the (Mosaic) law . . . They believed their living temple, consisting of people, rendered a better service to the God than the Jerusalem sanctuary made of stones. The chosen 'stones' of the Qumram community were witnesses to the truth of God and made atonement for the land of Israel."[2] Other values such as celibacy, asceticism, research on healing of disease and communal sharing of goods are described in the writings of Josephus and others.

The Dead Sea Scroll discoveries show that the Qumram Essenes sought to justify their position through intensive scrutiny and interpretation of ancient Hebrew scriptures, leading to an apocalyptic understanding of the historical process involving "last days," "final judgment," and a new Kingdom after God had vented his wrath. In general, of course, this apocalyptic message had its roots in the historical and prophetic tradition of Israel recorded in ancient scripture. But readings of the Dead Sea Scrolls are making it increasingly likely that the continuing transmission of the message had become mainly the intellectual property of the desert community of Qumram. Their understanding encompassed the extraordinary notion that they (the Essenes) were the loyal remnant of "sheep" destined to achieve their rightful heritage in God's new Kingdom, while all the non-remnant "goats" (the rest of humankind) would be punished for their sins by God. Naturally, they were much concerned about discovering when this upheaval would take place, and how it would come about, and it is quite possible that the astral phenomena of 7-6 B.C.E. signified to them that a messianic leader was being born and that the "last days" were imminent. According to Josephus, King Herod the Great favoured the Essenes (Antiquities 15:373-78), and there is archaeological evidence to suggest that the Qumram site was abandoned during his reign, only to be restored at the end of it.[3] Perhaps the evil behaviour of Herod the Great, and profanation of his great new Temple convinced the Essenes to renew their community at Qumram.

Into this setting arrives John the Baptist, probably born in Judea about the time of the astral phenomena. Neither Josephus nor any other ancient source has suggested that John the Baptist was an Essene. However, Josephus does mention that in order to renew their ranks, the Essenes "adopt other men's children . . . and mould them in accordance with their own principles" (Jewish War: 2:119-161). Luke's birth myth which refers to John "growing in the wilderness" (Luke 1:80), is consistent with formative years among the Essenes. Certainly the evidence indicates that his public mission functioned in close geographic proximity to Qumram.

By the time John launched his mission as "a voice crying in the wilderness" with a special message, he had clearly distanced himself from the Qumram community. And yet he evidently shared their strict observance of Mosaic Law, their asceticism and sharing of goods, their apocalyptic view of the "end days," and the idea of a living temple of the "saving remnant" surviving into the Kingdom of God; and he believed with them that "the time was at hand." However, instead of holing up at Qumram to await the divine action plan, he had come to believe that the message should be brought to the general public. And he also believed that all righteous people could be saved through sincere repentance for all past sins—not only the Qumram remnant. And God in his mercy would permit this to be accomplished (according to the canonical gospels) through a one-time ritual baptism—not requiring all the daily ritual minutiae of the Qumram devotees. Judging by his reputation as a desert hermit "clothed in camel hair and subsisting on locusts and wild honey" it is quite possible that John was expelled from the Qumram community for his views. His genius was to invent one-time flowing water baptism in the Jordan River as a symbol of God's interest in ordinary people.

The portrait of John presented by Josephus is that of a pious man who reached out to all Jews to encourage righteous lives as a necessary preliminary to a new water baptism, acceptable to God. According to Josephus, John's focus was on the overall cultivation of virtue "by righteousness towards each other, and piety towards God" (Josephus—Antiquities 18). "Immersion must be practiced, not as an expiation for specific sins, but for the purification of the body, when the soul had already been thoroughly cleansed by righteousness." Thus, the interpretation of Josephus was that John's water baptism was a sort of extension of bodily purification ritual intended to intensify righteous behaviour; it was not a substitute for the detailed ritual requirements of Mosaic Law. Such an interpretation seems to be consistent with John's continuing emphasis on fasting, asceticism, and strict observance, noted in the canonical gospels. He was simply offering an additional ritual immersion focused on total body readiness for the forthcoming Kingdom of God.

The catch was, however, that this baptism had to be administered by John using Jordan River water, which implied both his own special authority from God, and the Essene view that the sacrificial cult of the Temple was unnecessary.

The Temple cult of animal sacrifices, as the official sanctioned method for the remission of sins, provided enormous revenues for the Jerusalem establishment. The Qumram community, a small select group, had replaced animal offerings with "offerings of the lips" (i.e. prayers) and various ritual "works," but without impinging on the principle of repetitive sacrifices to achieve ongoing purity. John's new baptismal rite, on the other hand, was more threatening; it could be perceived as a cheap one-time alternative for all Jewish people that (potentially at least) could threaten the financial viability of Temple arrangements. It may have been particularly attractive to the large hinterland underclass of poor villagers and dispossessed peasants.

Perhaps a role model for John the Baptist was the Teacher of Righteousness, described in the Dead Sea Scrolls as founding leader and revered teacher of the Qumram community. A few scholars have attempted to directly identify John the Baptist with the Teacher of Righteousness, but the vast majority favour the opinion that the Teacher dates back to 150 years earlier. His quoted prayers and views seem not unlike the views of John the Baptist, and he too was subject to persecution.

Another aspect of John the Baptist's activities may have been a shamanic healing role. According to Josephus the Essenes "make investigations into medicinal roots and the properties of stones . . . with a view to the treatment of diseases" (Josephus—*The Jewish War*). The Q2 Gospel has the enemies of John say "he has a demon," a standard put-down of exorcizing healers (Luke 7:33). And Mark's Gospel describes three incidents of exorcism of demons, attributed to Jesus (the unclean demon at Capernaum—Mark 1:21-28; the demon of Gerasa—Mark 5:1-20; and man with mute spirit—Mark 9:14-29), each of which have characteristics that may indicate a story originating from John rather than Jesus. For example, the expulsion of the demon named Legion and the accompanying "suicide" of the Gerasene Swine, reads as a symbolic destruction of the occupying Roman Army, a story appropriate to a Zealot-inclined prophet like John.

Why was John arrested and executed by King Herod Antipas—a fact acknowledged by all biblical sources, and by Josephus? The synoptic gospels (particularly Mark 6:14-24) focus on a purported public condemnation by John of King Herod's sin of marrying his brother's wife, as the reason for John's arrest. Could John have been so foolishly outspoken, whatever his private opinion? Mark's source was probably Peter, whose version of the arrest and execution may have been coloured by his apparent anti-female bias (recorded in Thomas 114 and the Gnostic Gospel of Philip). Another explanation could be John's public denunciation of penitents coming for baptism (supposedly Pharisees and Sadducees) as "the spawn of Satan," recorded in the Q2 Gospel; however, this exaggerated picture of John's imprudence reflects later Matthewan rhetoric emphasizing extreme condemnation of opponents. The "Early John" component of the Gospel of John fails to confirm any such publicly militant attitude on the part of John the Baptist. In any event, an apocalyptic scenario which placed punitive action by God in the indefinite future was not likely to alarm the authorities. Their concern was with the immediate present.

The immediate present for Herod Antipas included the intense displeasure of the Arabian King Aretas at the divorce of his daughter by Herod to marry another woman. In fact, according to Josephus, King Aretas went to war with King Herod over this issue, which placed John the Baptist on the other side of the fence in a family feud.

According to Josephus (Antiquities 18:116-19), John's arrest and execution by King Herod Antipas was a consequence of John's extraordinary impact on public opinion in Israel. "Eloquence that had so great an effect on mankind might lead to some form of sedition . . . Herod decided therefore that it would be much better to strike first and be rid of him before his work led to some form of revolt." In other words, Josephus perceives John's arrest as a pre-emptive strike against the anti-establishment consequences of traditional prophetic zeal. He does not mention, however, the marriage issue and John's condemnation of Herod recorded in Mark's Gospel, which could be seen as sedition in the King Aretas war situation.

My conclusion is that "priests and Levites" described in "Early John's" Gospel (John 1:19) probably did meet with John the Baptist in an effort to assess his intentions. The new baptism along with any oblique reference by John to a new Kingdom (implying a new king) would be perceived as a threat both to the Temple cult and to King Herod Antipas. Obviously, as clearly stated by Josephus, John had to be eliminated.

---

[1]   None of the scrolls deciphered so far (1998) contain a self-designation for the Qumram community members, other than "Sons of Zadoc," the High Priest.

[2]   Betz, Otto, *Understanding the Dead Sea Scrolls*, pp. 210-212, Random House, New York, 1992.

[3]   Reisner, Rehmer in *Jesus and the Dead Sea Scrolls*, pp. 206-207, Doubleday, New York, 1992.

CHAPTER 12

THE EARLY YEARS OF JESUS

Jesus was probably born about the same time as John the Baptist in the final years of the reign of King Herod the Great (circa 6 to 7 B.C.E.). Whether this happened at Nazareth in Galilee or Bethlehem in Judea, all canonical gospel accounts concur that Jesus was perceived to be a Galilean.

The mother of Jesus was presumably named Mary, despite "Later John's" possible assignment of the name Mary to the sister of Jesus' unnamed mother (John 19:25). And the father of Jesus was presumably named Joseph, despite Mark's striking failure to mention any father in a context where sons were normally identified by reference to their fathers (Mark 6:3). The traditional Holy Family consisted of Joseph, Mary and Jesus.

Paul of Tarsus confirms that the early disciples claimed genealogical descent of Jesus from King David of Israel "according to the flesh" (Romans 1:3)—meaningless in terms of heredity shared by thousands of other Jews, but meaningful because it implied physical conception, as distinct from conception by the Holy Spirit proposed by the later synoptic gospel writers, Matthew and Luke. These two scribes, each with their own story, both made the point that Jesus, the Son of God according to Paul and Mark, must have been conceived through special divine intervention. The supposed fatherhood of Joseph, who had lineal descent from King David, acted as a cover-up for Jesus' "secret" mission (the hypothesis of Matthew). This link to King David, along with birth in Bethlehem (despite upbringing in Nazareth) provided a traditional scriptural mandate for assigning to Jesus the title Messiah, or in the larger sense Christ (in Greek translation) as proposed by Paul.

The Matthewan story of birth in Bethlehem may have a kernel of credibility, insofar as it locates the birth of Jesus in King Herod's reign at the time of (recently confirmed) astral phenomena (see Chapter 10).[1] If one assumes that the "carpenter" Joseph played a role in Temple construction, he might have fled Jerusalem at some point in response to Herod's crimes. The mention of Joseph's avoidance of King Archeleus in Jerusalem, when he returned to Galilee from Egypt after the death of Herod is suggestive of authenticity (Matthew 2:22). Such a hypothesis opens up the possibility that Joseph and Mary might have had connections in Jerusalem (including nearby Bethlehem and Bethany) that could have continued after they moved to Galilee.

Contradicting the notion of the Holy Family threesome is the mention of "brothers" of Jesus in all gospels including Thomas. The traditional explanation is that Joseph was much older than Mary and had children by a previous wife. As Mary was a virgin, she could not herself have other children. On this basis, all the brothers and sisters of Jesus were half-brothers and sisters, older than himself and descendants of King David. But if the virgin birth is treated as imaginative (note that Paul mentions the birth of Jesus "according to the flesh," as well as brothers), the possibility follows that Mary had various other children, probably younger than Jesus, fathered either by Joseph, or by a second husband. The chances of a second husband for Mary are enhanced by the absence of any reference in any writings to the brothers or sisters of Jesus as descendants of King David, which seems to rule out Joseph as their father. Thus, Mary would be the mother of all of them; they could be half-brothers and half-sisters of Jesus. In the early gospels of Thomas and Mark, Mary is connected closely with the siblings of Jesus.

"The disciples said to him: 'Your brothers and your mother are standing outside'" (Thomas 99).

"And his mother and his brothers came . . . and a crowd . . . said to him 'Your mother and your brothers and your sisters are outside asking for you'" (Mark 3:31-33).

Let us note also another possibility, which receives fuller discussion in Chapter 14. According to the Gospel of Matthew, Jesus had four brothers named James, Joseph, Simon and Judas. In the gospels of Mark and Luke, James and Joseph (albeit circuitously) are connected as sons of the same father (specified as Alphaeus), and are linked (albeit circuitously) with the nickname Justus (see Chapter 14). On the other hand, in the Johannine gospel, Simon and Judas are linked as possible brothers, with the nickname Iscariot, which implies strong traditionalist Zealot sentiments, and perhaps a different father (see Chapter 14). The possibility is that Simon and Judas had a different father, while Jesus, James and Joseph were sons of Joseph.

I conclude that Jesus grew up in a large family, and that he grew up in Galilee. His identity as a Galilean is confirmed by all sources. But what kind of Galilean was he? His father Joseph (and even his mother) may have been Judean with Diaspora connections in Egypt, if there are any facts underlying Matthew's nativity story. Moreover, the second husband of Mary (if there was one) and/or Mary may have been Samaritan (based on the accusation in John 8:48, and Jesus' failure to deny). Or he may have been an Essene Hebrew, based on the Zealot-related nicknames of the two brothers of Jesus.

An important clue to the early years of Jesus comes from a saying in Thomas' Gospel, which is repeated with additions in all four canonical gospels (Mark 6:4, Matthew 13:57, Luke 4:24 and John 4:44):

"Jesus said, 'A prophet is not acceptable in the prophet's own town; a doctor does not heal those who know the doctor'" (Thomas 31).

Unquestionably, this saying refers to the people of Nazareth, but the issue for my purposes is whether Jesus' unpopularity in his hometown arose from his own views and actions, or whether his family was unpopular to begin with. Both Mark and Luke relate contradictory stories of rejection of Jesus in Nazareth (Mark 6:1-6, and Luke 4:16-30) arising from his own personal claims; both stories fail tests of credibility (see Chapter 13). A more likely explanation would be long-standing animosity by the people of Nazareth towards a family of "outsiders," who had been previously in their midst. There are several possibilities that might have separated the family of Jesus from their neighbours: status as Judeans, status as Essenes, status as Greek-speakers, status as Samaritans, or some combination of the above. And various sayings by Jesus about family turmoil (e.g. Thomas 16) are suggestive of family disruption when he was growing up in Nazareth.

Another clue comes from the "Early John" Gospel quotation "Can anything good come out of Nazareth?" (John 2:46). Spoken by Nathaniel (a prospective disciple) to Philip (already a disciple of Jesus), it reflects an attitude of Hellenized Galileans, or of Samaritans. Could it mean that Nazareth was a centre of "Hebrew" Galilean nationalism?

An important event during Jesus' adolescence was the revolt led by Judas of Galilee in the year 8 C.E. Josephus describes a brutal Roman repression of the uprising (the crucifixion of 2000 rebels), a tragedy which must have made a deep impression on Jesus and his family and caused much turmoil. A sensitive young man might readily react with a burning desire to seek God's help to find a way of restoring Israel in peace and freedom, without going through the horrors of subjugation and war. Luke's story of Jesus (age 12) and the teachers in the Temple (Luke 2:41-51), is consistent with a strong desire by Jesus for answers in the Temple setting. "Did you not know that I must be in my Father's house?" (Luke 2:49) It seems a reasonable inference that Jesus would go to Jerusalem as a young adult to seek enlightenment and answers, in a setting peopled perhaps by family relatives.

My hypothesis of priestly connections for Jesus in Jerusalem, is not based on Luke's story of a twelve-year-old Jesus searching for enlightenment among priests at the Temple, but on an overlooked citation from "Early John's" Gospel, which begins with a visit to John the Baptist by a group of priests and Levites sent from Jerusalem. In responding to their inquiries John answers: "*Among you* stands one whom you do not know, even he who comes after me" (John 1:19-28, emphasis added). Since the author follows with "The next day he saw Jesus coming toward him" (John 1:29), I conclude that "Early John" wishes the reader to understand that Jesus was among the group of priests and Levites. Supporting evidence to this effect comes from Thomas 78 where Jesus seems to be addressing priests and Levites about John ("Why have you come out to the countryside" etc.—Thomas 78); and from circumstances surrounding the later Temple incidents, where Jesus seems very much at home in the Temple setting.

There appear to be three salient facts about the early years of Jesus, two of which involved later cover-up efforts. The first fact of Galilean identity could not be denied, although it was clearly somewhat of an embarrassment in terms of messianic qualifications. The second fact of close relationships and turbulence in a large family must also have been undeniable during his lifetime, although perhaps an embarrassment for his teaching, but required extensive cover-up later. The third fact (presumed here) of priestly background and Jerusalem connections would also have been very difficult to explain and fit into the interpretative framework of the synoptic and Pauline traditions. Nevertheless, a key point from the "Early John" Gospel is that Jesus appears to have roots in both Judea and Galilee, and connections with the Temple priesthood. This does not preclude close relationships as well with Essenes, Samaritans and Greeks.

---

[1]   Many aspects of Matthew's story are clearly mythological, such as the massacre of innocents and the adoration of the Magi. Luke's contradictory story relies on a Roman Census that occurred ten years after the death of King Herod, and a far-fetched idea that Joseph and Mary (nine months pregnant) would travel to Bethlehem from Galilee to register for a Roman Census.

CHAPTER 13

WHAT WAS JESUS UP TO?

While the outside observer Josephus credits John the Baptist with exercising major influence in Israel, he has much less to say about Jesus.[1] In fact his brief incidental mention of Jesus might be construed as supporting the canonical gospels' interpretation that the Jewish people paid little attention to Jesus, regarding him as a minor figure compared to John.

In the absence of any direct information on the activities of Jesus as a young adult, one must proceed by inference. The canonical gospels say nothing. However, we do have two early sources that outline the sayings of Jesus: Thomas and Q. If the ideas of Jesus evolved privately, these sayings may be used to infer what was going on in the mind of Jesus from an early date.

The teaching of Jesus is focused on the Kingdom of God (God's Plan for His People), a concept long pre-dating John the Baptist and Jesus. Historically, it referred to God's instructions to His people embodied for practical purposes in the scriptures and in the earthly Kingdom of Israel. However, using the Gospel of Thomas as our earliest valid source, the essential insight of Jesus seems to be that God's Plan is contained in the hearts and minds of His people—not in scriptures and institutions. God is Spirit, and the flow of that Holy Spirit through human beings constitutes the "real" Kingdom of God. This flow is a hidden spiritual Kingdom, always present in the world "but men do not recognize it" (Thomas 51). The activation of this Kingdom in the world arises from each individual's mystical identification with the Spirit of God through an inward-directed intuitive process of being "born again."

According to Jesus, as reported by Thomas, God is "Our Father," directly accessible to every member of his human family, and located as a spark of spiritual being within each person. God's fatherly compassion reaches out to every human being without distinction. When individuals enter His Kingdom (as "born again" children) they become transformed into a new way of life, which is God's Way. By contrast, the "old way" prescribed by ancient scripture and institutional structures has brokerage arrangements (purification rituals) for dealing with a distant God; these obscure the real Kingdom of God. These earthly structures are ephemeral, whereas God's spiritual realm is "real."

When an individual comes to "know" God's realm, he or she understands that God is within, and that he or she will return to God. Conventional human values are reversed. Access to the Kingdom changes human behaviour. God's Plan is for people to find inner peace, to abandon anxiety, to love one another without reservation, and "dance to the pipes in the market-place" (Luke 7:31-35). Optimism is the order of the day.

The essence of the Kingdom was to bring forth by human volition what is already within each individual. Within each person is a spiritual entity directly linked to divine authority. Through mystical knowledge of the Holy Spirit, human beings can activate and spread God's Kingdom in the world. "Jesus said, 'If you bring forth what is within you, what you have will save you. If you do not have that within you, what you do not have within you will kill you'" (Thomas 70). Here was a new shortcut to God's favour, through a transformation of consciousness that obviated the need for strict observance of Mosaic Law precepts as the specified expression of piety towards God. The catch, however, was the concept of gnosis, an unlikely intellectual step for the sinful majority of humankind.

There is an interesting connection between the Jesus concept of an "elect" group imbued with mystical knowledge of God's Kingdom, and the Essene view of themselves as a privileged "remnant" with special understanding of God's Plan. And in particular, the special Essene notion of the Holy Spirit, virtually non-existent in the Old Testament. According to J.H. Charlesworth, quoting from Qumram scrolls, "They claimed that 'the Holy Spirit' had left the polluted Temple and accompanied them into the wilderness. There 'the Holy Spirit' dwelt in 'the house of holiness.'" [2] Their living temple consisted of "people stones" (see Chapter 11), leading to the idea of God's Spirit dwelling within his chosen people. The novelty of Jesus, perhaps borrowing from neo-platonic thought processes, was to redefine the indwelling Spirit as being accessible to everyone. Proselytization could spread the good news. Traditional purification rituals could be by-passed through baptism "with the Spirit," and "people stones" would comprise the new Temple of the Kingdom of God.

Perhaps we may turn to the outsider Josepwhus to guide our perception: "About this time there lived Jesus, a man who was a *sophist* . . . for he was a doer of miracles, a *teacher of men who receive impiety with pleasure*" (Antiquities 8:63, emphasis added).

Note the word "impiety." Josephus does not apply this term to John the Baptist—only to Jesus. But how could a teacher of "impiety" be related in any way to the conservative Essenes? Josephus mentions many rigid ascetic practices and purification rituals, and the Dead Sea Scrolls seem to confirm a strongly traditional Qumram community, obsessed with the historic past and an apocalyptic future, hidebound by purification rituals, and the exact opposite of the revolutionary teachings of Jesus.

Clues to an answer come from the writings of Josephus and of Philo of Alexandria. Josephus describes Essenes as follows: "they occupy no one city, but settle in large numbers in every town," and "there is another order of Essenes that differs . . . in its views on marriage" (Jewish War 2:199-161). Philo describes Essenes as living "in villages, avoiding all cities on account of the habitual lawlessness of those who inhabit them." [1] A simple conclusion is that the community at Qumram was a special ascetic group, while the more numerous town-situated Essenes, distancing themselves from other Jewish groups, may have been influenced by some Hellenistic-type ideas. Indeed, Josephus may have been focused on the town-dwellers when he wrote: they "cultivate peculiar sanctity"; they "show a greater attachment to each other than other sects"; "riches they despise, and their community of goods is truly admirable"; "the individual's possessions join the common stock"; "on the arrival of any of the sect from elsewhere, all the resources of the community are put at their disposal just as if they were their own, and they enter the houses of men whom they have never seen before, as though they were their most intimate friends"; "they carry nothing whatever with them on their journeys"; "there is no buying or selling among them"; "they are freely permitted to take anything from any of their brothers without making any return"; *sharing the belief of the sons of Greece* . . . that the body is . . . impermanent, but that the soul is immortal and imperishable" (Jewish War 2:119-16, emphasis added).

What was the process by which Jesus became a teacher of "impiety"? According to Mark's Gospel, Jesus was a carpenter (Mark 6:3), but there is evidence that this is part of the Markan cover-up that I have described in Chapter 5; both Matthew and Luke delete this reference, and Matthew says instead that Jesus is the son of a carpenter (Matthew 13:55). "Later John" quotes Judeans as saying "How is it that this man has learning, when he has never studied?" (John 7:15); but this assertion of the illiteracy of Jesus is used by "Later John" to support the proposition that Jesus' words originate directly from God. Both Mark and "Later John" appear to be covering up the information that the articulate Jesus is an educated person. One reason for such a cover-up could be that the ideas of Jesus presented by the canonical authors might then be attributed back to his teachers rather than directly to God.

My contention that Jesus was well-educated is supported not only by the complexity and subtlety of his thought, but also by the discovery that a number of his disciples were scribes (see Chapter 14). Such a perception surely places Jesus in the Palestine "melting pot" of ideas where traditional Judaism faced the encroachments of the outside Gentile world. Priests, scribes, Sadducees, Pharisees and Essenes were in unavoidable contact with their Hellenistic and Roman surroundings. Jesus must have brought to this setting his youthful Galilean idealism and a determination to work out his own understanding of the meaning of it all.

The result, one may assume, was a calling as a Teacher of Wisdom, independent of all existing contending groups. We might even consider him somewhat like the secularized writer Josephus who had dallied also with many different schools of thought, except that Jesus' interest would have been intense and sustained. Josephus reports that as a youth he studied and carefully practiced the philosophies of the Pharisees, Sadducees and Essenes; he also lived for three years with a desert ascetic ("for purity's sake, I became his devoted disciple"—Josephus, Life 10-12), and he ended up as a Pharisee, and then a Roman-oriented pagan.

In the case of Jesus we know only that he became known as a teacher, that he was highly knowledgeable in both Jewish tradition and neo-platonic ideas, and that "Early John" refers to him as "standing among" priests and Levites from Jerusalem (John 1:26). If Jesus did train as a priest or was involved with the priesthood, it might help to explain some of his Jerusalem connections and his respect for the Temple. But obviously at some point Jesus became rather eclectic in rejecting traditional perspectives and accepting new ideas. Whether he experienced any special revelation from God, such as claimed by Paul from Jesus Christ, we do not know; in all likelihood, the symbolic story of revelation accompanying Jesus' baptism by John the Baptist in the synoptic gospels is fictional (see Chapter 15). Contrariwise, according to Thomas' Gospel, Jesus taught that enlightenment comes from an inner-directed process of self-discovery (Thomas 3). He most likely acquired his insights over time through a process of study, reflection and self-discovery.

One possibility, which might be termed the "Samaritan connection," is that Jesus was in some way influenced by Simon Magus, the Gnostic Samaritan leader mentioned in Acts 8:9-13. Particularly supportive of such speculation are references in the Johannine gospel (sourced from "Early John") to the recruitment of Nathaniel (John 1:45-51), the encounter with the Samaritan woman (John 4:5-42), and the accusation that Jesus was himself a Samaritan (John 8:48).

My speculative conclusion is that Jesus' teaching pre-dated his contacts with followers of John the Baptist and that perhaps he experienced ostracism from orthodox circles in Jerusalem, leading to a peripatetic lifestyle, and some secretiveness, since his ideas were generally counter to prevailing orthodoxies. The Thomas Gospel indicates clearly that at some point his ideas were rejected by the establishment, the rich and powerful (Thomas 63 and 64), by the Pharisees

(Thomas 39), and by some friends and family (Thomas 31). The initial impression among listeners may have been that Jesus was an eccentric.

The Thomas Gospel description of "hidden sayings" conveyed to a small group of followers seems plausible as an early teaching approach. I therefore infer that Jesus had disciples or "colleagues" before the commencement of his public teaching mission. A main candidate for such an early association is Thomas, presumably a "spiritual twin" of Jesus, who through long exposure had "become intoxicated with the bubbling spring that I have tended" (Thomas 13) and claimed to understand Jesus better than anyone else. And so just as the mustard seed parable (Thomas 20) expresses the growth of the Kingdom of God, the process begins as in Thomas 108 "Jesus said, 'Whoever drinks from my mouth will become like me; I myself shall become that person, and the hidden things will be revealed to that person.'" One may infer that Jesus began to attract some attention as he developed his storytelling abilities (through parables), created theatrical demonstrations, cultivated a talent for empathy with people in distress, and developed his mystical propensities.

All the gospels seem to agree that Jesus spent much of his time on the move, either with others or by himself. "Be passersby" (Thomas 42) is the most pithy of all his sayings, and seems to express advocacy of a wandering mendicant lifestyle, perhaps a reaction against the stationary Qumram and Temple communities. Such itinerancy might have been primarily passive, and relatively unnoticed, and fits a scenario of support for Jesus from Josephus' "second order of Essenes" in various towns and villages, who would provide an infrastructure of hospitality and sharing of goods with strangers.

My primary model of Jesus is that he was a Teacher of Wisdom, an itinerant "holy man," who brought a benevolent message of God's Plan for human beings. The Thomas and Q1 Gospels reflect most closely his sapiential understanding of the Kingdom of God: a spiritual ever-present ethical divine dominion, awaiting full participation by everyone through mystical engagement with the Holy Spirit of God. While opposed to many aspects of materialistic lifestyles and arrangements, the Gnostic Jesus did not seem to envisage the world as a battleground between good and evil, between God and Satan (as understood by Qumram Essenes, and proposed later by Paul and canonical gospel writers). Thus, his vision contrasted sharply with the apocalyptic view of an impending future Kingdom arising from destruction of evil forces by God to bring about justice and peace.

In regard to healing the sick, the available clues indicate private and incidental activity by Jesus prior to the arrest of John the Baptist. The absence of references in the Thomas Gospel and the emphasis on secretiveness in Mark seem to confirm itinerant healing without publicity. But when John is imprisoned, Jesus' public mission starts to include public cures and exorcisms, with Jesus saying to John "Blessed is he who takes no offense at me" (Luke 7:23).

To many readers the above paragraphs probably fail to capture the deep-seated mystical quality, compassionate nature, and charismatic potential of Jesus. His own consciousness of the divine Spirit within himself could not fail to communicate itself in encounters with others. There must have been an infectious enthusiasm about him as he went on his way teaching the mysteries of the Kingdom of God.

---

[1]   See Crossan, J.D., *The Birth of Christianity*, pp. 446-447, Harper, San Francisco, 1998.

[2]   See Charlesworth, James H., *Jesus and the Dead Sea Scrolls*, p.21, Doubleday, New York, 1992.

CHAPTER 14

DISCIPLES AND FAMILY OF JESUS

As a Teacher of Wisdom, Jesus gradually attracted disciples and followers. According to Mark and other synoptic gospels, he selected twelve of these disciples early in his teaching mission as a special dedicated inner group of apostles, chosen and commissioned to spread his message, with particular instructions on attire and comportment. Nevertheless, although such apostles are named explicitly, there are reasons for us to doubt that they were commissioned directly by Jesus during his lifetime.

Jesus undoubtedly did acquire an inner group of disciples, comprising both men and women, according to the Gospel of Thomas; there is no reference to apostles or to numbers of disciples in this gospel. Thomas 14 instructs them: "When you go into any region and walk through the countryside, when people receive you, eat what they serve you and heal the sick among them." There is no mention of identifying attire, which is described later in Mark's Gospel. The Markan details relating to staff, sandals, knapsack, shirt and money (Mark 6:7-12) are elaborated also by Matthew and Luke. My contention is that the Thomas Gospel version of instructions to the disciples was directed against strict observance of Mosaic dietary laws, and represents relaxed informal guidance to travelling disciples during Jesus' lifetime. Mark, on the other hand, translated this into a formal inauguration of missionary work by apostles, using information from the "Early John" text on the post-crucifixion appearance of Jesus "to all the apostles" (see Chapter 5). Mark then retrojected the description of the formal inauguration of missionary work back to the lifetime of Jesus. Originally, In "Early John," the twelve apostles were chosen mystically by the post-crucifixion Jesus as a symbolic replacement for the twelve tribes of Israel in the new Kingdom of

God. "Early John's" inferred original list of twelve named apostles, which was used as a source by Mark and Luke, was later eliminated from the Johannine text by "Later John" (see Chapter 9).

The information presented below, derived from the analysis in previous chapters, brings together inferences about individual disciples of Jesus, worked out from the references in the various writings. It is summarized in three tables. Disciples, of course, could be named in different ways using proper name, nickname, name of father, name of brother, etc., which would create legitimate confusion. Additionally however, references to individuals were affected by later political and leadership considerations, including a deliberate cover-up relating to the brothers and family of Jesus.

My candidates for "Early John's" original list of twelve apostles had the following names:

Simon and Andrew: brothers
John and James: brothers
Judas and Matthew
Philip and Nathaniel
James and Joseph: brothers
Simon and Judas: brothers

I will consider them in terms of three groups:
Group 1—Judas, Matthew, Philip, Nathaniel
Group 2—Simon, Andrew, James, John
Group 3—James, Joseph, Simon, Judas

Group 1 Disciples

Judas, Matthew and Philip are scribes, and Nathaniel seems to be a shaman. Judas is the author of the Thomas Gospel and Matthew is the inferred author of the Q1 Gospel, the two Sayings Gospels that precede any of the canonical gospels (see Chapters 1 and 2). Philip and Nathaniel were recruited by Jesus in a story contained in the "Early John" Gospel.

Evidence is presented below to suggest that these four (the middle group in all synoptic gospel lists) were probably early companions of Jesus, scribes or scholars, Hellenistically-oriented, and non-apocalyptic in ideology. Judas Thomas and Philip are named as authors of Gnostic gospels found at Nag Hammadi.

Judas is known generally by the nickname *Thomas*, meaning Twin in the Aramaic language. The only extant reference to the name Judas is in the prologue to the Thomas Gospel, which reads "These are the hidden sayings that the living Jesus spoke and Judas Thomas Didymos recorded" (Didymos means Twin in the Greek language). The synoptic gospels specify Thomas as one of the twelve, without any other mention. "Early John's" embedded material in the Johannine gospel does not mention Thomas; on the other hand "Later John" refers to Thomas Didymos several times. The nickname Thomas, presumably bestowed by Jesus, would be a way of distinguishing him from another disciple named "Judas." It also seems to suggest a sort of "spiritual twin" relationship with Jesus, which matches a self-described special understanding of Jesus set out in Thomas 13. Here Thomas records his own superiority to the disciples Simon Peter and Matthew, in terms of being the recipient of secret revelations from Jesus. Thomas 108 seems to confirm his own special status as scribal interpreter of the words of Jesus. Presumably his special understanding encompasses the whole approach of the Thomas Gospel in regard to Gnostic theological ideas and lifestyle implications. The sayings seem to fit a scenario of a peripatetic Jesus wandering around rural Palestine ("Be passersby" Thomas 42). One inference could be that Thomas was a very early companion of Jesus, prior to the John the Baptist events. Another inference is that he was a highly educated disciple with scribal status. A third inference is that he was deeply Gnostic in outlook.

Matthew seems to be another close associate of Jesus, named as part of the inner triumvirate in the Thomas Gospel (see also Chapter 19 for my interpretation of the reference to Matthew in Acts of the Apostles). He reputedly perceives Jesus in Hellenistic terms as a "wise philosopher" (Thomas 13), which is consistent with my inference of his authorship of the Q1 Sayings Gospel. As in the case of Thomas, Mark's Gospel makes no reference to Matthew, apart from his name. Perhaps Mark wished to avoid the implication that one of the chosen apostles was a former tax collector, as described in the Gospel of Matthew. This doesn't bother the author of the Gospel of Matthew, who explicitly attributes his gospel to a former tax collector, presumably because of his knowledge that Q1 was indeed written by Matthew. Certainly, the status of former tax collector and official is consistent with a Hellenistic outlook, a scribal background and a good education. It also implies that Matthew was wealthy, and converted to a completely alternative way of life. Whether this happened early or late in the teaching years of Jesus, is difficult to say. It is conceivable that Matthew was the official from Capernaum, whose son was "healed at a distance" by Jesus (John 4:46-54).

These two disciples, Judas Thomas and Matthew, as scribal authors, are primary sources of our information on the sapiential teachings of Jesus. Apparently, they were not interested in writing about miracle events, resurrection stories and apocalyptic prophecies.

NAMED APOSTLES CLASSIFIED BY NAME AND GOSPEL TEXT (GROUP 1)

GOSPEL	JUDAS	MATTHEW	PHILIP	NATHANIEL
"Early John"	-Judas Thomas[1] -Judas[3]	-Matthew the Tax Collector[1]	-Philip[1]	-Nathaniel[1] -Nathaniel of Cana[3]
Thomas	-Judas Thomas Didymos[5] -Thomas[3]	-Matthew[5]	-No mention	-No mention
Mark	-Thomas[2]	-Matthew[2] -Levi, son of Alphaeus[4]	-Philip[2]	-Bartholomew[4]
Matthew	-Thomas[2]	-Matthew the Tax Collector[2]	-Philip[2]	-Bartholomew[4]
Luke	-Thomas[2]	-Matthew[2] -Levi, the Tax Collector[4]	-Philip[2]	-Bartholomew[4]
"Later John"	-Thomas Didymos[5] -Thomas[3]	-No mention	-Philip[5]	-Nathaniel[5]

1. Inferred name in list of twelve apostles contained in inferred "Early John" text.
2. Name used by author in list of twelve apostles.
3. Other name mentioned elsewhere in gospel text.
4. Inferred cover-up name intended by author to suggest a separate person.
5. Name used by author.

Philip is a Greek name. The story of his recruitment by Jesus is ambiguous. According to the Johannine gospel (John 1:43-44), Jesus finds him directly and makes him the first disciple to respond to the words "Follow me." In this context, Philip seems to be a former disciple of John the Baptist, recruited in the desert at the same time as his friends Simon Peter and Andrew. But this may not be so. There is also contrary evidence that Philip was recruited by Jesus at an earlier time.[1] He is presented as a key disciple of Jesus who locates

Nathaniel (John 1:45), organizes the feeding of the multitude (John 6:5-7), is an intermediary to Greeks wishing to see Jesus (John 12:20-22), and asks a leading sceptical question of Jesus at the Last Supper (John 14:8). In this latter role, he is portrayed by "Later John" as failing to understand that "He who has seen me has seen the Father" (John 14:9). And Jesus says, "Have I been with you *so long*, and yet you do not know me, Philip" (John 14:9, emphasis added).

The point is that Philip has a different understanding of the identity of Jesus than does "Later John"; it is a Gnostic perception. This becomes very explicit in the Gnostic Gospel of Philip found at Nag Hammadi.[2] It is also interesting that the Acts of the Apostles portrays Philip as a missionary to the Samaritans and converter of the Gnostic teacher Simon Magus (Acts 8:9-13).

Nathaniel is a friend of Philip (John 1:45), who may be a Samaritan, described by Jesus as "an Israelite indeed in whom is no guile" (John 1:47); part of Nathaniel's response is to proclaim that Jesus is King of Israel (John 1:49). Note that Samaria regarded itself as the "true Israel." Perhaps this "Early John" dialogue is intended to convey the idea that a Samaritan can be as genuine an Israelite as anyone else. Jesus seems to recognize Nathaniel "under the fig tree" as a special holy man. His Nathaniel name is nowhere to be found in the three synoptic gospels, although it is likely that he is there under the name Bartholomew. It is interesting that the Son of Tholomew lacks a proper name and is paired with Philip in the synoptic gospel lists of names.

I assume that the name Nathaniel was an embarrassment to Mark (for unknown reasons), when he prepared the first synoptic gospel list. Mark also included Thomas, Matthew and Philip in his list, but they are only names; Mark has not a word of information about any of them, including Bartholomew. These Group 1 apostles may have shared the following characteristics: Hellenistic origins or connections, early colleagues or followers of Jesus, qualifications as scribes, Gnostic understandings, and probably not of peasant status.

Group 2 Disciples

The second group consists of Simon and Andrew who are brothers; and John and James who are brothers. These disciples are recruited as Jesus begins an active missionary program related in some way to John the Baptist. According to the Johannine gospel, the recruitment and mission was in Judea, when John was still actively baptizing in the Jordan Valley. According to Mark's Gospel, the recruitment and mission was in Galilee after the arrest and imprisonment of John by King Herod Antipas. In both instances Simon and Andrew are the first named recruits to join Jesus.

NAMED APOSTLES CLASSIFIED BY NAME AND GOSPEL TEXT (GROUP2)

GOSPEL	SIMON	ANDREW	JOHN	JAMES
"Early John"	-Simon Peter[1] -Simon, brother of Andrew[3] -Simon, son of John[3]	-Andrew[1] -Andrew, brother of Simon[3]	-John[1] -John, son of Zebedee[3]	-James, brother of John[1] -James, son of Zebedee[3]
Thomas	-Simon Peter[4]	-No mention	-No mention	-No mention
Mark	-Simon Peter[2] -Simon[3] -Simon bar Jonah[3]	-Andrew[2] -Andrew, brother of Simlon[3]	-John, son of Zebedee[2] -Brother of James[2] -Thunder brother[2]	-James, son of Zebedee[2] -Brother of John[2] -Thunder brother[2]
Matthew	-Simon Peter[2] -Simon[3] -Simon bar Jonah[3]	-Andrew[2] -Andrew, brother of Simon[3]	-John, son of Zebedee[2] -Brother of James[2]	-James, son of Zebedee[2] -Brother of John[2]
Luke	-Simon Peter[2] -Simon[3]	-Andrew[2] -Andrew, brother of Simon[3]	-John[2] -John, son of Zebedee[3]	-James[2] -James, son of Zebedee[3]
"Later John"	-Simon Peter[4] -Simon, brother of Andrew[3] -Simon, son of John[3]	-Andrew[4] -Andrew, brother of Simon[3]	-John, son of Zebedee[4]	-James, son of Zebedee[4]

1. Inferred name in list of twelve apostles contained in inferred "Early John" text.
2. Name used by author in his list of twelve apostles.
3. Other name mentioned elsewhere in gospel text.
4. Name used by author.

Simon is given the nickname Peter by Jesus, according to both "Early John" and Mark; it means "rock," signifying that Simon Peter is the first "stone" of the new Temple of God built with human stones, also a concept of the Essenes. This special distinction seems to derive from Simon Peter's status as a former disciple of John the Baptist (John 1:42). The recruitment of Simon as a disciple seems to mark the beginning of new directions in the story of Jesus.

Thomas reports that Simon Peter perceives Jesus as a "just angel" or messenger (Thomas 13), thus situating Jesus in the image of John the Baptist. From this "imperfect" perspective, Peter becomes an explicit sinner associated with violence, symbolized in the cutting off of Malchus' ear (John 18:10), and expressed as denial of Jesus at the time of his arrest in all the canonical gospels. It is interesting that the Thomas, "Early John" and Markan gospels all participate in denigrating Peter, while simultaneously acknowledging his status as an important disciple. Thomas puts him down for not understanding the teachings of Jesus. "Early John" locates him as a co-leader with "the other disciple," but again with inferior intelligence; Mark perceives him as a badly flawed leader among the disciples. But in the emerging post-crucifixion scenario, Paul specifies Peter as witness of the first appearance by Jesus; the Matthew Gospel allocates to him "the keys of the Kingdom"; and "Later John" elevates him to leadership when the resurrected Jesus tells him to "feed my sheep." As a former disciple of John the Baptist and a humble fisherman, Simon Peter tends to reflect a traditional Hebrew outlook.

Andrew, the brother of Simon Peter, is featured in the "Early John" Gospel as the first person, along with the unnamed "other disciple," to discover Jesus as the Messiah of Israel. Andrew is also shown working closely with Philip in assisting Jesus. The Markan gospel pinpoints him as a Galilean fisherman, along with his brother Simon Peter.

John and James, the Galilean fishermen sons of Zebedee, are featured by Mark as an inner triumvirate with Peter. These "Thunder Brothers," depicted by Mark as anticipating their own power role in a new messianic Kingdom of God in Israel, seem chosen to represent the wrong-headedness of the majority of disciples, unable to understand the total divinity and true mission of Jesus to the world outside Israel. However, according to Mark, they are privileged with Peter to witness the revelation of the Transfiguration, as well as prophecies of Jesus concerning his own resurrection and the approaching "end of days." Yet even while Mark sets up John and James as "inner three" members, he shows them asleep at the switch, along with Peter, when Jesus is about to be arrested. Evidently, according to Mark, the Thunder Brothers are cowards who run away just like all the other disciples.

I conclude that Andrew and Simon Peter were former disciples of John the Baptist, were inclined to strict observance (perhaps Essene), and were recruited by Jesus perhaps with the help of James, his brother (see below). Note also "James and John, sons of Zebedee, were partners with Simon" (Luke 5:10). These four were clearly Galilean "Hebrews" in contrast to the Group 1 disciples, who were perhaps more "Hellenized."

Group 3 Disciples

James, Joseph, Simon and Judas are the four brothers (or half-brothers) of Jesus, as discussed below.

According to Mark, the four brothers of Jesus are neither disciples nor apostles. His source document may have been "Early John," which shows "disciples" and unnamed "brothers" of Jesus (John 2:12) as separate entities. But when it comes to the post-crucifixion appointment of apostles, the inferred "Early John" Gospel probably included named brothers of Jesus on his list (see Chapters 3, 5 and 8). Insofar as Mark was aware that the four brothers of Jesus were among the named apostles, his efforts to hide this information constitute a cover-up. The other canonical gospel writers either took their lead from Mark (i.e. Matthew), or participated in a cover-up (i.e. Luke and "Later John").

Suspicion about the identity of *James* (not the brother of John) begins with his designation by Mark's Gospel as one of the twelve apostles, the son of Alphaeus (first letter of the Greek alphabet), and explicitly a brother of someone called Levi (Mark 2:14 and 3:18). Later Mark informs his readers that a James the Younger is the son of Mary and brother of Joses (Mark 15:40), and James is the brother of Jesus (Mark 6:3). According to Mark, an unnamed "young man" follows Jesus after his arrest by the authorities, and is humiliated when he is stripped naked and runs away (Mark 14:51). This latter event replaces the Johannine version of the "other disciple known to the High Priest," who accompanies Jesus to the palace of the High Priest after his arrest (John 18:15). The Johannine version later identifies the "other disciple" as "the disciple that Jesus loves," the first to see and believe in the resurrection of Jesus at the Empty Tomb. He is also identified as the author of the Gospel of John (John 20:2,8 and 21:24).

The term "disciple whom Jesus loved" is used by "Later John"; the term "other disciple" is the wording of "Early John." A reference to Lazarus as "he whom you love" (John 11:3) may have been written by "Early John," thus serving as "Later John's" source for use of the phrase. There is a strong possibility that Lazarus is the same person as the "disciple whom Jesus loved." The Thomas Gospel tells us that Jesus named *James the Just* (i.e. James the Righteous) to be leader when Jesus "had left the disciples," with the extravagant compliment "No matter where you are, you are to go to James the Just (or Righteous) for whose sake heaven and earth came into being" (Thomas 12). Note that the title "the Righteous" matches the name of the Qumram Essene Teacher of Righteousness, found in the Dead Sea Scrolls; and that the extravagant compliment about "heaven and earth" matches the significance of a revered founder leader. "Going to James no matter where you are" matches the historical likelihood that the disciples, having returned to their homes after the death of Jesus, later came back to Jerusalem to organize themselves under James and Simon Peter for a new missionary enterprise. This James is specified to be "the brother of the Lord" and "apostle" by none other than Paul (Galatians 1:19), who also states in other letters that Peter and James experienced post-resurrection appearances of Jesus, and were the leaders of the Jerusalem church.

Further details of the evidence that this James was the brother of Jesus are outlined in Chapter 3. Among the extraordinary conclusions that derive from this hypothesis are:

1. James, the brother (or half brother) of Jesus, became a follower of Jesus before Jesus' crucifixion.
2. James is the author of the "Early John" Gospel.
3. James refers to himself anonymously in accordance with Jesus' teaching that family members have no precedence in the Kingdom of God.
4. James borrows the name Lazarus to improve the credibility of the story of his rescue from the family tomb by Jesus.
5. James includes himself in the inferred "Early John" post-crucifixion list of the twelve apostles. Mark covers up by listing him as James, son of Alphaeus; Matthew and Luke repeat the cover-up designation. See Chapter 21 for more about James.

NAMED APOSTLES CLASSIFIED BY NAME AND GOSPEL TEXT (GROUP 3)

GOSPEL	JAMES	JOSEPH	SIMON	JUDAS
"Early John"	-"Other disciple"[4] -Lazarus[4] -James the Just[1]	-Joseph, brother of James the Just[1] -Joseph of Arimathea[4]	-Simon the Zealot[1]	-Judas, brother of Simon the Zealot[1]
Thomas	-James the Just[5]	-No mention	-No mention	-No mention
Mark	-James, son of Alphaeus[2,4] -James the Younger[3] -"Young man"[3] -James, son of Mary[3] -James, brother of Jesus[3] -James, brother of Joses[3]	-Levi, son of Alphaeus[4] -Thaddeus[2,4] -Joses, son of Mary[3] -Joses, brother of Jesus[3] -Joses, brother of James[3] -Joseph of Arimathea[4]	-Simon of Cana[2,4] -Simon the Leper[4] -Simon, son of Mary[3] -Simon, brother of Jesus[3]	-Judas Iscariot[2,4] -Judas, son of Mary[3] -Judas, brother of Jesus[3]
Matthew	-James, son of Alphaeus[2] -James, son of Mary[3] -James, brother of Jesus[3] -James, brother of Joseph[3]	-Lebbaeus[2] -Joseph, son of Mary[3] -Joseph, brother of Jesus[3] -Joseph, brother of James[3] -Joseph of Arimathea[4]	-Simon of Cana[2] -Simon the Leper[4] -Simon, son of Mary[3] -Simon, brother of Jesus[3]	-Judas Iscariot[2] -Judas, son of Mary[3] -Judas, brother of Jesus[3]

Luke	-James, son of Alphaeus[2] -James, son of Mary[3]	-Judas, brother of James[2] -Levi the Tax Collector [3,4] -Joseph Barsabbas Justus[5] -Joseph of Arimathea[4]	-Simon the Zealot[2]	-Judas Iscariot [2,4] -Judas, brother of James [2,4]
"Later John"	-"Beloved disciple"[4] -Lazarus[4]	-No mention	-Simon Iscariot, brother of Judas Iscariot[5]	-Judas Iscariot, brother of Simon Iscariot[5]

1. Inferred name in list of twelve apostles in inferred "Early John" text.
2. Name used by the author in his list of twelve apostles.
3. Other name mentioned elsewhere in gospel text.
4. Inferred cover-up name intended by author to suggest a separate person.
5. Name used by author.

That *Joseph* was both the name of a brother of Jesus, and also a disciple seems highly probable, despite incredible efforts by the synoptic gospel writers to show otherwise. The main proof comes from the transparency of these efforts. Mark seems focused particularly on Joseph, presumably because his name might point to Joseph as father of both Jesus and his brothers, thus rendering all of them descendants of King David. In fact, Mark omits any mention of Jesus' father, while describing Jesus as son of Mary; a most unusual omission. Among possible explanations are: 1) Mark's earlier definition of Jesus as Son of God; 2) a need to suppress the royal lineage of Jesus and his brothers as sons of David; or 3) a need to suppress the notion that Mary had more than one husband. So Mark replaces the name Joseph with Joses as brother of James. The author of Matthew, however, who solves the problem of Joseph the father with his virgin birth story, replaces the name Joses with Joseph in both instances where Mark mentions the sons of Mary, and adds that Jesus is known as "the carpenter's son." Luke and "Later John" avoid any problem by omitting to provide names for the brothers of Jesus.

The synoptic writers perform extraordinary antics to replace Joseph as a named apostle. Mark invents a new disciple named Levi who is a composite of Joseph and Matthew; that is to say Levi is the brother of James (son of Alphaeus) and a former tax collector (replacing Matthew in this new role). Levi is a disciple of Jesus and brother of James, but is excluded from Mark's list of twelve apostles; instead, there is Thaddeus, whose name may be a reversed duplicate of Judas Thomas (Thaddeus may be a condensation of Thomas Judas). The result is that Joseph (renamed Levi), is not one of the twelve, according to Mark. When the Matthew writer encounters Mark's text (Matthew has no access to the "Early John" text), he restores the status of the disciple Matthew as former tax collector, and transfers the name Levi back into the list of apostles by changing the name Thaddeus, which may mean Thomas Judas, to Lebbaeus, which may mean Levi Judas. Luke, on the other hand, has access to and utilizes the "Early John" text, but he also wants to continue the Markan cover-up of the role of Jesus' brothers. Luke therefore continues the Markan story of the disciple Levi as the former tax collector, but deletes the reference to Levi as Son of Alphaeus, transferring his status as brother of James back to Thaddeus. Luke then perceives that Thomas Judas (i.e. Thaddeus) includes a misplaced nickname, so he removes the nickname Thomas, leaving Judas, of James, which means Judas, brother of James (in Greek the expression can mean brother or son). Luke now has a second Judas among the apostles who is the brother of James, and a remaining Thomas (without the name Judas) who is not the brother of James. But what is Luke to do about Joseph, brother of James, mentioned as one of the twelve apostles in his "Early John" source? The solution for Luke is to "disappear" Judas Iscariot after the crucifixion of Jesus, and hold a replacement election between a second Matthew and Joseph (see Acts 1:15-26). The winner of the election is Matthew, who is designated Matthias by Luke to distinguish him from the other Matthew. The loser of the election is Joseph Barsabbas Justus, a title meaning Joseph, son of the father (i.e. Joseph) and nicknamed the Just (a transfer of the nickname from James the Just). The end result for Luke is an apostle James (son of Alphaeus) and a non-apostle Joseph, neither of whom are brothers of Jesus. "Later John" avoids the whole mess by simply removing the "Early John" list of apostles from his revised gospel.

Simon the Zealot is the brother of Judas Iscariot, as Joseph is the brother of James Justus. What we have in the inferred "Early John" text are two Justus brothers and two Zealot brothers, all of whom are brothers of Jesus. Such a hypothesis explains Mark's list of four named brothers (Mark 6:3) and Luke's decision to reduce confusion by excluding the names of Jesus' brothers (Luke 4:22) when devising an alternative story of the visit to Nazareth by Jesus.

The Johannine gospel's "Later John" text refers four times to Judas Iscariot as the son of Simon Iscariot. In the original Greek text this was written as Judas, of Simon Iscariot, an ambiguous rendering which could mean either son or brother of Simon.[3] In at least one instance "Iscariot" is written as "the Iscariot."[3] The meaning is Scariot or Zealot assassin. An important conclusion is that "Later John" was referring repeatedly to Judas as brother of Simon Iscariot, in order to distinguish him from the other Judas (not Iscariot). In his "Early John" source, the inferred references would be Simon, the Zealot, and Judas, brother of Simon; "Later John" changes this to the pejorative Iscariot. Mark, on the other hand wanted to disguise any implications of brotherly relationships among his last four apostles. He therefore borrows a Cana designation from Nathaniel, replacing Simon the Zealot with Simon of Cana (the Cananean); like Thomas, Nathaniel also loses his proper name and becomes Bartholomew (son of Tholomeus). The Matthew author accepts Mark's version, but Luke (being aware of the "Early John" text) compromises by changing Simon of Cana back to Simon the Zealot, which preserves his original nickname, but keeps him distinct from Judas Iscariot.

Judas Iscariot is not a villain in the "Early John" narrative, written by his own brother James. In fact, it seems more likely that the Judas who went out from the Last Supper to fetch the Roman soldiers was Judas Thomas, who could be relied upon to carry out the wishes of Jesus. The betrayal story of Judas Iscariot was invented by Mark, but without mentioning that a certain Judas was sent out from the Last Supper by Jesus. Mark also suppresses the name Judas that belongs to Thomas, and changes the nickname of Simon the Zealot to focus attention on Judas Iscariot as a non-brother of Jesus whose motivation for betrayal is money (see Chapter 5). The actual Judas, brother of Jesus, survives as an apostle into the post-crucifixion era, as reflected in Luke's reference to him as Judas, of James, and the canonical Letter of Jude.

Sisters and Mother of Jesus

The *sisters of Jesus*, according to Mark, numbered more than one; he assigns no names. If "Early John's" Lazarus of Bethany was actually James, brother or half-brother of Jesus, it follows that the sisters of Lazarus, Mary and Martha, were sisters or half-sisters of Jesus. For "Early John" (see Chapter 3), the disguise of family relationships continues into the Bethany meal/Last Supper story, and the crucifixion scenario. Lazarus becomes the "other disciple," Mary of Bethany becomes Mary of Magdala, and Martha of Bethany perhaps becomes Salome. When "Later John" separates the Bethany meal from the Last Supper, he integrates the former with the Lazarus story by re-identifying Lazarus and Mary of Bethany as participants in the Bethany meal.

The canonical Gospel of Mark deals with these matters by suppressing the Lazarus story, assigning unnamed protagonists to the Bethany meal story, replacing "the other disciple" with an unnamed "young man," and accepting Mary of Magdala and Salome as witnesses in later crucifixion events. Mark's acceptance of Mary of Magdala and Salome as followers of Jesus fits the text of the Gospel of Thomas, which describes "Mary" and Salome as female disciples of Jesus.

Do Mary and Martha of Bethany equate with Mary of Magdala and Salome? Logic would say yes. Why would female followers of Jesus witness the crucifixion and Empty Tomb, while sisters remain at home in nearby Bethany? This question is particularly compelling when we take into account the third woman at the crucifixion and Empty Tomb named by Mark as Mary, mother of James the Younger and Joses (i.e. Joseph). The probability is, therefore, that Mary of Magdala and Salome were sisters of Jesus.

---

[1]   I am interpreting the sentence in the Johannine gospel which reads "Now Philip was from Bethsaida, the city of Andrew and Peter" (John 1:44) as a "Later John" cover-up. The purpose may have been to suggest that Andrew and Peter brought Jesus to Philip, who in turn brought him to Nathaniel. This seems to contradict the previous sentence, written perhaps by "Early John," that reads "And he found Philip and said to him, 'Follow me.'" Philip is the first disciple to whom Jesus directs the pithy words "Follow me." My inference is that "Early John's" original text showed Philip and Nathaniel as earlier followers of Jesus, preceding the later recruitment of Andrew and Peter. Mark's later text confirms this by borrowing the words "Follow me" from "Early John" and applying them to Andrew and Peter, whom he designates as the first recruited followers of Jesus. Mark portrays Capernaum as the hometown of Andrew and Peter - not Bethsaida. Presumably, "Later John" wanted to conceal Jesus' earlier associations, by suggesting that his mission began with the recruitment of Andrew and Peter. They then brought Philip into the picture because he was their friend from the same hometown of Bethsaida.

[2]   The Gospel of Philip is a Gnostic sayings gospel written in the second century C.E., and found at Nag Hammadi. Its attribution to the apostle Philip is suggestive, although very little of its contents can be traced back to the time of Jesus.

[3]   See Eisenman, Robert, *James, the Brother of Jesus*, pp.712 and 812-815, Viking, New York, 1996.

CHAPTER 15

JESUS AND JOHN THE BAPTIST

According to the canonical gospels, the active mission of Jesus began when he received the Spirit directly from God, after coming to the place where John the Baptist was located. The synoptic gospels associate this revelation experience directly with water baptism of Jesus by John, a sort of consecration device symbolizing God's new intervention in the affairs of humankind. The Johannine gospel, however, fails to mention any water baptism, relying rather on verbal endorsement by John the Baptist of Jesus' special status. While John is quoted as describing a vision, "I saw the Spirit descend as a dove from heaven, and it remained on him," there is no reference by Jesus himself in either "Early John" or the Thomas Gospel to any defining moment or revelation from God. The reference to the descent of the Spirit may therefore represent an anti-Gnostic redefinition by the "Early John" writer of Jesus' own perception of the activated Holy Spirit within himself.

Many scholars have argued that the public water baptism of Jesus by John is one of the few certainties in the New Testament, because why invent something that seems to make John superior and Jesus sinful prior to being baptized. The Johannine gospel omits it, but may be argued as confirming it.[1] If the "Early John" Gospel was written fairly close to actual events, and was aimed (at least partially) at the former followers of John the Baptist (see Chapter 3), the author would likely suppress anything that appeared to contradict Jesus' superiority to John, as expressed in John's various endorsements of Jesus.

The contrary argument is that Mark couldn't find explicit mention of the baptism in his sources, and therefore invented it to fit a mythological analogy with the Old Testament prophet Samuel and King David. Any implied superiority of John the Baptist could be offset by the voice of God saying

"Thou art my beloved Son, with thee I am well pleased" (Mark 1:11), and by clarifying that the transmission of the Spirit came directly from God and not via John the Baptist's water baptism (Mark 1:9-11). Mark couldn't find mention of baptism, because it never happened. Although Jesus admired and supported some teachings of John, there must have been important differences and concerns. In practical terms, to have presented himself for baptism by John would have placed him in the subordinate role of disciple, whereas he wanted to proclaim an alternative approach, as shown in the words of Jesus about John expressed in Thomas 46.

The evidence for competition between Jesus and John the Baptist was largely suppressed in the synoptic gospels. The main way of doing this was to place the beginning of the public mission of Jesus *after* the arrest of John the Baptist by King Herod (Mark 1:14). In this way, Jesus' mission could be presented as a fulfilment of the advance work done by John, who is described as God's messenger even though differences of practice between Jesus and John (such as fasting) had to be acknowledged. If so, the synoptic gospels may constitute a later cover-up of what might be termed a "leadership race" between John the Baptist and Jesus, with Jesus entering the race as an underdog.

The existence of competition between Jesus and John the Baptist is fudged also in the "Early John" Gospel, but as it was written fairly close in time to the actual events, it could not deny the simultaneous activities of the two contenders. Instead, "Early John" tries to show that John the Baptist prophesied the coming of Jesus and endorsed him at first contact as the Lamb of God. "Among you stands one you do not know, even he who comes after me, the thong of whose sandal I am not worthy to untie" (John 1:26-27); this message was repeated in the synoptic gospels.

"Early John" had to deal with the simultaneous baptizing activity by John and Jesus in Judea (John 3:22), described as "Jesus was making and baptizing more disciples than John" (John 4:1).[2] The purported response by John the Baptist is to re-endorse Jesus with the quote "He must increase, but I must decrease" (John 3:30).

"Early John," however, fails to repress the evidence that the baptizing mission of Jesus in Judea was not a co-operative venture with John. The news is brought to John by his own disciples after they hear about it in a discussion with "a Jew over purifying" (John 3:25), implying perhaps a division of opinion between Jesus and John on the meaning of baptism. Josephus writes "John was a good man and had exhorted the Jews to lead righteous lives, to practice justice towards their fellows and piety towards God, and so doing to join in baptism . . ." (Antiquities 18:116-19). Jesus certainly agreed with John concerning righteousness and justice, but differed with him about the meaning of "piety towards God." The Thomas Gospel reports clearly on Jesus' sceptical attitude towards circumcision

(Thomas 53), fasting (Thomas 14) and food rituals (Thomas 14). John baptized with water for bodily purification in preparation for the forthcoming Kingdom, whereas Jesus baptized with the Spirit, signifying entry into a spiritual Kingdom already present in the world.

It is significant that Jesus attended the meeting at Bethany between John the Baptist and the priests and Levites from the Jerusalem Temple, who were attempting to assess John's intentions. But surprisingly, "Early John" quotes John the Baptist as saying that Jesus "stands among you" (i.e. among priests and Levites—John 1:26), indicating some sort of link between Jesus and the representatives of the Temple cult. And yet Jesus also perceives John as a highly righteous leader of the poor and oppressed, confirmed somewhat unexpectedly from a saying of Jesus in the Thomas Gospel, presumably addressed to the priests and Levites:

"Why have you come out to the countryside? To see a reed shaken by the wind? And to see a person dressed in soft clothes (like your) rulers and powerful ones? They are dressed in soft clothes, and they cannot understand truth" (Thomas 78).

Jesus appears disillusioned by the failure of the meeting to achieve some sort of reconciliation or understanding. In turn he is influenced to become more directly active in seeking a peaceful way towards the Kingdom of God. Quite possibly, Jesus may have hoped to deter violent action either by John or against John, by attracting followers away from him to forestall "some sort of revolt" (see Josephus, Antiquities 18:2).

So Jesus succeeded in recruiting some of John's disciples from directly under his nose (John 1:37-42), despite Jesus' own divergent views against strict observance of purification rituals.

Could it be that the unnamed disciple who accompanied Andrew in turning to Jesus (John 1:37-40) was James, brother of Jesus, and presumed author of the "Early John" text? Elsewhere in the Johannine gospel, there is evidence that other references to an unnamed disciple do mean the presumed author of "Early John" (see Chapter 3). And when Andrew says to his brother Simon "We have found the Messiah" (John 1:41), he is implying that the unnamed disciple and himself have initiated the discovery, which could mean that it is James who brings Andrew to Jesus. All of which opens up the possibility that brother James was helping Jesus become involved with activist Zealot-minded disciples of John. This line of thought also ties in with the nicknames of various disciples such as "Rock," "Thunder Brothers," and "Zealot or Iscariot." Another indicator that Jesus' change in direction could have been influenced by his brothers is the quote attributed to them: "no man works in secret if he seeks to be known openly" (John 7:4). The spread of the Kingdom of God, even though spiritual, had to involve public explanation to the people.

The next step was the public baptizing mission of Jesus in Judea, in direct competition with John for recruits. Whatever interpretation Jesus provided and whether or not he used water or the Spirit, he was moving to broaden perceived accessibility to the Kingdom; and he was moving from a quietist teacher to an activist figure.

The significance of baptism with the Spirit cannot be overstated, because it meant both that Jesus was filled with the Holy Spirit, a divine emanation, and that it could flow from him to others who qualified for entry into the Kingdom of God. Similarly, other activities such as healing the sick and table fellowship were expressions of the timeless presence of the Spirit flowing and connecting between persons. Note especially from "Early John" the element of surprise by recipients as they open up to the Spirit regardless of past sins, and experience a transformation of consciousness. They have moved directly into the Kingdom of God, bypassing Temple animal sacrifices, Essene purification rituals, and Jordan River water baptism by John the Baptist.

It is no surprise then that some of his followers, beginning with Andrew, perceived Jesus as specially anointed by God (John 1:41) to announce the presence of the Gnostic Kingdom of God, which equated with the activated presence of the Holy Spirit. This idea of "the anointed one" or Messiah, derived perhaps from the scriptural writings of the prophet Isaiah, was an important means of distinguishing Jesus from John the baptizer, and of implying his superiority to John. Initially, it may have been intended as an ambiguous nickname that permitted Jesus to be perceived either as a sort of spiritual philosopher King, or as God's choice for traditional King of Israel. The nickname Messiah probably came from former followers of John the Baptist, not from Gnostics such as Thomas. There is no convincing evidence that Jesus himself accepted it.

There is evidence, however, that Jesus may have played down his radical teachings in order to minimize his differences with John the Baptist, and to emphasize the openness of the new Kingdom to everyone. The "Early John" text contains only minimal information on the public teachings of Jesus, as if there was little to choose between Jesus and John as to their content. Nevertheless, the "Early John" text does imply that Jesus explained his views privately to his new disciples, after they turned away from John to follow him (John 1:37:39). The Gnostic teachings of Jesus in the Thomas Gospel are specified to be "secret" in that text, presumably partly replaced in public discourse by parables, signs and works in order to minimize controversy.

Jesus admired John the Baptist, not hesitating to praise him in Thomas 46: "From Adam to John the Baptist, among those born of women, no one is so much greater than John the Baptist that the person's eyes should not be averted." Yet the differences remain profound in the same passages: "But I have said that whoever among you becomes a child will recognize the Kingdom and will become greater than John" (Thomas 46, Matthew 11:9-11 and Luke 7:26-28).

John clearly had strong antipathy towards the Romans, the Temple establishment and King Herod Antipas, which was not matched by Jesus. According to "Early John," Jesus "stood among" the priests and Levites. A saying in the Thomas Gospel (later adapted by Mark) indicated his acceptance of the Roman domination, even in secret teaching to his inner-group followers.

"They showed Jesus a gold coin and said to him 'Caesar's men demand taxes from us.' He said to them, 'Give Caesar what belongs to Caesar, give God what belongs to God, and give me what is mine'" (Thomas 100).

---

1   Crossan, J.D., *The Historical Jesus*, pp. 234-235, Harper, San Francisco, 1992.
2   "Later John" tries to evade this by inserting "although Jesus himself did not baptize but only his disciples" (John 4:2).

CHAPTER 16

THE RESPONSE OF JESUS TO THE DEATH OF JOHN THE BAPTIST

The Gospel of Mark (Mark 1:14) states that Jesus commenced his public mission in Galilee, after the arrest and imprisonment of John the Baptist. His probable source was the "Early John" text, even though the edited Johannine gospel fails to mention it (see Chapter 5). Remember that "Later John" was covering up the Feast of Tabernacles insurrection story in his own way, which included disregarding the execution of John, which had happened many decades earlier (see Chapters 3 and 9). The Johannine text moves Jesus into Galilee after a successful public mission in Judea, first in Cana (John 4:46), a town not far from Nazareth, with his disciples and his brothers. Here Jesus is reported as performing a healing at a distance, and receiving a great reception by the people, despite (or because of) the immediately preceding comment "that a prophet has no honour in his own country" (John 4:44), presumably meaning Nazareth.

Since all canonical gospels and the Thomas Gospel concur that Jesus was rejected by his home village of Nazareth, the hostility of its residents may be taken for granted whether it was directed against the family of Jesus or arose from the actions or words of Jesus himself. But the stories by Mark and Luke, intended to illustrate this hostility, lack credibility. Mark's version seems intended to locate Jesus' family in Nazareth as part of the hostile population that perceives Jesus as a presumptuous fool (Mark 6:1-6). Luke, on the other hand, ignores the family of Jesus, while explaining the hostility as a response to public insults by Jesus to the local population (Luke 4:16-30).

In focusing on Cana, the Johaninne gospel implies the presence of both disciples and relatives. The disciples are with Jesus on the way to Cana (John

4:27, 31), and accompany him when he leaves Cana for Capernaum (John 2:12). His brothers and mother accompany him from Cana to Capernaum as well (John 2:12). Their presence in Capernaum is confirmed by Mark (Mark 3:20-21 and 31).

Jesus proceeds with his teaching and healing. Luke is our best guide, because he seems to omit quite a bit of Markan material that may have seemed too out-of-line with Luke's "Early John" source. For example, and significantly, Luke entirely omits Mark's follow-up stories to the feeding of the 5000 (Mark 6:45-8:26), with the exception of the Transfiguration, all of which precede the commencement of the journey to Jerusalem. He therefore seems to match "Early John" in closely sequencing the feeding of the multitude story and the trip to Jerusalem.

Was Jesus in touch with the disciples of John the Baptist while John was in prison before his execution? The available evidence deriving from the Q Gospel is flawed. The reported visit to Jesus by disciples of John, elaborated by both Matthew and Luke, seems designed to showcase Jesus as the expected Messiah with reference to the positive results of his teaching and healing activities; followers of John are congratulated for "taking no offence at me" (Luke 7:23). This appears to confirm that Jesus may have been perceived by John's disciples as taking advantage of John's imprisonment to push his own competitive vision of the meaning of God's Kingdom. Perhaps, therefore, Jesus was attempting to show empathy with John by downplaying the distinct features of his own teaching, and by avoiding Hellenized communities. Insofar as Jesus became identified with John's followers, of course, he risked incurring the wrath of King Herod Antipas. According to Luke (Luke 13:31), King Herod wanted to kill Jesus as well as John.

There is no direct comment by Jesus concerning the execution of John, but he must have been profoundly shocked. In the synoptic gospels, Jesus remains silent; in the Johannine gospel, there is not even a mention of John's death. Does this not suggest a cover-up of a link between John's death and subsequent actions by Jesus?

My inference is that Jesus actually reached out to the followers of John, just as he had reached out earlier to a few of John's leading disciples. The hypothesis, set out in Chapter 3, is that the lost "Early John" Gospel describes how, after the death of John, Jesus met a large number of his followers (and perhaps others) somewhere near Lake Galilee to persuade them that all was not lost, but rather that the Kingdom of God was already here, encompassed in the presiding presence of the Holy Spirit. Very significant here are the words "he had compassion on them because they were like sheep without a shepherd" (Mark 6:34), highly suggestive of a group who had lost their leader.

This was a new situation for Jesus. He was faced with a large group of relatively poor hinterland people who were looking for new direction and leadership, not just comforting words from an itinerant preacher. There may have been a sense of urgency at the time, arising from the probable turmoil and disturbance occasioned by John's execution. Some of Jesus' disciples, including his brothers, may well have urged Jesus to take some action. And what seems to have emerged, perhaps with reluctance from Jesus, is a less intellectual and a more action-oriented teaching approach, suitable to the predilections of his audience. The new medium for his public messages was the "sign," a sort of theatrical approach that went beyond ordinary healings and exorcisms. He used "surprise" as a teaching tactic, as in his earlier verbal messages. But now he invoked images of ancient scripture.

The feeding of the multitude of 5000 men was the first of a series of "surprises" intended to bring about an unprecedented revolutionary (but peaceful) change in the hearts and minds of the people of Israel. Jesus worked within the parameters of scriptural tradition, the only way to achieve meaningful rapport with his listeners. It would seem that the sharing of five loaves and two fishes among a huge crowd symbolically recalled the "manna in the Wilderness" that God provided to his hungry people as they wandered in the desert before reaching the Promised Land. Probably this gesture stimulated sharing of food by everyone present (why would they have assembled in the desert without bringing their own nourishment?) thus contrasting the bountifulness of Jesus' version of the Kingdom of God with the fasting ethic of John the Baptist. And this process, equated with the presiding presence of the Holy Spirit, expressed the values of open commensality, equal participation and sharing.

It also seems likely that this meeting represented a coming together of two divergent offshoots of the Essene community—the traditionalist-minded followers of John the Baptist, and the more Hellenistically-oriented original companions and followers of Jesus. There is indeed a hint of two separate Kingdom groups in "Early John's" explicit mention of Philip (Hellenist) and Andrew (Hebrew) as Jesus' main helpers in managing the feeding of the multitude (John 6:5-13). Mark's later deletion of the names of Philip and Andrew seems to drive home the distinctness of the participating groups, which Mark was intent on suppressing (see Chapter 5).

The response of the 5000 men was, however, somewhat more than Jesus may have anticipated. "Perceiving then that they were about to come and take him by force to make him king, Jesus withdrew to the mountain by himself" (John 6:15). Note the implication here that they wanted Jesus as a replacement for King Herod Antipas who had executed John the Baptist.[1] Perhaps they wanted to attack King Herod in Galilee. Jesus may have preached "loving your enemies" and "turning the other cheek"; he somehow redirected their attention toward Jerusalem. My inference is that Jesus negotiated with these people and persuaded many of them to join with him in celebration of the Feast of Tabernacles in Jerusalem, and a joyous demonstration with him through signs ("the works that you are doing"—John 7:3) of the presence of the Kingdom of God. He may also have implied that the Holy Spirit might preside over a "cleansing" of the Jerusalem Temple. The synoptic gospel writers suppressed the entire Feast of Tabernacles story to disassociate Jesus from the strict observance, Zealotically-inclined followers of John; "Later John's" Gospel achieved the same result by inserting an alternative explanation and scenario for the trip by Jesus to this particular Feast.

The fundamental reason for suppression and revision of these events by the canonical gospel writers was the insurrection in Jerusalem that occurred as a by-product. Both Mark and Luke (who had access to the "Early John" text), refer to the insurrection in other contexts. Mark feels compelled to mention it to explain the Barabbas matter: "And among the rebels in prison who had committed murder in the insurrection, there was a man called Barabbas" (Mark 15:7). And Luke elaborates slightly: "Barabbas, a man who had been thrown into prison for an insurrection started in the city and for murder" (Luke 23:19). And elsewhere Luke writes again "There were some present at that very time who told him (Jesus) of the Galileans whose blood Pilate had mingled with their sacrifices. And he answered them, 'Do you think that these Galileans were worse sinners than all the other Galileans, because they suffered thus? I tell you, no; but unless you repent you will all likewise perish'" (Luke 13:1-3).

Here is solid evidence that Jesus was warning his followers against the resort to violence that had occurred in Jerusalem. And with this background it becomes possible to understand another obscure quotation attributed to Jesus. "The law and the prophets were until John; since then the good news of the Kingdom of God is preached, and everyone enters it violently. But it is easier for heaven and earth to pass away than for one dot of the law to become void" (Luke 16:16-17). Thus, we find Jesus proclaiming the literal understanding of the Mosaic Law against the use of violence by his own followers: he is trying to instruct them that the Mosaic Law against violence and murder has not been overturned by the good news that he brings about the Kingdom of God.

We also find, unexpectedly, a parable in the Gospel of Thomas (Thomas 57) that reads as if Jesus were lecturing his followers about violence: "Jesus said, the father's Kingdom is like a person who had good seed. His enemy came at night and sowed seeds among the good seed. The person did not let them pull up the weeds, but said to them, 'No, or you might go to pull up the weeds and pull up the wheat along with them.' For on the day of the harvest the weeds will be conspicuous, and will be pulled up and burned." This parable of the weeds seems to read as an instruction against violence, possibly when talking to the former followers of John the Baptist after his death. The question of dealing with evil should be left for God to deal with at the appropriate time. The fact that Mark omitted this parable (available to him from Thomas) strengthens the argument for its connection with the violence that Mark was attempting to cover up. Matthew used it, thus indicating a Q Gospel version of the parable, but completely reinterpreted its meaning (Matthew 13:24-30).

And so, as outlined in the inferred "Early John" Gospel, Jesus came up to the Feast of Tabernacles in Jerusalem, accompanied by a mixed "crowd" composed of former followers of John the Baptist, as well as Hellenists and others. The "entry into Jerusalem," where Jesus was cheered by his supporters as a sort of king, probably merged with the general celebratory atmosphere of the festival, thus accounting for the lack of quick reaction by the Herodian and Roman authorities.

The "cleansing of the Temple" affair, postulated in Chapter 3 as occurring also at the Feast of Tabernacles, has been interpreted by some scholars as a contradiction of Jesus' strictures against violence. Some argue that this event was *intended* as a prelude to an actual overthrow by force of the Jerusalem authorities, and my hypothesis of the subsequent insurrection might seem to support such an interpretation. Did not Jesus really talk about destroying the Temple? And of course, in Mark's Gospel he prophesied its destruction. In Thomas 71, the earliest of all sources he is quoted as saying "I shall destroy this house and no one will be able to build it." The evidence also is strong that "Early John" originally quoted Jesus as saying: "I will destroy this temple made with hands, and in three days I will build another, not made with hands" (see Mark 14:58). Not wanting to associate Jesus with something that he did not do (destruction came much later via the Romans), "Later John" changed the wording, and Mark attributed the statement to false witnesses at the trial of Jesus.

But the actual description of the "cleansing" in the Johannine gospel reads more like a piece of theatre, responded to by onlookers with "What sign have you to show us for doing this?" (John 2:18). The ability to drive out animals and moneylenders without causing an immediate fight suggests a minor symbolic gesture, and a tactic of surprise. Jesus was making a statement with ambiguous meanings. For many Essenes and others the "overturning of tables" would symbolize the future destruction of the Temple by God, arising from the wickedness of the authorities, and previously of Herod the Great who built it. For local "progressive" Pharisees and other traditionalists, however, Jesus might appear as a moderate reformer who only wants to stop the commerce in the Temple precincts, and who is distancing himself from the image of John the Baptist as a destructive force.

The latter interpretation of Jesus' position tends to be confirmed by his reported meeting with the Pharisee Nicodemus, "a ruler of the Jews," who says: "Rabbi, we know that you are a teacher come from God; for no one can do these signs that you do, unless God is with him." "Early John" was trying to show that important Pharisees in Jerusalem endorsed Jesus, additional to important hinterland personalities; but whether or not this was so, it makes sense that Jesus would be seeking their support.

My conclusion is that the Johannine gospel accurately describes a sort of theatrical symbolic action, understood by onlookers as a protest against exploitative commercial activity conducted within the Temple's sacred precincts, but not against the animal sacrifice system as such, nor against the authority structure. It was simply a proposal that all the people in God's Temple should participate together in non-commercial common sharing of food and thanksgiving. Temple authorities, already familiar with the populist views of Jesus, failed to react immediately since the demonstration did not involve stealing of money or property. Also, the failure of the Temple authorities to react implies that Jesus was perceived to have authority in the Temple setting, and was presumably already well known in Jerusalem. Jesus used a "whip of cords" (John 2:15) as a symbol of his authority. "Later John's" efforts to depict Jesus as uneducated (John 7:15) to confirm that his words came from God rather than human teachers, only strengthens the likelihood that he was already an educated person of stature in Jerusalem. His demonstration expressed hinterland concerns about Temple financial corruption.

Perhaps Jesus was seeking a way to take advantage of the joyous atmosphere of the Feast of Tabernacles to bring contending reform factions together in a movement for change through celebratory food sharing under the guidance of the Holy Spirit. His preplanned entry into Jerusalem involved traditional messianic symbolism, simultaneously peaceful but triumphantly hopeful (John 12:13). The idea may have been both to pacify his new supporters and to reassure the Jerusalem establishment about their intentions. In this scenario, the cleansing of the Temple may have been a small theatrical demonstration but probably a tactical mistake. The subsequent insurrection was unplanned, which may explain its total failure. Whether it resulted from some followers of Jesus provoking the authorities, or the authorities provoking the followers of Jesus (or a combination of both), is impossible to know.

Both Mark and "Later John" muddy the waters in different ways. Mark transfers all the action to a later Passover Feast and reinterprets the cleansing of the Temple incident as a confrontational attack on the chief priests and scribes, with the "house of trade" aspersion (John 2:16) being rephrased as "a den of robbers" (Mark 12:17). Perceiving Jesus more in the image of John the Baptist, Mark writes that Jesus drove out all the people (both buyers and sellers) and "would not allow anyone to carry anything through the temple" (Mark 11:15-18). The Markan scenario leads directly to the arrest and trial of Jesus by the Sanhedrin.

"Later John" transfers part of the action, the Temple cleansing, to an earlier Passover Feast, and another part, the entry into Jerusalem, to a later Passover Feast as in Mark. As for the meaning of the Temple cleansing action, "Later John" proposes a non sequitur response by Jesus: "Destroy this temple and in three days I will raise it up" (John 2:19). Having disconnected the incident from the Feast of

Tabernacles, "Later John" produces a convoluted explanation of it as a metaphor for the death and resurrection of Jesus (John 2:19). At the same time, it forms a prelude for the launching by Jesus of his messianic mission.

My picture of what probably happened (based on the inferred "Early John" Gospel) is vastly different. Over several days of the Feast of Tabernacles following the cleansing of the Temple incident, Jesus preached in public about the presence of the Holy Spirit and Kingdom of God, using the healing of the paralytic and the blind man (John 5:1-9 and 9:1-40) as further signs or symbolic teaching devices.

Perhaps the essence of Jesus' message rests submerged in a passage from the Johannine gospel on the words of Jesus in the Temple during the Feast of Tabernacles: "If anyone thirst, let him come to me and drink. He who believes in me, as the scripture has said, 'Out of his heart shall flow rivers of living water.'" (John 8:37-38) Probably this text incorporates a change by "Later John" from belief in the teachings of Jesus to belief in the personhood of Jesus. In the original "Early John" text, Jesus would be expressing his teachings as comparable to the miraculous flow of water called forth from a rock in the desert by Moses to save the lives of the ancient Israelites (Numbers 20:2-13). Each person seeking spiritual insight may find it in the teachings of Jesus, and thereby become filled with the Holy Spirit.

The Sanhedrin responded to Jesus as described in the "Early John" Gospel (John 7:45-52), but were unable to exercise control because of strong support for Jesus among the people: "But this crowd, who do not know the law, are accursed" (John 7:49). Note how well the Sadducee-Pharisee charge of "not knowing the law" would fit a hinterland crowd of Hellenists and former followers of John the Baptist. My inference is that some form of insurrection began, leading to (or stimulated by) violent intervention by Roman soldiers (perhaps called in by the High Priest), and that herein lies the explanation for the departure of Jesus and his disciples to the Wilderness: "Again they tried to arrest him but he escaped from their hands. He went away again across the Jordan to the place where John at first baptized, and there he remained." (John 10:39-40) I also infer that the Romans succeeded in arresting some of the people who had participated in the disturbance. All the canonical gospels suppressed this event, which was probably described in the lost Gospel of "Early John."

We have already shown in Chapter 3 that a story of "the raising of Lazarus" was included by "Early John," then modified later in different ways by "Secret Mark" and "Later John." Evidence that something significant actually happened comes from the later Empty Tomb story in the Johannine gospel, which seems linked to the raising of Lazarus by the resurrection theme. I infer that the best explanation comes by equating Lazarus (i.e. James) of "the raising of Lazarus" story, with the "other" disciple (i.e. James) of the Empty Tomb story, who is also author of the "Early John" text. The sickness of Lazarus-James may have been clinical depression or some form of self-punishment arising from the failed insurrection, for which he may have had some responsibility. A hint comes from the Johannine passage in which Jesus' brothers urge him to go to Jerusalem "to show yourself to the world" (John 7:3-4). The rescue by Jesus of his brother James from attempted suicide in the tomb may have been pre-planned, or may have been fortuitous. In any case, the joy and private rebaptism of James described in the "Secret Mark" version would have been a personal sign of spiritual rebirth and the presence of the Holy Spirit. And this would account for his later intuitive understanding at the Empty Tomb, that God had raised Jesus from the dead, when "he (James) saw and believed" (John 20:8). Therefore, I infer that James perceived his own rescue from the tomb by Jesus as a sign that verified Jesus' mission.

Most twentieth-century scholars tend to regard the raising of Lazarus story as an embarrassing myth suppressed by other gospel writers because it had no basis in fact. I argue on the contrary that this event was suppressed by Mark and others because in highlighting Lazarus (the birth brother of Jesus) it didn't fit the synoptic revised storyline. In all likelihood, this private family resurrection event explains how Jesus restored his authority over his disciples to such an extent that they meekly acquiesced to his own decision to turn himself over to the Roman authorities.

---

[1]   Mark suppressed the reference to kingship, while "Later John" suppressed any mention of the execution of John the Baptist.

CHAPTER 17

THE ARREST AND CRUCIFIXION OF JESUS

The insurrection in Jerusalem during what should have been a joyful Feast of Tabernacles, must have disturbed both Roman and Jewish authorities, and provides an explanatory clue for the meeting of the Sanhedrin reported by "Early John" (John 11:47-53), where the High Priest Caiphas explains the executive (Caiphas—Pontius Pilate) view "that one man should die for the people, and that the whole nation should not perish."

The meeting and its decision is a logical response to a disturbance or insurrection, perceived perhaps as a continuation of sedition against the Herodian establishment. The link with John the Baptist is admitted when the Johannine gospel states that Jesus "went away again across the Jordan to the place where John at first baptized and there he remained." The synoptic gospels, using Mark's approach to concealment of the insurrection, changed the scenario to a later Passover Feast, where the governing authorities respond directly to a somewhat less credible description of the entry into Jerusalem and cleansing of the Temple. "Later John" sticks with the Feast of Tabernacles event minus an insurrection, but moves the Temple cleansing to an earlier Passover, and the entry into Jerusalem to a later Passover; the Lazarus story is transformed into a public event to provide an improbable explanation for the Passover entry into Jerusalem by Jesus, and the reaction of the authorities.

Pontius Pilate, Roman Procurator of Judea, maintained his official residence in Caesaria on the coast of Judea. Jerusalem was the holy city of the Jews, watched over by a Roman garrison. It is generally agreed by scholars that Pilate visited

Jerusalem only on special occasions. To visit during the Jewish Passover Festival perhaps implied special circumstances.

Sources such as Josephus and Philo of Alexandria indicate that Pilate was a crude army type, who would tend to react violently against Jewish unrest by "teaching them a lesson." Pilate therefore responded to the Feast of Tabernacles insurrection in his style by coming up to Jerusalem to attend the public crucifixion of one or more insurrectionists provocatively scheduled on the next Feast of Passover as a dire warning to the Jewish people against meddling with Rome. No gospel account attests directly to the prior intention of Pilate to crucify rebels. But all attest to the fact that two "others" were crucified with Jesus, although Barabbas was spared.

The mysterious Barabbas is surely one of the keys to the real story, despite the arguments of some scholars that he is a purely fictitious character created by Mark to slander the Judeans. Barabbas is a named character who is actually unnamed, because Barabbas means "son of the father," a meaningless designation except perhaps as a way of saying that the son has the same name as the father. Matthew's Gospel names him as Jesus Barabbas (Matthew 27:15). Combined with the possibility that Mark's source material (i.e. the Gospel of "Early John") may have used the words "father's son" in counterpoint to Jesus in the following passage, "Not this man, but his son" (John 18:40), the possibility emerges that Jesus was condemned by Pilate in place of his own son.

Be that as it may, a good case can be made that part of the purpose of spreading the word that "one man should die for the people" (John 11:50), was to persuade Jesus to surrender to the authorities. The drama would have been heightened by scheduling a crucifixion for the Passover Feast. Jesus may have been aware of Pilate's intention before deciding to return to Jerusalem from the Wilderness, as recorded in the Johannine gospel. The direct participation of Pilate in the whole affair is a strong indicator of a Roman response to a perceived insurrection.

"Early John's" lost Gospel may have shown that Jesus came back to Jerusalem privately, and perhaps attempted to negotiate a deal with Pilate. The record of the Johannine gospel does show that Jesus said "If you seek me, let these men go" (John 18:8), and that Barabbas, at least, was not crucified. In the end, Jesus may have concluded that it was his duty to accept responsibility for the insurrection, in order to offset the bloody intentions of Pilate. Perhaps there is an echo of this situation in the "Later John" verses "Greater love has no man than this, that a man lay down his life for his friends" (John 15:13).

Before carrying out the arrangements for his own arrest, Jesus dined in Bethany with friends, family members and disciples. While disciples such as Peter were uninformed of his plans, there are clues that family members understood to some extent what was going on. Mary of Bethany (his sister?) anointed his feet with costly ointment; the "other disciple" (his brother James?) accompanied him to the High Priest's interrogation; and Judas (perhaps his trusted associate Judas Thomas) appears to have been his go-between in negotiations prior to his arrest. The only real betrayal of Jesus (apart from the insurrection itself) was the violence of Peter's attack on Malchus, the slave of the High Priest (John 18:10). The Judas Iscariot story is an invention of Mark (see Chapter 5), which contradicts the Pauline version that it was Jesus who "handed himself over" (Galatians 2:20 and Ephesians 5:2).

The meals at Bethany and the Last Supper, carefully separated by all canonical gospel writers to rationalize a later revisionist interpretation, were actually one and the same meal, the Bethany meal occurring as stated by Mark, two days before the Passover Feast (Mark 14:1). There was no other special Last Supper with the disciples on Passover Day as reported in the synoptics, because that was the day that Jesus was crucified; hence his Johannine title Lamb of God. Paul's Letter to the Corinthians (1 Corinthians 5:7) confirms the early understanding of Jesus as "paschal lamb," thus reinforcing the likelihood that Jesus died at Passover, rather than the next day, an invention of the synoptic gospels.

My conclusion is that the "Early John" version of the Bethany "anointing" by Mary may well have occurred, as well as the foot washing of the disciples, and the departure of Judas Thomas (at the request of Jesus) to bring the Roman soldiers. Jesus then went out with his disciples from Bethany towards Jerusalem and to the Garden of Gethsemane, where he was arrested by pre-arrangement. It was evening, and he was taken to the residence of Annas, former High Priest, for preliminary questioning. The next day he was brought before the Sanhedrin where the main finding, probably, was that he was, like John the Baptist, guilty of "stirring up the people" (Luke 23:5).

The Sanhedrin, and particularly the High Priest were, by virtue of necessity, collaborators with the Roman authorities. Nevertheless, they were likely appalled by Pilate's intention to crucify a number of insurrectionists on the day of the Passover Feast, believing perhaps that such action could provoke further trouble, contrary to the intended effect. Having achieved the surrender of Jesus, John the Baptist's apparent successor, it was in their interest to work out a compromise. And such would certainly be done "behind the scenes," not in the public arena.

According to the Johannine gospel, Jesus was brought before Pontius Pilate on the Passover Feast Day. "Later John's" version, in which Pilate condemns Jesus to death and turns him over to the Judean population for crucifixion lacks all credibility (see Chapter 9). Luke's version is much more likely (he had access to "Early John"): that Pilate publicly decided "to chastise him and release him" (Luke 23:16), apparently having second thoughts about excessive harshness, considering the volatile crowds on the most important Jewish Feast Day of the year. Perhaps he was also giving credit to Jesus for turning himself in.

Pilate's apparent moderation may also have reflected the fact that the entry into Jerusalem and the insurrection had occurred months before. If these events had only been days before, Pilate would likely have taken a much more severe approach. The "normal" Roman procedure for crucifixion was to leave the crucified person on the cross for a period of days, both while still alive and after death as an object lesson to deter others. For the Jewish authorities however, it would make sense to fear that the intended deterrent would actually stimulate further violence; and they would be caught in the middle. Accordingly, it seems likely that they would look for a face-saving formula, and that a pre-arranged deal was in fact worked out. The key to the mystery of what actually happened would be the features of the deal.

In Chapter 3, I have outlined a hypothesis as to what was written by "Early John" about this matter, based on inferences from Mark, Luke and "Later John." The upshot suggests that the priests and officers favoured physical punishment and then release for Barabbas (but not crucifixion on Passover day) and a prison term for Jesus, "take away this man" (Luke 23:18).

All gospel accounts concur that Pilate decided to substitute Jesus for Barabbas. The synoptics claim that Barabbas was released, but this is not confirmed by the Johannine gospel; Barabbas disappears into the mists of history. Instead, Jesus was to be publicly "chastised," presumably for the insurrection, in which the insurrectionists tried to "make him King" by force (John 6:15). According to all gospel accounts, Jesus himself never admitted to being the traditional Messiah or King of Israel.

A popular alternative hypothesis among some scholars is that Barabbas was invented by the canonical gospel writers to shift responsibility for Jesus' crucifixion from Pilate to the Jewish authorities and people. Undoubtedly, they used Barabbas to suggest that the wicked Judean people wanted to save a murderer and to kill Jesus. But if Barabbas was an invention, we lack a reasonable explanation for the presence of Pilate, and the associated presence of Jesus in Jerusalem at Passover time. The reality of Barabbas fits the sequence of events contained in the inferred "Early John" Gospel.

In any event, the evidence from "Early John" seems to indicate that the "chastisement" of Jesus ordered by Pilate consisted of a severe beating, and a few hours on the cross, accompanied by two guilty rebels, but not Barabbas. The actual deal probably was that Jesus would accept severe physical punishment for the insurrection act, including the humiliation of being pinpointed by public notice on the cross as "King of the Jews"; but the crucifixion would end before sundown preceding Sabbath, thus enabling Pilate to seem responsive to Jewish sensibilities. Normally, Romans left crucified persons to die slowly over a period of several days. This time two rebels had their legs broken for a quick death. Jesus was spared the leg-breaking, but died quickly anyway. Since Jesus was offered "a sponge full of vinegar" to strengthen him for the ordeal of being taken down from the cross, his immediate death could be attributed to an act of God. He was probably given a quick-acting poison, so that Pilate could be rid of him while simultaneously appearing merciful. Later, Pilate could express innocent surprise that Jesus had died so quickly (Mark 15:44). The reported piercing of his side by a spear was probably done simply to ensure that he was dead (John 19:34).

The strategy worked, because there is no evidence in the written record of riots or violent protest. Of course, the Romans undoubtedly forestalled any possible protest with a show of strength for as Mark writes: "they called together the whole battalion" (Mark 15:16). This would also mean that spectators were "far off" and that nearby "bystanders" were Romans.

And what were the disciples of Jesus doing while he was being arrested, judged, and crucified? According to the Gospel of Mark "they all forsook him and fled" (Mark 14:50), except perhaps Peter and a "young man wearing a linen cloth." But the "young man" was grabbed, and "he left the linen cloth and ran away naked"; Peter entered the courtyard of the High Priest, and "denied" Jesus three times. Nothing more is heard of any of the inner-group disciples in Mark's story. Jesus has been abandoned completely by his own disciples. In actuality, such a reaction by the disciples seems unlikely. The situation was probably much more complex. In the Johannine gospel (John 11:16), Thomas speaks for the disciples in relation to the dying Lazarus, "Let us also go (back to Jerusalem), that we may die with him," thus expressing Gnostic philosophy about death as a return to God, the timing being appropriate for all the disciples. In bringing Lazarus back to life, however, Jesus is instructing his inner-group disciples to continue living actively in this world to spread the message of the Kingdom of God. Jesus has restored his own authority to such an extent that his disciples acquiesce (except for Peter) to his response of turning himself over to Pilate. The disciples understand that they are not to die, and can only hope that Pilate may be merciful to Jesus. His death, however, is an unexpected shock, because they had expected God to ensure his safety.

There seems no reason to doubt the story that Pilate granted the body of Jesus to Joseph of Arimathea and Nicodemus, particularly if Joseph was actually Joseph, brother of Jesus. These two may already have been waiting to care for Jesus after his physical punishment. "Early John" could simply say that Joseph was a disciple of Jesus, who along with Nicodemus took down his body, bound it in pieces of linen cloth with spices, and placed it in a new tomb. "Later John" revises this in several ways: Joseph is a secret disciple "for fear of the Jews," and the tomb was in a garden in the same place where he was crucified. It is a tomb where nobody had ever been laid. Mark adds further cover-up information: he specifies that Joseph is a member of the Sanhedrin "looking for the Kingdom of God"; he has a centurion confirm to Pilate that Jesus is "already dead"; he omits Nicodemus and the spices; he has Jesus wrapped in a linen shroud (unlike the pieces of linen cloth described by "Early John" for both Lazarus and Jesus); and he omits that Joseph is a disciple of Jesus. Remarkably, Matthew seems to go back in some ways to "Early John" by contradicting Mark: he restores Joseph as a disciple of Jesus, and says nothing about his membership in the Sanhedrin; he omits any confirmation to Pilate that Jesus is dead, and he mentions significantly that Joseph places Jesus "in his own new tomb." From all this, it becomes reasonable to conclude that Joseph is the brother of Jesus, who places his body in a new family tomb, perhaps the same tomb where Lazarus was temporarily located.

What happened to his body over the weekend will probably remain an impenetrable mystery forever. Despite the enormous amount of ink that has been spilled in imagining various scenarios, there is no real evidence that Jesus was still alive in the tomb, or that any particular individual or group removed his body. Paul's version makes no mention of an empty tomb, and states that Jesus "was buried," before "being raised on the third day in accordance with the scriptures" (1 Corinthians 15:3).

PART III

THE MISSIONARIES

CHAPTER 18

THE EMPTY TOMB

The empty tomb is a mystery that in all probability will never be solved, except as a matter of faith. Some scholars argue that the tomb story (in its various versions) is imaginative fiction created later by the canonical gospel writers as supporting evidence for the physical resurrection story. In their opinion, the body of Jesus was disposed of directly by the Romans in the normal manner for a crucified person—it was dumped somewhere without burial.

However, it is not reasonable to regard the crucifixion of Jesus as a normal crucifixion, even from the point of view of Roman authorities. Certainly, the two insurrectionists crucified with Jesus suffered normal crucifixion procedure, and their bodies may well have been dumped for consumption by birds and animals. But Jesus was a special case, and all available evidence from the canonical gospels points toward some degree of special treatment by the Romans involving permission for burial. Such permission is particularly likely, if the ostensible intention of Pilate's verdict was physical punishment without death, as I proposed in Chapter 17.

Permission for burial would normally be granted to members of the victim's family, if such family members were available. This seems to have created problems for all the canonical gospel writers, and probably also for "Early John." While each writer admitted the existence of a living family for Jesus, no mention is made of their presence in Jerusalem at the time of his crucifixion, except for his mother. Such an unlikely absence of family members is especially inconsistent with the Bethany meal/Last Supper scenario (see Chapter 3), where inferred brothers and sisters of Jesus are among those present.

If Pontius Pilate granted permission for burial to a family member, it is possible that Joseph of Arimathea was actually the brother of Jesus named Joseph, and that the intent was to bury Jesus in a family tomb, presumably in Bethany. If such was the case, even the author of "Early John" would have perceived the need to conceal such details to support the plausibility of any Empty Tomb story.

Since Paul's Epistles make no explicit reference to an empty tomb (although he mentions "burial"), he apparently did *not* consider this to be essential in order to verify his particular concept of Jesus' resurrection. Such a lack of mention by Paul is consistent with the theory that the Empty Tomb stories were a later development worked out by the canonical writers in support of later concepts of Jesus' physical resurrection.

On the other hand, there is evidence that the first Empty Tomb story was written by "Early John" at a very early date; there are curious linkages between Mark's story and the Johannine version (see Chapter 5). As pointed out elsewhere, Mark's story reads as a refutation of the Johannine story, which therefore must have been proposed prior to Mark. This proves only that there was an early story, perhaps true, or perhaps a fabrication.

An empty tomb is an essential concomitant of resurrection, defined as a reconstitution of a dead body back to life. This would apply regardless of whether the concept involves restoration to life on earth, or is limited to raising up the physical body to Heaven or the afterworld. By contrast, the Gnostic idea of a "real" spiritual self that returns to God without "tasting death," by "casting off" the physical body, does not require an empty tomb. Jesus' "real" spiritual self could be "raised up" by God; such an idea had been taught by Jesus, and believed by his followers when he was physically alive.

It seems highly probable that there was an early Empty Tomb story that stimulated a change of thought among some followers of Jesus. For other followers, an empty tomb would be irrelevant, because the body might easily have been moved by anyone to another unknown location. And this opposing view would account for the Thomas Gospel's complete abstention on the matter. Even the experience of visions or the spiritual presence of Jesus could be consistent with the opposing Gnostic view, which regarded the physical body as ultimately artificial or "unreal."

In the "Early John" Gospel it is Mary of Magdala, along with at least one other woman, who first discovers the Empty Tomb (see Chapter 3). Their reaction is that someone has removed the body of Jesus to another location (John 20:2). Then Mary alone experiences the first vision of Jesus, according to the Johannine gospel. Mary seems to have had a spiritual vision rather than an encounter with a physical bodily presence. According to the Gnostic Gospel of Mary (a later non-canonical document), Mary reports that she received the vision of Jesus "through the mind." When "Later John" recreates the encounter with Jesus saying to Mary "Do not hold me" (John 20:17), he seems to be confirming an earlier version of the story that implies such a non-physical presence. If so, "Early John" presumably claimed only a spiritual vision for Mary. Note that both Mark and Luke, who had access to an "Early John" text (see Chapters 5 and 8), make no mention of a physically resurrected Jesus appearing to Mary. Neither does Paul.

I infer that "Early John" elaborated his own details of the Empty Tomb event to provide credibility for a resurrection interpretation. Mary fetches Peter and "the other disciple" (i.e. James, brother of Jesus), and they both confirm the Empty Tomb; but "the other disciple saw and believed" (John 20:8). In other words, it is James who first understands that Jesus (as vindicated Messiah) "must rise from the dead" (John 20:9), in the sense of being raised up to Heaven in his physical body, in accordance with unspecified scripture (John 20:9). The absence of Jesus' body confirms his Messiah status and vindication by God. Note especially that this interpretation connects with the belief of the Pharisees in an eventual resurrection of the body at the "last days." It could be a sign from God of a forthcoming physical resurrection of all the dead, and of other astounding events to come. But in itself the event implies nothing definitive about the divinity of Jesus himself.

Thus, in the original "Early John" story, Mary discovers the fact of the empty tomb and interprets it as meaning that someone has removed the body of Jesus (John 20:2). Then, she experiences a spiritual presence of the dead Jesus, which she understands perhaps as the lingering of his spirit, before returning upward to God "on the third day." It is James who reinterprets the scenario as meaning that the physical body of Jesus has been raised up or "resurrected," an interpretation that fits his own earlier experience (as Lazarus) of being physically rescued from a tomb by Jesus, through divine intervention. Mary sticks to her version, which is spelled out in the Gospel of Mary and represents the Gnostic interpretation. Later, when Mark's Gospel deals with the matter, Mary and her friends are shown to be uncomprehending when "a young man" at the tomb expresses the interpretation of James.

CHAPTER 19

THE APPEARANCES OF JESUS

Following the discovery and confirmation of the Empty Tomb, the Johannine gospel states that "the disciples went back to their homes" (John 20:10), presumably an "Early John" statement of fact, which "Later John" turns into a prophecy by Jesus: "The hour is coming . . . when you will be scattered, every man to his home" (John 16:32). What really happened at this point is obscure, but it is quite likely that the feeling of loss and sorrow among the disciples was accompanied by recriminations and dispute.

The earliest source on what happened next is the famous quotation from Paul's Epistle to the Corinthians: "Christ . . . appeared to Cephas (i.e. Simon Peter) then to the twelve. Then he appeared to more than five hundred brethren at one time . . . Then he appeared to James, then to all the apostles" (I Corinthians 15:5-7). An alternative translation from the Greek is that "Christ was revealed to . . ." This information was conveyed to Paul presumably by Simon Peter and James, brother of Jesus. I have proposed (in Chapter 3) that it matches what was written in the Gospel of "Early John," based on embedded material in the Johannine, Markan and Lukan gospels; except that Paul omits mention of Mary of Magdala's (Johannine) vision of Jesus at the Empty Tomb. Significantly, however, neither Paul nor the inferred "Early John" text mention various other appearances of the spiritual Jesus to different disciples recorded by later Gnostic writers in the Nag Hammadi documents. This implies that the new Jerusalem leadership of the Jesus people in the early years had decided which appearances were authentic, and which were not.

The available evidence supports the proposition that the disciples considered these appearances to be consistent with the Gnostic teachings of Jesus (see Chapter 1) about spiritual life after death, divine mysteries, and communication through the Holy Spirit within. In "not tasting death," Jesus had become holistically united with the Spirit, and mystically supplied revelatory knowledge to living members of the Kingdom of God. As when Jesus was alive, understanding (gnosis) could come to individuals through private insight or publicly to groups or communities through sharing of the Holy Spirit (now linked to the spiritual form of Jesus).

Clues from the Markan and Johannine gospels indicate that the first three revelatory moments mentioned in Paul's Epistle happened in Galilee, which if so, supports the argument that Simon Peter and other disciples returned there soon after the crucifixion. Mary of Magdala's vision of Jesus at the Tomb "on the third day" (where other women are present but do not "see" Jesus) had occurred, but apparently was not accepted as authentic by most disciples.

Simon Peter's visionary experience on a mountain in Galilee, known as the Transfiguration (see Chapters 3 and 5), matches Paul's reference to an appearance to Cephas (i.e. Peter) and may have impacted Peter in a manner similar to Paul's own purported revelatory moment on the road to Damascus. Whether or not Peter already knew of Mary's appearance event at the Tomb, his own moment of epiphany may have transformed his own troubled feelings. If he already knew of Mary's vision, it would be "just like a man" not to believe it until the same sort of thing happened to him. Note that while Peter is accompanied by the sons of Zebedee as witnesses, only Peter attempts to speak to the transfigured Jesus dressed in intensely brilliant white, as the three of them awake from their sleep (Mark 9:2-8 and Luke 9:28-36). Presumably, Paul's later understanding was that the vision was exclusive to Peter.

The Transfiguration (or private appearance to Peter) then propelled a get-together with other disciples. One day (or one night at dawn, according to John 21:4), while fishing together on Lake Galilee, they had an unusually large catch of fish, accompanied by a collective perception of the spiritual presence of Jesus urging them to become "fishers of men." Perhaps there were four of them (Mark and Luke), perhaps seven ("Later John"); probably not twelve as stated by Paul. According to "Later John's" story edited from "Early John," they included Group 1 disciples (Judas Thomas and Nathaniel), Group 2 disciples (Simon Peter and the sons of Zebedee) and two others. The spiritual presence of Jesus may have seemed very much like the presence of the Holy Spirit that Jesus described when he was alive.

In turn, the collective experience of Jesus' spiritual presence at the fishing expedition leads to an attempt to reassemble a larger group of "brethren," in order to experience again the "feeding of the multitude" under the joint guidance of the spiritual Jesus and the Holy Spirit. Paul's reference to "five hundred brethren," and the second feeding of the multitude event recorded in the Gospel of Mark are the clues to this occurrence. The significant link is the number seven which is the number of disciples at the Sea of Galilee reported by the Johannine gospel (John 21:2), and the number of loaves symbolically representing apostles, reported by the Markan gospel (Mark 8:1-10). In other words, seven inner-group disciples presided over the second feeding of the multitude and followed it up with another journey to Jerusalem from Galilee, accompanied by other followers of Jesus.

Note how the progressive enlargement of the "appearance" experience continues to fit a Gnostic understanding of a spiritual being in ongoing mystical communication with his earthly companions of the Kingdom of God. There is not yet necessarily a notion of a resurrected physical body, or of Jesus' return to Earth in a physical body. But the revelatory visions are experienced as signs from the divine spiritual realm that vindicate and verify the teachings and mission of Jesus, and his spiritual survival after death.

The purpose of the new journey to Jerusalem was consultation. The disciples had experienced the spiritual presence of Jesus on a mountain, on Lake Galilee, and at another "feeding of the multitude." The next step was a return to Jerusalem for further guidance. Particularly enlightening in this regard is the Gospel of Thomas, which reflects the Gnostic understanding of what had happened: "The followers said to Jesus, 'We know that you are going to leave us. Who will be our leader?' Jesus said to them 'No matter where you are, you are to go to James the Just, for whose sake heaven and earth came into being'" (Thomas 12). Other evidence from the canonical gospels indicates that by this time members of Jesus' family lived in Bethany, near Jerusalem.

The next thing that happened, according to Paul, was the appearance of Jesus to James. James was "the brother of Jesus" according to Paul; he may also have been Lazarus and "the other disciple" mentioned by "Early John" and "the disciple that Jesus loved" mentioned by "Later John." He is also the leading candidate for authorship of the "Early John" Gospel (see Chapter 3).

The only recorded event in the canonical gospels that fits an appearance to James is Luke's story of the encounter with a stranger by two disciples on the road to Emmeaus (Luke 24:13-33). A point to note is that all appearances to individuals in the canonical gospels involve the presence of others as witnesses who are aware of the happening, but explicitly or implicitly do not share the revelatory understanding. The following are four examples:

1) Mary of Magdala has a vision of Jesus at the Tomb, which is not shared by other women present (inferred "Early John" account);
2) "The other disciple" is accompanied by Simon Peter to the Empty Tomb, but only "the other disciple saw and believed" (John 20:8);
3) Simon Peter is accompanied by the sons of Zebedee during the Transfiguration vision, but only Peter speaks to Jesus (Mark 9:2-8 and Luke 9:28-36);

4) Paul, on the road to Damascus, experiences the risen Lord as light and voice, but his companions "see no one" (Acts 9:3-7).

Similarly in Luke, the two disciples walking in the countryside report to others that "The Lord has risen indeed, and has appeared to Simon" (Luke 24:34), despite the fact of two persons involved, Cleopas and another (Luke 24:13-18). Here in this latter story rests the crux of the whole resurrection question, which explains the confusion surrounding Luke's story described earlier in Chapter 8. The substitution of the name Simon for the name James is an attempt by Luke to square this story (which denies any return of the disciples to Galilee) with the tradition (confirmed by Paul) that Jesus "appeared first" to Simon Peter; unfortunately it contradicts the story in the same Lukan text that Peter visited the Empty Tomb on the same day as the road to Emmeaus incident, found nothing, and went home (Luke 24:12). The reference to the two persons in the countryside as Cleopas and an unnamed disciple is a further attempt to conceal the presence of James, brother of Jesus; the original version of the story being presumably from "Early John's" account of post-crucifixion appearances by Jesus (see Chapter 3). It follows that James himself first wrote it (see Chapter 8). Luke rearranged it.

A key feature of the story is that unlike the spiritual-type appearances in Galilee to Peter and the larger groups of disciples, this appearance to James involves the physical body of a person who talks and "breaks bread" with the two travelers; however they do not recognize him as Jesus until he vanishes from their sight. In the meantime, he talks to them, and "interprets to them in all the scriptures the things concerning himself" (Luke 24:27). Here surely is the genesis of the idea that Jesus will return to earth, the Parousia. "We had hoped that he was the one to redeem Israel" (Luke 24:21). The stranger turns out to be a physical reincarnation of Jesus, bringing a message of hope to be transmitted to the other followers by James. This is one step further than the spiritual appearances of Jesus in Galilee, which are more akin to the ongoing presence of the Holy Spirit in support of members of the Kingdom of God. The Gospel of Mark had suppressed information on post-crucifixion appearances by retrojecting these events back to the lifetime of Jesus (see Chapter 5). In so doing, Mark removed the story of an appearance to James, but retained the message of the Parousia as part of a prophetic speech by Jesus on the Mount of Olives (Mark 13:24-37). Luke repeated Mark in suppressing the three post-crucifixion appearance stories in Galilee, but contradicted Mark with two elaborated stories of appearance events in and near Jerusalem "on the third day" after the crucifixion of Jesus (see Chapter 8).

The road to Emmeaus story (inferred as the appearance to James) moved the meaning of physical resurrection one step further ahead. Not only had the physical body of Jesus been raised up from the Jerusalem tomb to the realm of

God, but the resurrected spirit of Jesus had returned temporarily to earth in a body, as a sign to his disciples that he would return in the near future to restore the Kingdom of Israel and implement God's Plan. But note that Jesus is occupying an apparent body, a body for the job of conveying a message to James; this remains consistent with the Gnostic concept of a disposable body, which differs from the later more pharisaic idea of resurrection of one's own physical body. Thus, James had become the source of two stories: the first concerned the raising up of the physical body of Jesus from the Empty Tomb—acceptable to Pharisees who believed in physical resurrection; the second concerned the occupation of another physical body by the spiritual Jesus, perhaps acceptable to Gnostics who denied the possibility of the first story.

But for James and Hebrew traditionalists, it was important also that the raising up of Jesus be in accordance with the scriptures. The stranger on the road to Emmaus confirms this to be so. Prior to this event the disciples "did not know the scripture that he must rise from the dead" (John 20:9), clearly an "Early John" quote. Now the post-crucifixion Jesus had explained to James the meaning of the scriptures.

The fifth reference by Paul to an appearance by the spiritual Jesus "to all the apostles" happened after the other four appearances, and certainly *not* on the third day after the crucifixion of Jesus as stated in the gospels of Luke and "Later John." The appearances in Galilee preclude it. Probably it took place some months or years after the crucifixion of Jesus, and probably not before 36 C.E. (despite contrary evidence from the Pauline epistles) when Pontius Pilate was recalled to Rome, and King Herod Antipas was in eclipse following his losing war with King Aretas of Arabia.

For the followers of Jesus, assembled in Jerusalem, the appearances or visions proved that God had vindicated Jesus and his mission, by raising him up to His divine realm. It meant that God was endorsing the teachings or words of Jesus concerning the presence of the Kingdom of God, and its implementation by his followers who would become "fishers of men." Additionally, for many of them inspired by James' Emmaus story, it proved that Jesus was God's anointed Messiah prophesied in Hebrew scripture, who would soon return from death somehow "in power." All seem to have agreed initially that the starting point for them was to establish an organized group, a church (or assembly) in Jerusalem, to exist as a model of the coming Kingdom, and to spread the good news. Why in Jerusalem? Because here God's Temple of stones would merge with God's new Temple of people stones into a new dispensation.

Unlike the separated Essene and Samaritan groups, the church of Jesus would be an active proselytizing church, open to everyone who accepted and practiced his teachings. It would represent the forthcoming "new Israel," to be headed by the Messiah, equivalent to High Priest and King, assisted by twelve apostles, equivalent to the Sanhedrin (or Council), and a body of members across the world. The commissioning of these apostles took place in Jerusalem at the time when the spiritual Jesus "appeared to all the apostles."

It is true of course that the synoptic gospels (based on Mark) are emphatic in asserting that Jesus arranged a structure of twelve apostles during his lifetime, but the evidence against such a scenario is strong, and the reasons are set forth in Chapters 5 to 9 of this book. But if "the twelve" were not explicitly pre-selected by Jesus as apostles during his lifetime, how indeed were they chosen?

Part of a normal answer to this question would be that the twelve apostles were elected by a larger body of disciples or members of the Kingdom of God assembled for the purpose. Indeed, the Acts of the Apostles begins its account by describing an electoral process termed "the casting of lots" (Acts 1:21-26), used to select a successor for a deceased Judas Iscariot, purported to have been one of the twelve original apostles chosen by Jesus during his lifetime. No such election process is mentioned for the other eleven, since they were supposedly pre-chosen by Jesus. What is more likely to have happened is that the seven disciples that led the post-crucifixion return to Jerusalem by followers of Jesus qualified themselves as future apostles by virtue of their leadership in this regard, and their collective experience of the spiritual presence of Jesus in Galilee. Their inferred names were: Peter, Andrew, James and John ("Hebrew" traditionalists), and Thomas, Nathaniel and Philip ("Hellenist" Gnostics). The next four were James the Just, Joseph, Simon and Judas; they qualified by virtue of their status as brothers of Jesus (see Chapter 14). This makes a total of eleven.

Which brings us back to the story in Acts about the election of a twelfth apostle to replace Judas Iscariot. The name of the elected replacement is Matthias, which is another form of the name Matthew. In other words, Matthew, not included in the Galilean "seven," is the twelfth apostle; he seems to be a "Hellenist" closely identified with the teachings of Jesus (see Chapter 2). The result is twelve apostles with a balance between four "Hebrews," four "Hellenists" and four brothers of Jesus (see Chapter 14).

But there is more to it than that. I have argued elsewhere that the story of the traitor Judas Iscariot is a myth (see Chapter 5). This Judas was actually Judas, the brother of Jesus, who was designated one of the twelve apostles, and wrote a letter that is part of the New Testament Canon (the Letter of Jude). It follows, therefore, that the election of Matthias was intended to replace another Judas i.e. Judas Thomas. How can this be, since Thomas was clearly one of the twelve apostles? And why would he resign at this initial stage? The strange yet compelling answer is that the election described in Acts probably refers to an election to an inner triumvirate, not an election to the group of twelve apostles. The person to be replaced, Judas Thomas, resigns from the triumvirate (perhaps in disagreement about the meaning of the visionary appearances of Jesus) but remains one of the twelve apostles. Similarly, the loser of the election described in Acts as "Joseph called Barsabbas, who was surnamed Justus," also remains as one of the twelve apostles, for this man is Joseph, brother of Jesus (see Chapter 14), perhaps referred to later in Acts under the name Joseph Barnabas. The winner of the election to the triumvirate, Matthias, is already an apostle named Matthew.

The situation implies that initially there was an executive threesome to start the ball rolling; indeed, in describing the election of Matthias, Acts uses the terminology "his office let another take" (Acts 1:20) when referring to Judas as the previous holder of the office. Although Acts never explicitly confirms a triumvirate, all the other canonical writings (with one exception) refer to three inner-group persons. In the Epistles of Paul, which relate to a context some years after the death of Jesus, the three "pillars" are James (brother of Jesus), Cephas (Simon Peter) and John (son of Zebedee). Contrariwise, in the synoptic gospel stories of the lifetime of Jesus, the "inner three" are Simon Peter, James, son of Zebedee, and John, his brother. The Thomas Gospel refers to three close colleagues of Jesus with varying viewpoints: Simon Peter, Matthew and Thomas (Thomas 13), and to James the Just as single leader during the absence of Jesus (Thomas 12). It is here that the Thomas Gospel links with the Johannine gospel in focusing on a single leader. This person is "the disciple that Jesus loves" (see Chapters 3 and 9); "Later John" claims this disciple to be the author of the Johannine gospel.

The commissioning of apostles in Jerusalem, which I have inferred as being described originally by "Early John," matches the fifth reference by Paul to an appearance by the spiritual Jesus "to all the apostles," which may be alternatively described as a group meeting under the joint guidance of the spiritual Jesus-Holy Spirit connection. It may have occurred as a kind of "love-in" around the time of the Feast of Pentecost. A single event was then divided into two parts by Luke in Acts of the Apostles in order to have a physically resurrected Jesus appear to the apostles on "the third day" and ascend to Heaven, with the separate Holy Spirit descending later upon the apostles at Pentecost. A more plausible scenario is that the Pentecostal meeting, supported by the presence of the spiritual Jesus-Holy Spirit connection, generated a burst of creative energy involving the selection of an inner group of twelve apostles, and the beginnings of organization, procedures and rituals: "And they devoted themselves to the apostles' teachings and fellowship, to the breaking of bread and the prayers" (Acts 3:42).

It is important to note the initial emphasis on fellowship, eating together, and sharing of goods: community lifestyle rather than unanimity of belief. The disciples' self-designation as "the Way" implied an open commensality based on the teachings of Jesus, linked to divine authority, or "the Way of the Lord." The term "Way" was broad enough and vague enough to encompass traditional perceptions, ideas from John the Baptist and the Essenes, and neo-platonic influences. It focused attention on the common practice of works of righteousness and piety that previewed the coming Kingdom of God.

Before proceeding, it is necessary to deal with the credibility of the canonical Acts of the Apostles, the prime source of information on the post-crucifixion activities of Jesus' followers, apart from Paul and the outside observer Josephus. For many scholars, this second book of Lukan material is primarily fantasy, intended to mythologize the early exploits of the followers of Jesus for a Gentile audience. Yes, there can be little doubt that the author embellishes or invents certain stories. Frequently, he seems to contradict both himself (compare Acts 1:1-3 with Luke 24:50-53) and other sources. And he performs the remarkable feat of describing the missionary activities of the apostles without clarification of the identity and role of James, without mention of the violent deaths of Peter, Paul and James (although the deaths of James, son of Zebedee and Stephen are described), and without an inkling of the calamitous Roman-Jewish War.

Nevertheless, although the author evidently fudges certain events with imaginative distortion, there are reasons for taking seriously some underlying features and details of the text. To some extent (Acts 16-28), the author claims to be an eyewitness, when he refers to "we," in describing the travels, ordeals and adventures of Paul during the later years of his career. And in regard to Acts 1-15, there are hints of embedded material from an earlier written source.

Can it be mere coincidence that a man named Joseph "surnamed Barnabas by the apostles" (Acts 4:36), is significantly present at all the major turning points of Acts 1-15? Was he initially called Joseph Barsabbas Justus, the loser in the first apostolic election? Joseph Barnabas is the first to sell his property and bring the money to the apostles; then Barnabas introduces the converted sinner Saul to the apostles in Jerusalem; next Barnabas brings Saul from Tarsus to begin his teaching mission at Antioch; and then Barnabas accompanies Paul on his early travels, until they quarrel and separate in Antioch for unstated reasons. And who is Joseph Barnabas, supposedly "a Levite from Cyprus" (Acts 4:36)? Some evidence suggests that he may be Joseph, brother of James and Jesus, possibly referred to by "Early John" as Joseph of Arimathea. Keep in mind that Levi, the tax collector (thereby a man of wealth) was designated by Mark as Son of Alphaeus, and therefore brother of one apostle named James (Mark 2:14); and that Luke retained Levi in his text outside the circle of twelve apostles, but carefully deleted his identification as "son of Alphaeus" (Luke 5:27). And note the equivalence of Levi, man of wealth, with Luke's unusual identification of Joseph Barnabas as "a Levite" who was a property owner (Acts 4:36-37). This man, who may have been originally surnamed Justus (Acts 1:23), was re-surnamed "Barnabas by the apostles" (Acts 4:36), presumably to re-allocate the name Justus to James. All of which supports the proposition that Joseph and James were brothers. One purpose of such a convoluted cover-up may have been to disguise the origins of source material from Joseph Barnabas that had been overwritten by Luke, just as both Mark and Luke disguised the origins of source material from "Early John" (James), which had been overwritten by both of them (see Chapters 5 and 8). The hypothesis of some source material authorship by Joseph, brother of Jesus, cannot be confirmed by reference to being embedded in any other canonical gospel. However, it does suggest the possibility that some of the events and details in "Acts of the Apostles" may be derivative from eyewitnesses.

CHAPTER 20

JUDAS THOMAS AND
THE HELLENISTS

The Gospel of Judas, a remarkable 2nd century Gnostic script recently found in Egypt and published in 2006[1], purports to explain the real story of the betrayal (handover) of Jesus by Judas Iscariot. According to this story Jesus asked him to do it, in order to perform a sacrificial act that would return Jesus to the divine realm of transcendent Deity, and elevate Judas Iscariot to the status of "thirteenth" above the other twelve disciples. Interestingly, along with his instructions, Jesus speaks privately and exclusively to Judas about the secret mysteries of God's immortal realm, separating Judas from the other disciples, in a manner parallel to the way Jesus exalts Judas Thomas with exclusive secret knowledge in the Thomas Gospel (Thomas 13). The special role of Judas as messenger to the authorities in the newly found gospel is consistent also with the passage in the canonical Gospel of John where Jesus tells Judas Iscariot "what you are going to do, do quickly" (John 13:27), but is otherwise totally inconsistent with the evil Judas portrayed in all four canonical gospels.

Let us now consider the puzzle of the two Judases.

All four canonical gospel texts and the Acts of the Apostles admit to the existence of two men named Judas. One Judas named Judas Iscariot, the man who betrays Jesus, is "one of the twelve"; in the Johannine Gospel he is also brother (or son) of Simon Iscariot (or Zealot). The other Judas is brother of Jesus, James, Joses and Simon, and is *not* mentioned as one of the twelve (Gospel of Mark); he is brother (or son) of James, and is one of the twelve (Gospel of Luke); he is "not the Iscariot" (Gospel of John); and he is "brother of James," author of the canonical Letter of Jude, which is essentially a diatribe against "false teachers" (probably Gnostic) that had infiltrated the Christian community. Note that there is no third Judas in the canonical gospels; the disciple Thomas (a nickname) is never assigned a proper name, a most unusual omission.

In the found Gospel of Thomas (see Chapter 1), the Prologue states "These are the hidden sayings that the living Jesus spoke and Judas Thomas Didymos recorded." Apparently, the proper name of Thomas is Judas. Taking this into account, I have proposed that the lost "Early John" Gospel named this disciple as either Judas or Judas Thomas to distinguish him from Judas of Simon Iscariot (see Chapters 3 and 14).

From this premise I have argued that "Early John" referred to a man named Judas at the Bethany meal, who objected that the costly ointment used by Mary to anoint the feet of Jesus should have been given to the poor (John 12:3-5). The "Later John" author amended the name of this man to Judas Iscariot; the Markan author changed the reference to "some disciples" (Mark 14:3-6), and Luke simply eliminated the Bethany story. All the above supports the possibility that the Judas involved in this dialogue was Judas Thomas.

"Early John" is also the author of the Last Supper story element (see Chapter 3) in which Jesus sends out a man named Judas to the Roman authorities to arrange his arrest (John 13:26-30). The "Later John" author changed the name to Judas, of Simon Iscariot, while explicitly stating that another Judas remained at the Supper (John 14:22). Note that "Later John" tries to imply that the "other Judas" is a brother of Jesus by having him ask a question of Jesus (John 14:22) that harks back to the same question attributed earlier to the brothers of Jesus (John 7:4). Note also that Thomas continues to be present at the Last Supper because he asks a question after Judas has gone out (John 14:5), and note his name, Thomas Didymos (John 11:16) which carefully shows that Thomas is his proper name, and Didymos (Greek for twin) is his nickname. Thus, neither Thomas nor a brother of Jesus was Judas Iscariot, according to "Later John."

This eminently successful cover-up effort by "Later John," together with the total disappearance of the "Early John" text (apart from embedded portions) seems to point towards Judas Thomas as collaborator with Jesus in arranging Jesus' arrest. Somehow the author of the 2nd century Gnostic Gospel of Judas was aware of such a tradition, but was unaware that the arrangements were carried out by Judas Thomas and not by Judas Iscariot. Apparently, the story of Judas Iscariot fabricated by Mark (see Chapter 5), and used by the other synoptic gospels was what was available to the anonymous author of the Gospel of Judas, who used it to propagate a complicated later Gnostic version.

What does all this mean in terms of historical probability? Simply that Judas Thomas carried out his instructions from Jesus, the "Early John" account being suppressed later by all canonical gospels (see Chapter 17). Writings of Paul say nothing about Judas, while hinting that Jesus "handed himself over" (Galatians 2:20 and Ephesians 5:2).

Judas Thomas, reputed "spiritual twin" of Jesus, was steeped in gnostic-type neo-platonic wisdom. He was explicitly present at a post-crucifixion appearance of Jesus in Galilee (John 21:2), and was presumably elected to and resigned from the first triumvirate leadership of the Jesus people in Jerusalem (see Chapter 19). His perspective was "Hellenist."

According to the Acts of the Apostles, both "Hellenists" and "Hebrews" participated, at least initially, in the setting up of a new sharing community in Jerusalem (with some Essene-type features), established "in the name of Jesus Messiah of Nazareth" (Acts 3-6). "Hellenists" in the broadest sense encompassed all persons, both Jew and Gentile, who spoke Greek and followed some Greek customs. In the narrower sense, the term referred probably to those "people of Israel," both in Palestine and the Diaspora, who used Greek language and customs, accompanied by varying degrees of detachment from Mosaic Law and ritual. In regard to the disciples and followers of Jesus, such Jewish "Hellenists," influenced by neo-platonic ideas, were probably supporters of the gnostic-type teachings of Jesus recalled in the Sayings Gospel of Thomas. The presence of such "Hellenist" followers of Jesus is noted in the Johannine gospel, when some of them try to see Jesus after his public entry into Jerusalem (John 12:20-22). See also Chapter 14 for a review of clues that Thomas, Philip, Nathaniel and Matthew were "Hellenist" disciples of Jesus.

In the Thomistic understanding expressed in the Gospel of Thomas (non-canonical but pregnant with authenticity), the revelations or words of Jesus represent his own "gnosis" or intuitive self-discovery of the Spirit within, the divine spark already present and accessible within every human being. Through inward-directed insight, each person can discover the "hidden truth" and achieve direct mystical reunification with God the Father through the Spirit. Temple cult observances and ritual purification are acceptable to God, but insight ("gnosis") into the divine Spirit trumps the "strict observance" written messages from God in Hebrew scriptural tradition. "Jesus said, 'Whoever drinks from my mouth will become like me; I myself shall become that person, and the hidden things will be revealed to that person'" (Thomas 108). The Kingdom of God on Earth spreads from the Spirit within individuals—not through action by God from without.

The Thomas Gospel and other Gnostic writings regarded physical or bodily resurrection as inconsistent with the teachings of Jesus. The body was a cast-away feature of life on Earth. Direct knowledge of God comes through mystical identification with the divine spark inside each human being. Transformation of individual consciousness by becoming "a child of the living Father" brings divinity into the World. Entering the Kingdom of God equates with being filled with the Holy Spirit within. The significance of the Holy Spirit is highlighted by Thomas and Q Gospel sayings in which Jesus forgives blasphemies against God the Father and himself (son of Adam) "but whoever blasphemes against the Holy Spirit will not be forgiven, either on earth or in heaven" (Thomas 44).

It was the expression of that Spirit which singled out Jesus, locating him at the fringe of society—a "marginal Jew" influenced by neo-platonic Hellenistic ideas, and quintessentially a wandering Holy Man and teacher of divine Wisdom. His teaching, reflected in Thomas, implies that Jesus perceived himself as no more divine than anyone else, the term "messiah" being simply a nickname (albeit a dangerous one) suggestive of authority when preaching his public message.

In the post-crucifixion scenario, the Gnostic teaching of Jesus prevailed in the form of visions and interior revelations that provided inspiration and guidance to his disciples. What was the meaning of these revelations for Thomas and other Hellenists? Simply that the spiritual Jesus had returned to God from whence he came, confirming life after death, and that his teaching should be spread to all humankind. Beginning with Mary of Magdala's vision near the Empty Tomb, the Hellenist disciples could explain that the spiritual Jesus, now mystically unified with God the Father and the Holy Spirit, remained in communication. Then when Simon Peter and James experienced their own private appearances, the whole group began to realize that the death of Jesus was a positive turning point in the growth of the Kingdom of God, underpinned by an ongoing spiritual Jesus-Holy Spirit connection within themselves. The "living" spiritual Jesus prefigured their own destiny. They could best prepare for the future by getting together in community in Jerusalem.

However, if the Jesus people were to function in Jerusalem on a continuing basis, they had to find an image of acceptability in a relatively hostile environment. In particular, with or without the physical presence of their leader, they could not continue the "take these things away" approach regarding commercial activities in the Temple. Moreover, any proselytization that seemed to threaten Temple culture and Mosaic Law would be doomed to failure; a determinedly "Hebrew" posture was essential. How it played out is outlined in Chapter 21.

In organizing themselves to model the coming Kingdom, there was discord between "Hellenists" and "Hebrews" according to Acts; ostensibly because of discrimination by "Hebrews" in daily distribution to widows of "Hellenists" (Acts 6:1); but probably because of disputes on issues of belief and appropriate action. Presumably, the gnostic-oriented Hellenists were preaching "the Way" of Jesus underpinned by the Holy Spirit within; scriptural tradition was largely irrelevant to them. The Hebrews tended to focus on the resurrected Jesus as God's chosen Messiah of Israel, scripturally mandated to return soon with God's promised Kingdom. Apparently, the initial compromise arrangement (Acts 6:1-6), was to assign seven Hellenists (persons with Greek names) "to serve tables," which meant the organization of common meals and property—the inward life of the church.

The apostles (mainly Hebrews) took on the burden of prayer and teaching, of spreading the "good news," the external face of the church. According to Acts, the division of responsibility "pleased the whole multitude."

These arrangements existed for a while, bringing new "Hebrew" recruits including "many of the priests" (Acts 6:7). My inference is that such an influx would have increased tensions about traditional Mosaic ritual and Temple cult requirements. The text of Acts goes on to describe proselytization or teaching activity by Stephen (one of the Hellenists assigned to "serve tables") among Hellenists or Diaspora Jews present in Jerusalem, in apparent contravention of the agreement that preaching was reserved to the twelve apostles. My interpretation is that the previous agreement to separate responsibility for "serving tables" and proselytization had been replaced. Now "Hebrews" and "Hellenists" would eat at separate tables; Hellenists would proselytize Hellenists, and Hebrews would proselytize Hebrews. Hence the beginning of separate streams of missionary activity with the Hellenist Gnostics sticking to their understanding of Jesus' teaching, which involved changing traditions and eventual Temple replacement, while the Hebrews were constrained by Mosaic Law and Temple rituals. Perhaps it was the agreement by priestly authorities to cease persecution of the Jesus people (see Chapter 21), on condition of "good behaviour," which became a stumbling block for those Jesus people who regarded the Kingdom of God as a replacement for traditional values. Note how discord is inadvertently mentioned in Acts of the Apostles when the converted Paul in Jerusalem "spoke and disputed against the Hellenists" (Acts 9:29).

Before long, many of the Hellenists, perhaps headed by Philip and Thomas, were persuaded to undertake missions to Greek-speaking Jews and others outside Jerusalem, beginning in Judea and Samaria, and spreading to the cities of the Diaspora. Acts makes specific reference to the presence of such missionaries in Phoenicia, Cyprus and Antioch (Acts 11:19). This would be a way of avoiding internal confrontation in Jerusalem over both the principles and the tactics of the Jesus Kingdom of God movement. Whether or not there was accompanying persecution of Hellenist disciples by the Herodian authorities is an open question. Acts' description of the Great Persecution, the stoning to death of Stephen and Paul's role seem highly imaginative (see Chapters 21 and 22). The credibility of a violent expulsion from Jerusalem of all followers of Jesus "except the apostles" (Acts 8:1) is difficult to accept, although it may have happened later under King Herod Agrippa I (see Chapter 22). It would not be surprising if most of the Hellenist Gnostics left voluntarily.

The first mission by the Hellenist Apostle Philip was to Samaria, long since alienated from traditional Hebrew understandings. Acts of the Apostles reports that Philip converted both the people of "a city of Samaria," and their messianic leader Simon Magus (Acts 8:4-13); but immediately "the apostles" sent Peter and John to expose Simon Magus as a liar and sinner (Acts 8:14-24). Peter, John and Philip continue preaching the gospel, but Philip goes to Caesarea, while Peter and John return to Jerusalem. What becomes of the Samaritans remains unstated. However, a reasonable inference would be that the Jerusalem headquarters had responded to news of Gnostic teaching by Philip in Samaria by attempting to counter it with their own version of the resurrected personhood of Jesus as Messiah of Israel. Whether they succeeded is doubtful, in light of the long historical alienation of Samaritans from traditions centred on Judea and the Jerusalem Temple.

Further evidence of the Gnostic missionary effort, and of Jerusalem headquarters' efforts to counter it is the reference to Antioch (Acts 11:19-26) where "the disciples were for the first time called Christians." Apparently, when the Jerusalem Church heard that "men of Cyprus and Cyrene" were preaching in Antioch to Hellenists, they sent Barnabas who recruited Saul to help him in teaching (presumably the correct version) to these people. But the Gnostic teachers moved on, as evidenced later from Paul's letters showing that the message about the Kingdom of God had already reached Corinth, Rome and other cities before he got there. In particular, the Corinthians encountered by Paul were apparently functioning as if the Kingdom were already there, living a libertarian interpretation of its meaning in their lives. An individual named Apollos (mentioned in 1 Corinthians and Acts 18:24-28), who "knew only the baptism of John," seems to have sowed much confusion in this regard.

Of course, the second century doctrinal controversies, and the discovery of the Nag Hammadi Gnostic Library in the twentieth century, are the ultimate proof of the survival of the Gnostic teachings of Jesus. The most significant evidence of their early importance (apart from the Thomas Gospel itself), is the embedded elements of the Thomas Gospel contained in the gospels of Mark and Luke, the Gnostic components in the Letters of Paul, the clues in Acts of the Apostles, and the gnostically-related concepts in the Gospel of "Later John." We may speculate that Gnostic teaching activity was rejuvenated after the Roman-Jewish War wiped out the Jerusalem Church. It may indeed have been such a revival that contributed in part to the response of the four (ultimately canonical) gospels in rebuttal of the Gnostic tendency.

Judging by the Nag Hammadi documents,[1] many variations on Gnostic understandings of Jesus, God and humanity survived into the second century as an alternative approach in conflict with the emerging Pauline-oriented Christian Church. Just as Paul and the Johannine gospel reacted to and absorbed many Gnostic ideas, later Gnostic writers accepted some of the insights of Paul and "Later John" into their interpretive understandings. In fact, it is the absence of Pauline or "Later John" traces in the Thomas Gospel that further supports its dating as very early after the crucifixion of Jesus (see Chapter 1). The importance of gnosis as "secret Wisdom," or superior Divine Wisdom received by Jesus, moves outward from the Thomas Gospel as a sort of advanced spirituality beyond simple "faith." Later Gnostic writers, in their efforts to mystically imitate Jesus, could see themselves as superior to others in their understanding of "truth." And so it came to be that Gnostic interpretation, which perceived Jesus as teaching the paradox that true knowledge of suffering releases the believer from it, alienated those who required a Divine Saviour to rescue them from sin. The Gnostic outlook, vested with a timeless sensibility, was not well-equipped to deal with the urgency of immediate anguish and suffering in everyday existence. The hidden "good news" that the divine dwells as "light" within all human beings was an idea that remained potent but dormant over the centuries.[2]

---

[1]   Rodolphe Kasser, Marvin Meyer and Gregor Wurst (editors), *The Gospel of Judas*, National Geographic Society, Washington, D.C., 2006.

[2]   See Pagels, Elaine, *The Gnostic Gospels*, Random House, New York, 1979, and *Beyond Belief*, Random House, New York, 2003.

CHAPTER 21

BROTHER JAMES AND
THE HEBREWS

James was a younger brother of Jesus "in the flesh," implying quite a different relationship to Jesus than that of Jesus' "spiritual twin" Thomas. Judas Thomas had a special mystical understanding of Jesus (Thomas 13), while recognizing in his gospel that Jesus had selected James the Just (brother of Jesus) to be leader while Jesus was away (Thomas 12). Indeed, James served as first leader of the Jerusalem Church (or member of a leadership triumvirate) for a time span lasting about 26 years until his death in 62 C.E. The evidence is strong, also, that he was the mysterious "disciple whom Jesus loved" credited by "Later John" as being the author of the Johannine gospel (see Chapters 3 and 14).

The main sources for understanding the viewpoint of James are the canonical Letter of James, and the embedded elements of the "Early John" Gospel situated in canonical Mark, Luke and John, some letters of Paul, and Acts of the Apostles.

Essentially, while James embraced the ethical teachings of Jesus, he sought continuity with Hebrew tradition and Mosaic Law. After the crucifixion, he reached back to ancient scripture to identify Jesus as the newly vindicated Messiah of Israel chosen by God to announce the coming of His Kingdom on Earth. Jesus had chosen martyrdom as an atonement sacrifice for the sins of Israel. James envisaged his resurrection and elevation by God, and his return in bodily form in the near future to implement God's Plan. In the meantime, he emphasized "doing the words of Jesus," good works which equated with traditional commandments from God about righteousness towards fellow human beings. In regard to piety towards God, James struggled to maintain traditional Jewish values of ritual expression, while allowing non-circumcised followers of Jesus to be excluded from ritual requirements within certain limitations.

The lost Gospel of "Early John" (written by James or a close associate) may be interpreted in part as a rebuttal of the views of Thomas and his fellow Gnostic "Hellenists." It tells the story of Jesus' mission and death. The post-crucifixion appearances of Jesus are perceived not only as a verification of his teachings about the Kingdom of God, but as proof of his imminent return "in power." Thomas understands the Kingdom to be unfolding from the divine Spirit (or Light) within each human being, bolstered by a mystical communication from the spiritual Jesus. "Early John" has a different revelation of imminent external action by God through Jesus the Messiah, as proven by Jesus' witnessed resurrection. For both gospels, the task is to spread the "good news" of Divine Light that is (or will be) coming back into the world to reclaim the children of God.

By unraveling the embedded "Early John" source material in the canonical gospels, clues become available on the role of James and his siblings, which challenge the misleading conventional portrayal of their opposition to Jesus during his lifetime. The trick about James is to realize that the "disciple whom Jesus loved" is also Lazarus of Bethany whom Jesus loved (John 11:3) and also "the other disciple known to the high priest" (John 18:15). In writing his gospel, James apparently conceals his own role as family member in the story perhaps because in the new Kingdom of God all participants are children of the Divine Father, with no family privileges (Thomas 99). Enlarging on this precedent the later canonical writers distinguished between brothers and disciples, trying to conceal the presence of brothers of Jesus as disciples. Nevertheless, the Thomas, Johannine and Markan gospels all state that family members, particularly his brothers, accompanied Jesus during at least some of his travels. Acts of the Apostles places his mother and brothers in Jerusalem with the disciples immediately after the crucifixion of Jesus (Acts 1:14). And in the post-crucifixion situation, Paul acknowledges that James is an apostle, and complains that the brothers of Jesus do have special privileges.

An interesting theory is that one or both parents of Jesus were Essenes, which could account for the hostility of the villagers of Nazareth towards Jesus, recorded or hinted at in most gospels. Caught up in the antagonisms of rural Galileans, Hellenists in the nearby city of Sephoris, Samaritans blocking the way to Jerusalem, and the Herodian establishment, the family of Jesus may indeed have been divided in allegiance as the five brothers grew to maturity (note Thomas 16). Available evidence suggests a move to Bethany near Jerusalem by some family members, and a peripatetic search for new insights by others, much in the manner recorded by Flavius Josephus about his own youthful self.

James' inferred "Early John" narrative begins with the meeting between John the Baptist and the Jerusalem priests and Levites, which is a clue that James was present as the unnamed "other disciple," a follower of John the Baptist who accompanied Andrew in turning to follow Jesus (John 1:37). His later nickname Justus (the Righteous) is a clue that he may have been an admirer of the Essene Teacher of Righteousness. Presumably, James had been checking out the ideas of John the Baptist about God's Plan, when he turned to Jesus along with Andrew and Simon Peter and "they stayed with him that day" (John 1:39). Both his mentors taught (in the language of Josephus) "righteousness of men towards each other," but differed in respect of "piety towards God." John was a strict observance Hebrew traditionalist, while Jesus endorsed Gnostic spiritual communication with the Spirit of God as superior to ritual purification.

The supposed endorsement of Jesus by John the Baptist, recorded in "Early John," may have been wishful thinking by those who were seeking to enroll John's followers after his death. Multiple sources show that John was rooted in Hebrew tradition and asceticism, fasted regularly, and baptized with water. Jesus, on the other hand, "baptized with the Spirit," and the Thomas Gospel states clearly his Gnostic ideas, along with his indifference towards circumcision, fasting, and food rituals and taboos. "Early John" admits that Jesus was competing with John the Baptist when he began his baptizing mission in Judea. But when King Herod Antipas arrested and executed John to forestall "some form of revolt" (Josephus Antiquities 18:2), the situation changed. Jesus had become politically involved in a crisis-engendered effort "to gather into one the children of God" (John 11:52).

The "feeding of the multitude" was a milestone event in bringing together hitherto separated Galilean traditionalists and Gnostic radicals, in a symbolically loaded food-sharing experience that pointed toward Jerusalem and the Feast of Tabernacles as the next step. Jesus was trying to find ways of bridging differences between hinterland people and the Herodian establishment, between followers of John and King Herod Antipas, between Essenes and the Temple cult, between "Hebrews" and "Hellenists" in his new Kingdom of God movement (see Chapters 15-17). This speeded-up proselytization may have been intended to prevent violence and civil war, but inevitably directed attention to the personhood of Jesus, evidenced by an attempt to "take Jesus by force to make him King" (John 6:15). Trace elements of Jamesian influence can be detected; he was probably keen to attract "strict observance" Jews into the movement. The reference to the brothers of Jesus debating with him on how best to inform the people and cope with the Herodian establishment (John 7:1-9) implies their participation in the enterprise, despite the "Later John" cover-up (see Chapter 3).

The tumultuous scenes of the entry into Jerusalem, the "cleansing of the Temple" and the healings and preaching in the Temple, do not prove that Jesus was seeking to overthrow the Herodian establishment. His utopian objective may simply have been a "change of ways" mediated by the Holy Spirit within Jesus; a demonstration of a completely non-commercial model of the Kingdom of God, in which all the people in the Temple setting (God's sacred space) could participate together in egalitarian sharing of food, sacrifice, and thanksgiving. Instead, the truth suppressed by the canonical gospel writers was that violence reared its ugly head; Roman soldiers intervened; the project failed; some "insurrectionists" were arrested. Jesus and his closest disciples escaped "across the Jordan to the place where John at first baptized" (John 10:40).

The story of Lazarus "whom Jesus loved" (John 11:3 and 5) makes sense when understood as a "happening" in the life of James, who had upper-class connections, being "known to the High Priest" (John 18:15). Perhaps James had been expecting some kind of Temple reform agreement to result from the preaching of Jesus in the Temple. The resurrection of Lazarus can then be understood as implying a psychological depression experienced by a young James appalled by the failure of the mission to Jerusalem, who is rescued from the tomb in Bethany by a forgiving Jesus. This would be a defining moment for James.

My interpretation is that the emergence of the entire Christian enterprise hinges on the impact of the "Lazarus" rescue on James and his sister Mary, both of whom perceive it as saving forgiveness by Jesus, the agent of God's compassion. Divine power has intervened to save James. Later, at the Last Supper in Bethany with disciples and family members, Jesus explains his forthcoming surrender to Roman authorities with an implied expectation of his future return, naming James as interim leader (Thomas 12). They acquiesce to his decision, perhaps expecting some sort of divine intervention leading to a peaceful outcome. Pontius Pilate, with forced collaboration from the Herodian establishment, orders flogging and public crucifixion of Jesus (of temporary duration) to be followed by his release; his actual death (perhaps by poison) can then be assigned to the will of God. Jesus' body is placed in a tomb (see Chapter 17). Such inferences are deductions about what may have happened, deriving from inferred "Early John" material embedded in the Johannine gospel, and the gospels of Mark and Luke (see Chapters 3,5,8, and 9).

When Jesus dies unexpectedly on the cross, despair among the disciples is succeeded by befuddlement engendered by the Empty Tomb and Mary's vision of Jesus near the tomb. For Mary (we may speculate), her vision meant not only confirmation of Jesus' teaching about life after death, but also ongoing communication from the spiritual Jesus, now united with God the Father and the Holy Spirit. For James (we may speculate), the combined "Lazarus" experience and Empty Tomb setting meant something closer to his own physical "resurrection" from a tomb. Perhaps the Empty Tomb and Mary's vision were signs that Jesus and his mission were still very much alive and part of the Divine Plan. And later, after encountering the mysterious stranger on the road to Emmeaus, James realized that Jesus had appeared to him in a physical body and "interpreted in all the scriptures the things concerning himself" (Luke 24:27).

The spiritual Jesus, therefore, had not only joined God above, but had returned temporarily to Earth in a bodily form to explain God's Plan. Here was a physical presence of Jesus that promised the return of a messianic Jesus "in power" during "the present generation" (Mark 13:30, Luke 21:32 and John 21:23). For James and other "Hebrew" disciples, the encounter likely indicated some sort of divine personhood previously "in Jesus" and now "of Jesus" encompassed by the Hebrew terms "resurrection" and "Messiah." The teaching message of "Early John" (reflected also in Acts 5:31), was about a human Jesus Messiah exalted by God "to give repentance to Israel and forgiveness of sins." An essential point, revealed to the author on the road to Emmaus, was that the whole story was foretold in Hebrew scriptures. Jesus was a worthy son of God, like Moses and other prophets, but specially chosen to be resurrected and later returned to life as traditional Messiah of Israel.

The lost Gospel of "Early John," therefore, was the first creative written attempt to restore direct action by God the Father as the governing principle in human affairs, in denial of the "gnosis" of Thomas, Jesus' "spiritual twin." Instead of Jesus' discovery of the secret Wisdom of God (the Holy Spirit) already within himself (and potentially within everyone else), James surrendered to traditional scriptural opinion that God would anoint a new Moses to carry out the Divine Plan, a descendant of King David who would "redeem Israel." He proposed that "a man sent from God" (i.e. John the Baptist) had observed "the Spirit descend as a dove from heaven" to permit Jesus to baptize with the Holy Spirit (John 1:31-33). This key endorsement was a sign of God's intervention that promised forthcoming rescue and salvation of God's children if they understood and responded to the challenge. Jesus had shown the Way and his sacrificial martyrdom, as well as subsequent resurrection as confirmed by his spiritual appearances, demonstrated the coming fulfillment of God's Plan.

The visions and revelations experienced by the disciples were consistent with Jesus' teachings about spiritual survival after death, and the ongoing presence of the Spirit of God. A Gnostic perception of divinity and spirituality (beyond charismatic personality), provides a handy explanation for the mystical exuberance and enthusiastic response of Jesus' disciples, as compared, for example, with the downcast followers of John the Baptist after John's death (Mark 6:34). But accompanying this was a new sense of urgency about accessing the Kingdom of God proclaimed by Jesus to all the peoples of a restored Israel, regardless of their traditional beliefs and practices. Keep in mind, though, that both Gnostics and traditionalists shared a common neo-platonic interpretation of spiritual being and ethical activity. The Q1 Gospel, probably written by the disciple Matthew, expresses the common ground between the two groups. Only shared viewpoints can explain the unequivocal endorsement in the Thomas Gospel of James the Just as leader after Jesus "leaves us" (Thomas 12). Acts of the Apostles states: "And they devoted themselves to the apostles' teaching and fellowship, to the breaking of bread and the prayers" (Acts 2:42).

But the Gnostic perception was also a cause of division because mystical revelations could take many contradictory forms. When disputes broke out between Hellenists and Hebrews, the chosen apostles took on responsibility "for the ministry of the word" (Acts 6:4) (see also Chapter 20), the beginning of "apostolic authority" by Hebrew-oriented leaders of the Jesus people. The result was a time-limited and male-limited definition of "authentic appearances" of Jesus. According to Paul's Letter to the Corinthians (1 Corinthians 15:5-7), five visionary experiences of the deceased Jesus had been defined as valid witness of his resurrection; apart from Paul himself, only Simon Peter and James had received valid private revelations.

From the "Early John" Gospel, we learn that Simon Peter had been a follower of John the Baptist, presumably interested in social change and overthrow of Herodian hegemony. Along with "another disciple" and Andrew, he moves to Jesus as a perceived Messiah who will restore Israel. According to the Gospel of Thomas, he regards Jesus as a "just messenger" or prophet from God. But James' "Early John" text denigrates Simon as a violent man who uses his sword to cut off the ear of Malchus, the high priest's slave, and then falsely denies being a disciple of Jesus to save his own skin. Subsequently, at the Empty Tomb, Simon fails to understand, while James "saw and believed." Nevertheless, the transfiguration scene in the synoptic gospels (which derives from Simon's post-crucifixion vision of the spiritual Jesus reported by Paul, and presumably reported also by James in the "Early John" text) is an acknowledgment that Simon Peter was a major player among the disciples, particularly as first male recipient of direct visionary revelation of the spiritual resurrection of Jesus.

The tendency of the "Hebrews" was to perceive Jesus' teachings as evolutionary rather than revolutionary, a continuity with God's Word contained in scripture, tradition and Temple practice. If Jesus was going to return to Earth, the new Temple of people comprising members of the Kingdom of God would be reintegrated with the physical Temple of stones in Jerusalem, under the new Messiah in an alternative church that could "take over" whenever God chose to act. The most immediate requirement would surely have been to demonstrate credibility as a non-violent Essenic movement steeped in traditional values of Judaism. The external face of the movement would have to be determinedly "Hebrew" to overcome the previous image of hinterland insurrection by "those who do not know the law" (John 7:49). Herein is the explanation for the immediate attention devoted to Temple attendance by "Hebrew" followers of Jesus for purposes of prayer, preaching and healing of the sick, which is described in Acts of the Apostles.

Acts presents Simon Peter speaking to assembled multitudes in the image of a John the Baptist calling the people "to repentance and baptism for the forgiveness of sins" (Acts 2:38). He said: "save yourselves from this crooked generation" (Acts

2:40). It is clear that traditionalist Hebrews are leading the charge "in the name of Jesus Messiah" (Acts 2:38). Jesus is described as the prophet, foretold in scripture, as God's appointed Messiah; "every soul that does not listen to that prophet shall be destroyed from the people" (Acts 3:23). Unmistakably, the apostles, through Peter and John speaking in the Temple, are invoking Moses and the Law, "and proclaiming in Jesus the resurrection from the dead" (Acts 4:2). This is an appeal to traditional Judaism, and particularly the Pharisees. "And fear came upon every soul" (Acts 2:43), as they "attended the temple together" (Acts 2:46). The arrests of the apostles (Acts 5:18) by Temple officials and the Sadducees is not surprising, since by proclaiming the dead Jesus as Messiah of Israel, they were implying the illegitimacy of both King Herod Antipas and the High Priest. Jesus had been crucified for sedition, and his followers were still around. Reason enough to explain the initial persecutions of the Jesus people by the Temple authorities. Peter was arrested three times. The situation was dire, but other mitigating factors were also at work.

Perhaps of first importance was the losing war that King Herod Antipas had been fighting with King Aretas of Arabia over Herod's insulting divorce of Aretas' daughter. As reported by Flavius Josephus, many people saw Herod's defeat by Aretas, his exile to Spain by Roman Emperor Caligula, and his death circa 38-39 C.E., as punishment for his unlawful execution of John the Baptist. This turn of events undoubtedly weakened, at least temporarily, the position of the Annas-Caiphas "Herodian" high-priestly establishment in Jerusalem. Secondly, in 36 C.E., the Roman Governor Pontius Pilate was recalled to Rome; one may speculate (although not mentioned by Josephus) that the crucifixion of Jesus may have been a factor. In any case, the Roman Emperor Tiberius died in 37 C.E., to be succeeded by Caligula and four years of chaos in Rome. No successor to Pilate was sent to Judea, and responsibility was assigned to the distant Governor of Syria. In the meantime another "Herodian," King Herod Agrippa, who had lived nearly all his life in Rome, was awarded certain territories in Palestine (excluding Judea) by his friend Caligula. He visited Jerusalem briefly in 38 C.E., long enough to depose the High Priest Theophilus (of the Annas-Caiphas family) in favour of Simon Cantheras from a different family. Herod Agrippa then returned to Rome for the next three years. Such changes, which left both Roman Governors and Herodian Kings at a distance, and the Annas-Caiphas family out of power, must surely have been good news for the Jesus people. Perhaps the Roman Empire and the Herodian establishment were falling apart.

These circumstances offered an opportunity to someone, presumably James, "the other disciple who was known to the High Priest" (John 18:16), to achieve an accommodation with the Temple authorities. The outcome of the deal between the "Hebrew" followers of Jesus and the priestly establishment (brokered by the Pharisee Gamaliel—Acts 5:27-42), may have been a new alliance between Jesus

people and some Pharisees impressed by the story of Jesus' resurrection as a sign
of the approaching end of Satanic domination of Israel by the Roman Empire.
Certainly, the Acts of the Apostles refers several times to the fact that Zealots for
the Law, including some Pharisees and priests of the Temple, joined the ranks of the
disciples of Jesus. Apocalyptic feelings were probably intensified during the period
from 38 to 41 C.E. by the rumoured intention of the Roman Emperor Caligula
(reported by Josephus) to install a gigantic statue of himself in the Jerusalem
Temple. During this period, no Roman governor had been appointed, the High
Priest was no longer from the family of Annas-Caiphas, King Herod Antipas was
exiled and died, and King Herod Agrippa remained in Rome after a brief visit to
Jerusalem in 38 C.E.

Things may have been progressing quite well for the Jesus people until King
Herod Agrippa I returned to Jerusalem in 41 C.E., having been restored as King
of all Israel by the new Roman Emperor Claudius. He appointed Matthias,
another member of the Annas-Caiphas family, as High Priest. Then, according
to Acts, "King Herod . . . had James, the brother of John, killed with the sword,"
arrested Simon Peter, and "laid violent hands upon some who belonged to the
church" (Acts 12:1-4). Chances are that this was the "great persecution" (Acts
8:1); if so Saul could not have been involved. Thus, if the story of the martyrdom
of Stephen is a fabrication (see Chapter 22), the first martyrs of the Church were
"Hebrews" involved in reactions to persecution by King Herod Agrippa I. Relating
to this period, Josephus describes the execution of Theudas who attempted to
lead a group of followers across the Jordan River, and the crucifixion of two sons
(or grand-sons) of Judas of Galilee, presumably as preventive measures against
rebellion. There was also a famine in Palestine. Finally, the death of Agrippa I circa
44 C.E. may have raised the spirits of the persecuted Jesus people, but Rome then
appointed new governors and the Annas-Caiphas family continued their control
of the priesthood.

How did the Jesus people continue to survive in Jerusalem within the corrupt
and chaotic environment that existed after the death of King Agrippa I? One
reason was that the Roman Emperor Claudius allowed only minimal responsibility
to Agrippa II, son of the dead king. Roman governors maintained stability, and
it was understood that ongoing pacification of the Jewish people required some
compromise with Hebrew nationalism, and limitations on suppressive action
by Herodian extremists. When Roman Governor Cumanus nearly provoked
armed rebellion in 52 C.E., Emperor Claudius replaced him, while retaining the
High Priest Ananias (47-59 C.E.), who seems to have been relatively tolerant of
nationalist attitudes. Somehow James emerges in Acts as leader in Jerusalem of
"the sect of the Nazarenes" (Acts 24:5), apparently tolerated and understood to
be a distinct group—although not mentioned as such by the writer Josephus, who
may have considered them to be a sub-group of Essenes.

Helpful in explaining the staying power of the Nazarenes in Jerusalem is the Q1 Sayings Gospel, probably written by the disciple Matthew. It is a purist version of the remembered teachings of Jesus, lacking any framework of Hebrew scripture or of Gnostic ideology. Note that it includes the Lord's Prayer. As a public teaching document, it expresses the joy of living the Kingdom of God in this world. It fits well into a Jamesian strategy of avoiding conflict over varying interpretations of God's Plan, and correlates well with the profound ethical sensitivity of the canonical Letter of James. In his letter, James concentrates on "righteousness," which is in effect the "works of the law," whose essence is "to love your neighbour as yourself" (James 2:8). But "for whoever keeps the whole law but fails in one point has become guilty of all of it" (James 2:10). "What does it profit, if a man says he has faith but has not works? . . . If a brother or sister is ill-clad and in lack of daily food . . . without giving them the things needed for the body, what does it profit?" (James 2:14-17) Remember that James designated the apostles as "the poor ones," according to the letters of Paul. The Letter of James is a paean of praise for the poor, and a condemnation of the sins of the rich. It shows beyond any doubt the deep compassion of James, who defines pure religion as follows: "to visit orphans and widows in their affliction, and keep oneself unstained from the world" (James 1:27).

Essentially, the Sect of the Nazarenes took on the burden of "the poor" in Jerusalem, which for practical purposes made things easier for the Herodian and Roman establishment. James and the apostles offered the Kingdom of God to those who shared their wealth for the benefit of the downtrodden poor. The original Essenes had made themselves separate and economically self-sufficient at Qumram. But the Sect of the Nazarenes, following Jesus' teaching, came face to face with poverty in the city, without the means of caring for "widows and orphans." Hence a strong economic motivation to proselytize and obtain material support from converts in all parts of the Roman Empire. The clue as to how this worked comes from the Letter of Paul to the Galatians. "They agreed that we should go to the Gentiles . . . only they would have us remember the poor, which very thing I was eager to do" (Galatians 2:10). And so over the years Paul collects money from his new converts in city after city, to bring it eventually for the "poor ones" in Jerusalem.

The new centralized missionary effort required follow-up actions by "Hebrew" apostles to maintain control over the "Hellenist" missionaries to the hinterland (see Chapter 20). For example, "when the apostles at Jerusalem heard that Samaria had received the word of God (i.e. from the apostle Philip), they sent them Peter and John" (Acts 8:14). And "News of this (i.e. missionary activity among the Hellenists) came to the ears of the church in Jerusalem and they sent Barnabas to Antioch" (Acts 11:22). In other words, after the first step of encouraging Gnostic Hellenists to proselytize outside Jerusalem, the next step was to send

Hebrews to counter the Gnostic interpretation of the message. The reluctant third step was to attempt authoritative definition. Apparently, at a special meeting in Jerusalem circa 49 C.E., James rendered a "judgment that we should not trouble those of the Gentiles who turn to God, but should write to them to abstain from the pollution of idols and from unchastity and from what is strangled and from blood" (Acts 15:19). James remained deeply committed to the maintenance of Hebrew traditions, but equally committed to proselytization of non-Hebrews into the Kingdom of God.

Undoubtedly, James was a mediator, struggling to encompass both Jews and Gentiles in a common community, pending direct action by God. Recognizing that Gentiles could belong to the Kingdom of God without adopting Jewish identity and traditions, he insisted only that they avoid certain pagan Temple and food practices, and immorality. At the same time, Jews who continued to be obligated by strict observance of Mosaic Law and tradition could also be followers of Jesus, even though unable to eat together with non-observant Gentiles. He was one of them, a "strict observance Hebrew," and apparently evaded the problem by not traveling away from Jerusalem. While Paul argued that circumcised Jews had the option of ignoring Hebrew ritual and tradition when eating with Gentiles, more and more Nazarenes in Palestine were "Zealots for the Law." Their hostility towards Paul for undermining the ritual integrity of Jewish Diaspora communities explains the attack on Paul during his visit to Jerusalem circa 58 C.E. Perhaps they suspected also that Paul was a "Herodian" interloper who was trying to hijack the Jesus movement.

In Jerusalem, increasing recruitment of "poor ones" and zealous anti-Romans tended towards confrontation with Herodian corruption and Roman power, by the sect of the Nazarenes and many others. According to Josephus, during the fifties there was increasing disorder in the city, and a Zealot group known as the Sicarii assassinated various officials and members of the establishment. When one of them assassinated the former High Priest Jonathan (a member of the Annas-Caiphas family) in 59 C.E., it eventually touched off the arrest and stoning to death of James. The account by Josephus provides no explanatory details for James' arrest and condemnation, except the hint that it was part of a reprisal for the earlier assassination. The implication in the text of Josephus as well as in the text of Acts (as related to Paul's final visit to Jerusalem), is that Zealot members of the Jesus people had become "freedom fighters" ready to assassinate and kill enemies, instead of "loving their enemies." There is no evidence, however, that James himself subscribed to their views. To the contrary, his proposal to Paul in Jerusalem, for example, to visibly confirm his attachment to Judaism (Acts 21:22-24), reaffirms his mediating propensities.

Josephus reports that the sentencing of James and "certain others" to death for "transgressing the Law," was accomplished in 62 C.E. by Ananus the Younger, a

High Priest of the Annas-Caiphas family, when a new Governor (Albinus) and King (Agrippa 2) were absent from Jerusalem. A significant point is that important "strict observance" citizens protested strongly to both Albinus and Agrippa 2 (after the event), which resulted in the dismissal of Ananus the Younger after only three months in office. Evidently, his repressive action, however motivated, was very unpopular, and was symptomatic of the circumstances that led to the outbreak of the Roman-Jewish War a few years later. Josephus' eerie follow-up story about the lamentations of *Jesus* ben Ananias over the coming fate of Jerusalem resonates back to Jesus' own prophecy about Jerusalem in the Gospel of Mark. This Jesus ben Ananias is arrested by Herodian authorities in the same year as the death of James, brought before the Roman Governor and sentenced to heavy flogging. He stoically says nothing except "Woe, woe to Jerusalem, to the people, to the city and to the Temple"; he is then released (Josephus, War 6, 302-04).

After the killing of James, the disastrous Roman-Jewish War, and the failure of Jesus to return, it was left to others to pick up the pieces. James was reviled and forgotten. His story of Jesus fell into the dustbin of history. Is it not a profound irony that it was probably James who first "saw and believed" (John 20:8) the resurrection of Jesus, and first received the revelation "in all the scriptures" (Luke 24:27) of Jesus' messianic destiny?

Very little is known about the fate of the Jerusalem Nazarenes. No documents have yet been found that can match the Nag Hammadi Gnostic Library or the Dead Sea Scrolls of the Essenes at Qumram. Josephus did not identify the Nazarenes separately in the context of the Roman-Jewish War. All other references are embedded in the canonical gospels, and other orthodox Christian writings in subsequent years. One thing is clear, however. The role of James and the "Hebrews" was critically important in the foundational years of Christianity. And their surviving descendants continued within the Jewish polity as the Ebionites or "poor ones." Through sources dating from the second to fourth century, we know that the Ebionites understood themselves to be "Hebrew" followers of Jesus, who followed the original teachings of James, brother of Jesus, and Simon Peter. They followed Mosaic Law, believed in Jesus as the traditional Messiah of Israel, and practiced circumcision for males, traditional food rituals and observance of the Sabbath. Interestingly, they apparently believed that the atoning sacrifice of Jesus replaced the traditional ritual sacrifice of animals. They were vegetarians.

CHAPTER 22

PAUL AND THE GENTILES

Perhaps the best way to approach the mission of Paul (also known as Saul) is to begin with his own self-evaluation. "I have become all things to all men, that I might by all means save some" (1 Corinthians 9:22). "To the Jews I became as a Jew, in order to win Jews . . . To those outside the law I became as one outside the law . . . that I might win those outside the law" (1 Corinthians 9:20-21). As a person inside the law, he was known first as Saul and later as Paul. As a person outside the law he was known as Paul.

In his earlier incarnation as Saul, all sources agree with his own statement in the Letter to the Galatians: "For you have heard of my former life in Judaism, how I persecuted the church of God violently and tried to destroy it, and I advanced in Judaism beyond many of my own age among my people, so extremely zealous was I for the traditions of my fathers" (Galatians 1:13-14).

The suggestion by Paul himself that as a young man he "tried to destroy the church of God violently" certainly implies that he had significant status in the Herodian establishment, and indeed there are references in Acts (13:1) and Romans (16:11), that hint at Herodian family connections. Other clues to his earlier allegiance include his claim to be a Roman citizen, his emphasis on being a zealous Pharisee, his self-reference as a Hebrew of the Hebrews from the tribe of Benjamin, and his dramatic switch to faith in Jesus Messiah, possibly signaling a prior youthful infatuation with the Herodian dynastic destiny to restore Israel, as symbolized by the Temple built by King Herod the Great. Remember that the Jesus people were proclaiming in the Jerusalem Temple setting that Jesus had been resurrected by God as a sign that he was indeed the traditional Messiah of Israel, which of course implied the illegitimacy of the Herodian line of kings.

The problem is that Paul seemingly denies in his Letter to the Galatians any connections to persecutions in Jerusalem, or preaching there after his conversion on the road to Damascus. Apparently in that letter he is responding emotionally to criticism that his later teaching to the Gentiles is in serious conflict with what he was taught by the original apostles and disciples of Jesus in Jerusalem. He writes, "But when he who had set me apart before I was born, and had called me through his grace, was pleased to reveal his Son in me, in order that I might preach him among the Gentiles, I did not confer with flesh and blood, nor did I go up to Jerusalem to those who were apostles before me, but I went away into Arabia; and again I returned to Damascus. Then after three years I went up to Jerusalem" (Galatians 1:15-18). He then proceeds to deny being "known by sight to the churches of Christ in Judea" (Galatians 1:22), or by the apostles other than Peter and James, brother of the Lord (Galatians 1:18-19), until another visit to Jerusalem "after fourteen years" (Galatians 2:1). Furthermore, he insists, as he does several times in other letters, "In what I am writing to you I do not lie" (Galatians 1:20).

Many scholars continue to argue that Paul's own statement of facts should prevail over the contrary material in Acts of the Apostles that places violent persecution by Saul in Jerusalem, which was after all the initial location of the church. But how could Paul destroy the Jerusalem church by violence in Damascus (or elsewhere)?

A difficult problem for the Jerusalem hypothesis is posed by the story of Stephen, regarded as fraudulent by many scholars; I concur that it is a rather clumsy interpolation of a story of the actual death by stoning of James, twenty years later, mentioned by Josephus in Jewish Antiquities (Antiquities 20:197-203). The story of Stephen is used by the author of Acts to dramatize the wickedness of the persecutor Saul, and to explain the "scattering" of "Hellenist" followers of Jesus to the hinterland as being the consequence of "a great persecution" (Acts 8:1) conducted by Saul. However, this seems to be a mix-up with the later severe persecution by King Herod Agrippa (41-44 C.E.), much too late for the participation of Saul (see Chapter 21). Circumstantial evidence does not support the notion of a "Hellenist" martyr like Stephen between 38 and 41 C.E., when the Jesus people were riding high (see Chapter 21). A more plausible scenario would be that Saul participated actively in the first persecutions of "Hebrew" Jesus people by the Herodian establishment of the Temple in Jerusalem, until a combination of circumstances (circa 37-38 C.E.) involving the Pharisee Gamaliel, the High Priest, King Agrippa I, and the Roman Emperor Caligula brought temporary respite. When the Pharisee Gamaliel (teacher of Saul according to Acts 22:3), brokered an arrangement that stopped the persecution (reflecting the weakness of the Herodian establishment at this point), Saul seems to have been given a new assignment by the Herodian High Priest to investigate the situation in Damascus.

An important clue is a casual reference by Paul to his dramatic escape from Damascus, when boasting in a letter about his own youthful tribulations: "At Damascus, the governor under King Aretas guarded the city of Damascus in order to seize me, but I was let down in a basket through a window in the wall, and escaped his hands" (2 Corinthians 11:30). There seems little reason to doubt the veracity of this statement, which is unconnected to any context, and contradicts the version in Acts that says that Saul was rescued by Jesus people from Jews in Damascus "plotting to kill him" by "letting him down over the wall, lowering him in a basket" (Acts 9:23-25). The point is that, according to the outside observer Josephus, King Aretas of Arabia, incensed (like John the Baptist) with the marital affairs of King Herod Antipas (his daughter was the unfortunate divorcée) declared war and defeated Herod; the outcome signified to most Jews that King Herod had wrongfully executed John. The significance for understanding Saul is that King Aretas was on the same side of the fence as the followers of John the Baptist, and by extension the Jesus people. According to his own story, Saul when in Damascus was perceived as an enemy by King Aretas, and presumably was rescued by Herodian supporters.

It seems likely that Saul's investigative mission to Damascus was a failure, and that his vision of Jesus Messiah (coinciding with a perception that the Herodian dynasty was out of favour with God) occurred on the road *from* Damascus, after he "was let down in a basket." The vision, an external act of God, perhaps reflected an initial "Hebrew" understanding by Saul of a Jesus who would be returning to Earth soon to take over as Messiah of Israel. He then "went away into Arabia, and again returned to Damascus" (Galatians 1:17) as the beginning of a new effort to be reconciled with former enemies.

The upshot of my assessment is that some of the text in Acts of the Apostles, probably based on source material written by Joseph Barnabas, is more credible than Paul's own defensive account of his earlier life. Relevant quotes are: "When he had come to Jerusalem (after the Damascus vision), he attempted to join the disciples; and they were all afraid of him, for they did not believe that he was a disciple. But Barnabas took him and brought him to the apostles . . . So he went in and out among them at Jerusalem preaching boldly in the name of the Lord. And he spoke and disputed against the Hellenists" (Acts 9:26-29). If these statements derive from source material written by Barnabas, their credibility is acceptable (excluding the Stephen material), along with the implication that Saul retained his Hebrew Pharisee convictions while believing in the resurrection of Jesus in opposition to the Gnostic Hellenist interpretation. Note that "he spoke and disputed against the Hellenists." And note that in the text of Acts, twenty years later, Paul is quoted as saying: "I am a Pharisee, a son of Pharisees" (Acts 23:6), apparently still claiming that he retains his allegiance to this group. Note also that Saul's early missionary travels with Barnabas support the proposition that Paul and Barnabas at this time shared the same convictions as James and Peter about Jesus as the Messiah of Israel.

Such a hypothesis of continuing fidelity to Mosaic Law (at least when in the presence of "Hebrews") seems confirmed by the story in Acts that Saul was recruited by Barnabas to preach the gospel in Antioch, in reaction to news reaching Jerusalem that Hellenist teachers were preaching to Hellenists there. Presumably, the Jamesian leaders in Jerusalem believed that a converted Greek-speaking Jew such as Saul was well qualified to teach the Hebrew version to persons who were Gentiles or Hellenists with weak attachment to Jewish tradition. And for some considerable period of time, Saul was accompanied by Barnabas in missionary activities that still reflected the Hebrew perspective. There are no letters from Saul in this early period to confirm this one way or the other, but the fact that Barnabas accompanied Saul, only to break up with him at a later date, is supportive of such a hypothesis. So also is the absence of surviving letters from this period. Obviously, the issues of Mosaic Law and circumcision for Gentiles began to intrude, but somehow Saul (now renamed Paul) managed to maintain relationships with the "Hebrews" by working out compromise understandings. *In other words, the progression of Saul towards his own idiosyncratic interpretation of Jesus and of his own mission to the Gentiles was a gradual process, not a blinding flash of revelation.* By the time that he was undertaking his journeys without Barnabas in the late forties, and writing his epistles, his ideas had become fully formed, and his attitudes had firmed. In crisis-stimulated explorations of the Spirit within himself (unacknowledged "gnosis"), he discovered his own version of Jesus within himself, as distinct from the external Road to Damascus vision. Both Gnostic and pagan influences had been incorporated into his thinking, and the new Pauline interpretation was on its way.

It is a plausible hypothesis that Saul's rejection in Jerusalem after his conversion experience ("they were seeking to kill him," Acts 9:29), combined with contacts with Gnostic Hellenists as he traveled abroad, helped to generate his re-imagination of the divine personhood of Jesus in a novel breakthrough linkage of Jewish tradition and Hellenistic ideas. His intellectual starting point may have been the Pharisaic belief in resurrection of the dead at the "end times," which connected to his visionary experience of Jesus as a direct personal revelation of the truth of the resurrection. This may have signaled initially to Paul the status of Jesus as the Messiah who would return to Earth to redeem Israel, as taught by the apostles in Jerusalem to the local people. However, by appearing to a miserable sinner such as Paul, Jesus was demonstrating much more in that he had died "for our sins" to redeem all sinners, therefore all humankind.

Paul claimed special revelation, communicated directly to him by the spiritual Jesus, as the basis for his own teaching. This "secret and hidden wisdom" (1 Corinthians 2:7) was not relayed to him by the apostles. As in Gnostic mystical ecstasy, he was "caught up to the third heaven" where "he heard things that cannot be told, which man may not utter" (2 Corinthians 12:2). But he also received gnostic-type revelation of Jesus as a pre-existent divine cosmic figure, the Christ, Lord of Heaven, and Son of God, sent by his Father to announce the Kingdom and die a sacrificial death "for our sins."

For Paul, the word Messiah as translated into the Greek Christ, had taken on a new expanded meaning beyond the traditional Messiah of Israel. Jesus Christ represented the entry of God into the material world. The physical body of the human Jesus had, through resurrection, been transformed into the holistic mystical Body of Christ, which equated to the spiritual Son of God, an emanation of God the Father. In terms of Gnostic vocabulary, Jesus had recovered his original spiritual undivided self in returning from whence he came as the pre-existent Son of God. However, for Gnostics, Jesus was simply *a* son of God returning to God, as would all other humans who achieved enlightenment or gnosis. For Paul, on the other hand, Jesus Christ was *a spiritual form of God*, divinely distinct from fleshly human beings. Jesus Christ took on the "likeness of human flesh" (Romans 8:3) thereby "becoming sin" (2 Corinthians 5:20), and moving to the "poverty of bodily life" (2 Corinthians 8:9), as in Gnostic vocabulary. But Jesus had a special role as sacrificial Saviour, to rescue all humans from their bondage to Satan and his evil spirits.

The resurrection therefore was a cosmic event, confirmed by time-limited appearances of the resurrected Jesus to his disciples, and to Paul himself. The word "appearances" served as shorthand for lumping together a variety of specified visionary experiences that avoided the issue of Jesus as a risen corporeal body or as a risen spirit. For Paul, these post-crucifixion encounters were events related to a fully divine Jesus Christ, who now was disseminating the fruits of his sacrifice through the Holy Spirit connection. The spiritual resurrection of Jesus (his physical body had been raised and transformed) proved that the "end times" were at hand, whereas the Gnostics believed in a timeless Kingdom, always present, and already here. Paul was reaching back in time to Jewish-type prophecy about an apocalyptic ending just around the corner. When the message had been brought to "all the nations," God would take action.

And who qualified for this spiritual Kingdom reached by "not tasting death"? According to the Thomas Gospel, entry was for persons achieving self-knowledge or gnosis. Paul changed this to the word "faith" meaning committed belief in the resurrected Jesus Christ. In other words, the Hebrew notion of having a right relationship to God (defined by biblical tradition) took precedence over right understanding (based on experience). Here was a change from relatively elitist gnosis to simple faith in Jesus Christ, open to all repentant sinners regardless. All human beings are sinners requiring divine intervention (the grace of God) to be saved.

Another underlying idea developed by Paul was the New Covenant (or new deal) between God and his people, designed to replace the old arrangement described in Hebrew scriptures. The new deal was between God and the "new Israel" made up of all humankind. The new "chosen people" comprised all who have faith in Jesus Christ. Such faith (committed belief) replaced the "works" of the Mosaic Law. The New Covenant event occurred "on the night when he was betrayed," when Jesus broke bread and drank wine with his disciples, prior to his crucifixion by the Romans. Paul was not present at the event, so how did he know about it? "I received it from the Lord" he wrote (1 Corinthians 11:23-26; see also Chapter 4).

Along with "faith" was an authority structure, headed by Jesus Christ in heaven, and corresponding apostolic authority on Earth; Paul was a self-designated apostle. There was, of course, friction between Paul's authority, and the authority of James and other apostles in Jerusalem. All of them expected the return of Jesus in some form, but Paul had the foresight to bypass the scenario of a return to Jerusalem, and to envisage an apocalyptic "end of days" setting in which all Christians would be resurrected together, rising up in their bodies and being transformed into their spiritual being. In this cosmic setting, God would achieve final victory over Satan, and the world as we know it would end.

Paul was insistent on the (Gnostic) distinction between spiritual transformation and traditional observances or "works of the law" which he identified "with the flesh." James, on the other hand, wrote about good works (with or without traditional ritual) as the essence of righteousness. The Jamesian interpretation was that followers of Jesus could optionally observe whatever forms of traditional Jewish ritual they wished (excepting certain obligatory moral requirements), while Paul claimed that in a mixed community with Gentiles, Jewish followers could be exempted from Mosaic Law obligations. Many "strict observance" Jesus people took the opposite tack that pagans had to be circumcised into Judaism before qualifying as Jesus people. For Paul, "baptism in Christ" was the "new circumcision."

Through vigorous proselytization, Paul's ideas became rather dominant in Gentile reaction to "Hebrew" interpretations of Jesus' death. Because of his Pharisaic background, Paul was able to incorporate many strands of Jewish tradition into his new elaboration of God's Plan. This probably helped to promote his version among some Diaspora Jews as well as Gentiles (see also Chapter 4). Paul died in the city of Rome in the sixties. Little did he know that within a few years the Roman-Jewish War would bring about the Fall of Jerusalem and destruction of the Temple in a way that seemed to match what he said, and to refute the expectations of James and company in Jerusalem about Jesus as the Messiah of Israel.

CHAPTER 23

CONCLUDING COMMENTS

During the chaos of the ten years following the death of James in Jerusalem in 62 C.E., and the presumed deaths of Paul and Simon Peter in Rome about the same time, the Jesus Kingdom of God movement was in a state of crisis. The Roman-Jewish War (66-73 C.E.) seemed to confirm that God the Father was taking action against his previously "chosen people." The city of Jerusalem was destroyed. The Temple was demolished and its cult destroyed. The Herodian establishment was finished. The Essenes disappeared. The Sect of the Nazarenes was fragmented, no longer in charge of managing the missionary church. The Jewish face of the Kingdom of God had been broken, and the story that Jesus Messiah would return "to redeem Israel" (Luke 24:21) had lost its credibility.

The Gospel of Mark

Mark's Gospel, written circa 70 C.E., was a sort of emergency response designed to show that Jesus was not an anti-Roman anointed Messiah of Israel, but rather the fully divine Christ, Son of God, sent into the world to rescue all human beings from the consequences of their sins. It seems likely that the author of Mark, evidently well acquainted with varying points of view among the followers of Jesus, was jolted into rethinking the story of Jesus by the crushing evidence of God's anger against the Jews in the Roman-Jewish War. God's action proved that the apocalyptic age had begun, the Gnostics were wrong, and the people of Israel had failed.

Mark's Pauline-influenced perception was that scriptural prophecy was about the coming to Earth of a God-Man, the fully divine Son of God and Son of Man, for the redemption of all human beings. He carefully distinguished the Son of

Man personhood of Jesus from the outdated concept of a human Davidic Messiah linked with the salvation of Israel. As Son of Man, Jesus was fully human, but he was not a human Davidic Messiah; he was the divine Messiah, the Christ.

The Pauline cornerstone of Mark's belief system was the cosmic conflict between God and Satan—between Good and Evil. Jesus Christ comes with "secret wisdom" for a new set of "chosen people," the elect who believe (who have a committed faith) in Him. As a dying sacrificial Saviour, He will share their sufferings to rescue them from sin.

Mark was seized by the tragic horrors of the Roman-Jewish War, which he could picture in parallel with the sufferings and humiliation of Jesus during his crucifixion. Just as the divine suffering of Jesus was followed by his resurrection, so would the apocalyptic tribulations of humankind be followed quickly by the redemptive hope of the return of Jesus Christ, Son of Man and Son of God. "The time is fulfilled and the Kingdom of God is at hand" (Mark 1:15).

Using the "Early John" Gospel as basic source material, Mark reorders events in a radical way to fit his scripturally-grounded perception of the identity and mission of Jesus. *The first part* of the story, placed in Galilee, is framed by his astonishing manoeuvre of retrojecting four post-crucifixion appearances of Jesus back into his lifetime: the transfiguration, the Sea of Galilee recruitment of disciples, the appointment of apostles, and the second feeding of the multitude. *The latter part* of the story in Jerusalem is reconstituted by the transfer of the entry into Jerusalem event and the cleansing of the Temple incident from the Feast of Tabernacles to the Passover Feast.

The backbone of Mark's account is that Jesus explained God's Plan to his uncomprehending disciples during his lifetime, while preserving "secrecy" against outsiders in order to foil Satan. Presumably, for Mark, the post-crucifixion spiritual appearances, visions and revelations of Jesus were Thomas-inspired deceptions intended to mislead his followers away from the Divine Truth. Mark replaced these happenings with parallel lifetime stories, and apocalyptic prophecy by Jesus to refute the Thomastic interpretation. At the same time he did not hesitate to select many sayings and parables of Jesus from the Gospel of Thomas for his new gospel, while carefully omitting "secret mysteries" at the heart of the Gnostic belief system.

Mark also omitted key elements of the "Early John" narrative that seemed to link Jesus with an attempted insurrection in the Temple at the Feast of Tabernacles, and to link siblings of Jesus with events in Jerusalem. He thereby needed an alternative explanation for the arrest and crucifixion of Jesus. No hint of anti-Roman activities could remain.

From the beginning of the story, Jesus is identified by God as his Beloved Son, and Satan plots to destroy Him throughout the narrative. The concept of anointed Messiah is a sort of confusion device, which keeps the people of Israel, the family of Jesus, and the disciples from understanding Jesus' identity as the True Christ, Son of Man and Son of God. They simply *don't get it*, for they are predestined not to understand.

And when Jesus acknowledges finally to the High Priest of Israel that he is the Son of God who will return again as the Son of Man "they all condemned him as deserving death" for his "blasphemy" (Mark 14:62-64).

Reflecting the tragic mood at the end of the Roman-Jewish War, Mark's dénouement is an extraordinarily moving portrait of the Satanic crucifixion of a "despised and rejected man" who cries out "My God, my God, why hast thou forsaken me?" (Mark 15:34). The disciples abandon him, Simon Peter denies him, Judas Iscariot betrays him. The people of Israel reject him

Readers of Mark's Gospel are urged to believe what Jesus said while still alive. He had told his disciples that he would be "raised" after his death. He would "go before you into Galilee" (Mark 14:28). "There you will see him as he told you" (Mark 16:8), perhaps a backhanded reference to the visions in Galilee which Mark had retrojected to Jesus' lifetime. The unnamed young man at the Empty Tomb is perhaps James, brother of Jesus, bringing Mark's message as witness against his own "Early John" Gospel version. Presumably, Mark's message was denial that Jesus had promised to return to Jerusalem to implement God's Plan as anticipated perhaps by James and other disciples (possibly in the "Early John" text). Rather, it was that those with committed faith "who endure to the end" will be saved when the Son of Man comes "before this generation has passed away" to "gather his elect . . . from the ends of the earth to the ends of heaven" (Mark 13).

The Gospel of Matthew

The author of the Gospel of Matthew (circa 80-90 C.E.), was strongly impressed by the Gospel of Mark, particularly by the way Mark told the story of Jesus as God's action to defeat Satan, infiltrator and corruptor of the people of Israel.

His lyrical rendering of the ethical teachings of Jesus in the Sermon on the Mount, suggests the fervour of a deeply committed convert, inspired by the Q1 writings of the disciple Matthew. Contrariwise, his intensive search of Hebrew scriptures for prophetic texts, and his stubborn insistence on Mosaic Law indicate a scribe steeped in traditional Hebrew patterns of thought, suggestive of a Qumram Essene background. From Mark he realizes that the "secret" mission of Jesus is the fulfillment of God's Plan, discoverable in ancient prophetic scripture that reveals the full dimensions of the people of Israel's failure to accept God's Messiah and God's Plan.

The first response of the author to his reading of Mark's Gospel seems to have been the expansion of the Q1 Sayings Gospel to include some dark statements about the fate of sinners who fail to accept Jesus' teachings. Then came another idea, when he noticed shortcomings in the Markan gospel that could be improved by adding a birth narrative, matching events more closely to scriptural prophecy, adding rewritten Q material on the teachings of Jesus, and by correcting, omitting and/or expanding certain Markan statements to answer objections by sceptics.

In so doing, the author of Matthew searched the Hebrew scriptures to find continuity and connectedness between the old and the new. The coming of the Son of God, and details of his life and mission were foretold in particular scriptural passages. The ethical teachings of Jesus were not replacements of Mosaic Law, but higher forms of the Law. The New Covenant, too, was not a replacement; it was an extension of the Covenant in new format to all the peoples of the world. The Matthew Gospel writer sharpens the distinction made by Mark between the evil Jews who had failed God (particularly Pharisees, Scribes and Sadducees), and the "saving remnant." He revels in the everlasting guilt of the Jews in murdering prophets and crucifying the Son of God; he describes the horrors of the Last Judgment that await all evildoers. And then he demonizes the Jews in Jerusalem at the time of the crucifixion. "His blood be upon us and on our children" (Matthew 27:25).

But paralleling the authority of the past encased in scripture and Mosaic Law, was the need for apostolic authority against the Gnostic tendency, which Mark had weakened by downgrading the apostles chosen by Jesus to a bunch of fools. The Matthew author stresses their rehabilitation as repentant sinners, and the special delegation of authority to them by Jesus, particularly to Simon Peter as leader (Matthew 16:17-19). And he revises Mark's post-crucifixion story to include an "appearance" in Galilee, (although "some doubted") where the apostles' baptizing and teaching authority is confirmed, pending "the close of the age" (Matthew 28:16-20). Presumably the reference to doubters was an ambiguous way of acknowledging controversy about alleged "appearances" in Galilee. And the "end of days" was now less imminent than in Mark: "those days will be shortened" (Matthew 24:22) instead of "already shortened" (Mark 13:20).

The most significant change to the post-crucifixion story, however, was the Matthewan response to criticisms of the Empty Tomb story by Gnostics and others. He describes a resurrection moment accompanied by a "great earthquake," terrified tomb guards, and a messenger "angel of the Lord" (Matthew 28:2-4); in addition, women at the tomb provide witnessed proof of the physical resurrection of Jesus in an encounter where they "took hold of his feet and worshipped him" (Matthew 28:9). Mary of Magdala was now specified as a witness against the earlier accounts of what had transpired. Jesus' physical body had been seen and touched momentarily on its way back to God, thus verifying the bodily nature of his resurrection.

The Gospel of Luke

The scribe Luke, writing from a "Hellenist" perspective in counterpoint to Matthew's "Hebrew" orientation (at about the same point in time), was also enthused by Mark, but had access to a remarkable variety of other sources such as an updated Q (as elaborated by the Gospel of Matthew writer), Thomas, "Early John," Barnabas, some Essene writings, and presumably direct contact with Paul.

Infused with a Pauline-inspired image of Jesus as Divine Saviour incarnated as the perfect human teacher, totally empathetic with all repentant sinners, Luke's grandiose aim went beyond Matthew's concept of Jesus Messiah revealed in traditional Hebrew scriptural prophecy. It was intended as a unified account of God's intervention in human history through his Son and the Holy Spirit, beginning with the Jews, Israel and Jerusalem, and culminating with the Gentiles, all the nations, and presumably Rome.

By the time Luke was writing, the main challenge to the Pauline outlook in the Hellenist world was no longer the Jerusalem Church and the Jamesian "Hebrew" tendency; the challenge was the Gnostic missionary effort. From sources such as Q1 and Thomas, Luke derived a rich supply of sayings and parables of Jesus, including some of the all-time favourites that have not been found elsewhere. His gospel pays a lot of attention to living the Kingdom of God in this world. For unlike Mark and Matthew who characterize it as a future Kingdom, the Lukan Jesus says "Behold, the Kingdom of God is in the midst of you" (Luke 17:20); it is timeless and always present in the form of the Holy Spirit. This Gnostic emphasis helps to reduce apocalyptic tension about the second coming of Jesus. For example, when using Mark's prophetic text about "the Son of Man coming in clouds," Luke deletes the reference about "gathering the elect from the four winds" (Mark 13:27) which reflected the Pauline idea of "the second coming" as meaning the end of the material world.

In a sense, Luke's beautifully crafted sayings of Jesus about living in this world were an invitation to Gnostic Hellenists to participate in God's unified Plan as a linked continuity with biblical history. He concurs with Mark's storyline but wants to improve it with a birth narrative, Q selections and even some information from "Early John"; simultaneously he omits (more extensively than Mark) certain undesirable elements of the "Early John" story.

In fact, Luke effectively bypasses any explanation of why King Herod Antipas killed John the Baptist and "wants to kill Jesus" (Luke 13:31), and totally ignores the eventual war between Israel and Rome, in Acts of the Apostles. But by writing the latter, he was forced to come to grips with the obvious fact that the disciples had settled in Jerusalem in expectation of the return of a resurrected Jesus "in power" to that city "before this generation will pass away." Instead of Mark's view that this was all part of a wrong-headed misunderstanding by his dim-witted Jewish followers that Jesus was the traditional Messiah-King of Israel, Luke understood it as a transitional phase of God's Plan. For Luke, Jesus had lived as an observant Jew, and after his death he told his apostles to remain in Jerusalem and worship in the Temple.

We can imagine Luke puzzling over the contradictions between Mark and "Early John." Obviously Jesus had explained his identity and prophesied the future when he was alive. The disciples had received the message but failed to understand it, even though it was foretold in ancient scripture. In the post-crucifixion scenario, both "Early John" and Mark continued the confusion. For Luke, the spiritual appearances in Galilee were irrelevant, as they were for Mark. By implication, Jesus could only be distinguished from the Holy Spirit by some element of physical identity. All that mattered to Luke were the real resurrection events that occurred in Judea, "real" because they conveyed essential new messages from Jesus about staying in Jerusalem and organizing a missionary church. The whole point was the historical manifestation of the physical resurrection of Jesus in bodily form "on the third day" before ascending to God.

Thus, Luke uses "Early John" in a rebuttal of both Mark and the Gnostics. He ignores the appearances in Galilee, but rewrites the appearances in and near Jerusalem as physical resurrection events, retrojected to the third day after Jesus' crucifixion, and witnessed by the apostles. Apostolic authority is confirmed by Jesus who then ascends to God; the Holy Spirit descends later at the Feast of Pentecost to provide ongoing support, pending the eventual unfolding of apocalyptic events.

Luke's description of the descent of the Holy Spirit on the apostles was his penultimate refutation of the Gnostic idea of a primordial Spirit present in every human being since the Creation. Derivative from the "Early John" claim that John the Baptist witnessed the descent of the Holy Spirit on Jesus, it strengthened the concept of divine action from without rather than from within. Now the gift of the Holy Spirit given to the apostles was connected to faith in Jesus Christ, and disconnected from gnosis.

The Gospel of John

"Later John's" Gospel, composed later than the three synoptic gospels (circa 100 C.E.), comes at the story of Jesus from another direction, that of a gnostically-trained follower of Jesus, converted to the Pauline outlook.

Paul had reacted against his own traditional Hebrew understanding of Jesus as Messiah of Israel by redefining and divinizing his personhood into Son of God and Lord of Heaven. "Later John" reacted against his own Gnostic perception of the words of Jesus, by redefining Jesus as "the Word," the totally divine Redeemer descended from Heaven—God made flesh—co-existent with God from the beginning of creation.

In his opening words, "Later John" agrees with the Gnostics that divine Light was located in human beings from the Beginning, but that the world did not grasp or recognize it (John 1:5-10). Only when "the Word became flesh and dwelt among us" (John 1:14), could those who "believed in his name" (John 1:12) be born again as children of God. From that time onwards only those who believe in Jesus Christ (i.e. God himself in human form) can find divine truth. The Thomas message of unmediated direct access to the Spirit of God within through gnosis, is replaced by exclusive access to God the Father through Jesus Christ the Son. The somewhat anarchic Gnostic Kingdom of God within each person is replaced by Christ, who embodies God's Word within each person. What remains from Thomas, however, is "eternal life" for members of the Kingdom of God.

"Later John" composes entirely new sets of words for Jesus (high poetry), which focus on his own divine identity and presence. The essential Gnostic message of love and compassion remains, but Jesus does not offer specific ethical sayings and parables, nor does he describe an apocalyptic "end of days" scenario.

The narrative framework is borrowed from "Early John" as in Mark, which accounts for some similarities in the two gospels, except that the drastic narrative changes by "Later John" are vastly different in detail from the changes made by Mark. The following are some common features of changes by "Later John" and Mark to the source material: omission of the insurrection in the Temple, re-assignment of certain events to Passover Feasts from the Feast of Tabernacles, and emphasis on hostility to Jesus by Jewish people. Fortunately however, "Later John," Mark and Luke retain enough embedded elements from the "Early John" source to permit reasonable reconstruction of this lost gospel.

For the same reasons as Matthew and Luke, the author of "Later John" is preoccupied with affirming the physical resurrection of Jesus on the third day after his death, but in a much more explicit put-down of Gnostic scepticism. The disciple Thomas is somehow absent when Jesus "appears" to commission the disciples and give them the Holy Spirit. Confirmation of the presence of his physical body comes eight days later at another appearance when doubting Thomas touches the prints of the nails in his flesh, and says "My Lord and my God." This is the ultimate triumph of the interpretation of "Later John"; Thomas, the Gnostic who does not believe in the physical resurrection, or that Jesus is God, has *become a witness against himself.*

The Johannine gospel author depicts himself as "the disciple that Jesus loved" whom we have identified as James, brother of Jesus. In other words, James' concept of the personhood of Jesus (redefined by "Later John") has prevailed over the Thomas Gnostic viewpoint. But in terms of leadership, the "disciple whom Jesus loved" is put to rest. Simon Peter (the rock) emerges as the symbol of weak and sinful humanity rescued and redeemed by the resurrection of Jesus Christ. His story resonates across all the canonical gospels as the struggle of an ordinary Hebrew Galilean fisherman towards enlightenment, understanding and leadership. "Jesus said to him, 'Feed my sheep'" (John 21:17).

APPENDIX 1

INFERRED SOURCES FOR MARK'S RE-INVENTION OF THE STORY AND SAYINGS OF JESUS

I Events (Exclusive of "Signs")

Chapter and Verse	Description	Inferred Source
Mark 1:1-8	Activities of John the Baptist	Simon Peter's notes; "Early John" (John: 1:19,23,26,28).
Mark 1:9	Baptism of Jesus	Mark's invention
Mark 1:10	Descent of the Spirit	"Early John" (John 1:32)
Mark 1:11	Voice from Heaven	Mark's invention
Mark 1:12-13	Temptation in the wilderness	Mark's invention
Mark 1:14	Entry into Galilee	"Early John" (John 4:3)
Mark 1:16-20	Recruitment of disciples	"Early John" (John 1:37-43;21:1-14)
Mark 1:21-28	Healing in Capernaum synagogue	Simon Peter's notes

Chapter and Verse	Description	Inferred Source
Mark 1:29-31	Healing of Simon's mother-in-law	Simon Peter's notes
Mark 1:32-40	Additional works	Simon Peter's notes
Mark 1:40-45	Healing of Leper	Simon Peter's notes
Mark 2:13-17	Recruitment of Levi	"Early John" material?
Mark 3:7-19	Commissioning of apostles	"Early John" (John 20:19-23)
Mark 3:20-21	Family seizes Jesus	Simon Peter's notes
Mark 4:35-40	Rebuking of wind and wave	Simon Peter's notes
Mark 5:1-20	The Gerasene demoniac	Simon Peter's notes
Mark 5:21-43	Jairus' daughter	Simon Peter's notes
Mark 6:1-6	Visit to Nazareth	"Early John" material?
Mark 6:7-13	Instructions to apostles	"Early John" material?
Mark 6:14-29	John the Baptist beheaded	"Early John" material?
Mark 7:31-37	Healing of deaf man	Simon Peter's notes
Mark 8:1-21	Feeding of 4000	"Early John" (John 21:13-14)
Mark 9:2-13	The transfiguration	"Early John" (John 21:15-19)
Mark 9:14-29	Healing of epileptic	Simon Peter's notes

Chapter and Verse	Description	Inferred Source
Mark 10:1	Trip to Judea & Jordan	"Early John" (John 7-10)
Mark 10:46-52	Blind Bartimaeus	?
Mark 11:1-6	Colt at Bethany	Simon Peter's notes
Mark 11:12-14;20-21	Cursing of fig tree	Simon Peter's notes
Mark 12:12	Attempted arrest	"Early John" (John 7:32)
Mark 14:1-9	Supper in Bethany	"Early John" (John 12:1-8)
Mark 14:10-21	Last Supper	Mark's invention (Pauline interpretation)
Mark 14:22-25	The Eucharist	Paul
Mark 14:26-42	Garden of Gethsemane	Mark's invention
Mark 14:43-45	The kiss of Judas	Mark's invention
Mark 14:46-52	Arrest of Jesus	"Early John" (John 18:8,10,15-16)
Mark 14:53-65	Trial by Sanhedrin	?
Mark 14:66-71	Peter's denial	"Early John" (John 18:25-27)
Mark 15:1-15	Trial by Pilate	"Early John" material
Mark 15:2	Trial by Pilate	"Early John" (John 18:33)

Chapter and Verse	Description	Inferred Source
Mark 15:9-10	Trial by Pilate	"Early John" (John 18:39-40)
Mark 15:16-40	Crucifixion	"Early John" material
Mark 15:16-20	Crucifixion	"Early John" (John 19:1-2)
Mark 15:22	Crucifixion	"Early John" (John 19:17)
Mark 15:24	Crucifixion	"Early John" (John 19:23)
Mark 15:26	Crucifixion	"Early John" (John 19:19)
Mark 15:27	Crucifixion	"Early John" (John 19:18)
Mark 15:36	Crucifixion	"Early John" (John 19:29)
Mark 15:42-47	Burial in tomb	"Early John" (John 19:38-42)
Mark 16:1-8	The Empty Tomb	"Early John" (John 20:1-10)

II Sayings (Exclusive of Signs, Prophecies and Events)

Chapter and Verse	Description	Inferred Source
Mark 1:15	Kingdom of God at hand	Mark's invention
Mark 2:18-20	Bridegroom and wedding guests	Thomas 104
Mark 2:21-22	Garments and wine	Thomas 47
Mark 2:23-28;3:1-6	The Sabbath	"Early John" (John 7:22-24, 32)
Mark 3:22-27	House divided	Thomas 35
Mark 3:28-30	Blasphemy against Holy Spirit	Thomas 44
Mark 3:31-35	Mother and brothers	Thomas 99
Mark 4:1-20	Parable of seeds	Thomas 9
Mark 4:21-23	Lamp under bushel	Thomas 33
Mark 4:24-25	Insiders vs outsiders	Thomas 41
Mark 4:26-29	Scattering of seeds	Thomas 21
Mark 4:30-34	Parable of the mustard seed	Thomas 20
Mark 6:4	Prophet without honour	Thomas 31
Mark 6:10	Instructions for traveling	Thomas 14
Mark 7:1-23	Teaching on food	Thomas 14
Mark 7:24-30	Let the children first be fed	Thomas 93
Mark 8:27-30	Who am I?	Thomas 13
Mark 9:33-35	Last will be first	Thomas 4
Mark 9:36-49	Children in Kingdom	Thomas 22

Chapter and Verse	Description	Inferred Source
Mark 9:50	Love one another	Thomas 25
Mark 10:2-12	Marriage & divorce	Apostle Paul and Thomas 22
Mark 10:13-16	Enter Kingdom like a child	Thomas 46
Mark 10:17-31	The first will be last	Thomas 4
Mark 10:35-44	Number one is servant of all	"Early John" (John 13:12-17)
Mark 10:45	Life as a ransom for many	"Early John" (John 11:50-52)
Mark 11:22-26	Ask and you will receive	Thomas 94
Mark 11:27-33	By what authority?	"Early John" (John 7:14-18)
Mark 12:1-9	Parable of the vineyard	Thomas 65
Mark 12:10-11	Stone which the builders rejected	Thomas 66
Mark 12:13-17	Tribute to Caesar	Thomas 100
Mark 12:18-27	Resurrection of the dead	Thomas 111 and Paul
Mark 12:28-34	Love your neighbour	Thomas 25 and Paul
Mark 12:35-40	Messiah as Son of David (polemic against)	"Early John" in general
Mark 12:41-44	The poor widow	Thomas 4

III Signs and Prophecies

Chapter and Verse	Description	Inferred Source
Mark 2 :1-12	Healing of paralytic (changed from sign to miracle)	"Early John" (John 5:1-16)
Mark 6:30-44	Feeding of 5000 (changed from sign to miracle)	"Early John" (John 6:1-15)
Mark 6:45-56	Walking on water (changed from sign to miracle)	"Early John" (John 6:16-21)
Mark 8:22-26	Healing of blind man (changed from sign to miracle)	"Early John" (John 9)
Mark 8:31-33	Prophecy of Jesus' death	Mark's invention (Pauline interpretation)
Mark 8:34-38	Saving or losing life	Mark's invention (Pauline interpretation)
Mark 9:1	Prophecy of Parousia	"Early John" material
Mark 9:30-32	Prophecy of Jesus' death	Mark's invention
Mark 10:32-35	Prophecy of Jesus' death	Mark's invention
Mark 11:7-11	Entry into Jerusalem	"Early John" (John 12:12-15)
Mark 11:15-19	Cleansing of the Temple	"Early John" (John 2:13-17)
Mark 13	Apocalyptic prophecy	Thomas 16 and Mark's invention
Mark 14:26-28	Prophecy of Parousia in Galilee	Mark's invention

APPENDIX 2

ANALYSIS OF THE GOSPEL OF JOHN

Chapter and Verse	Inferred "Early John" Text	"Later John" Changes and Additions	Comments
John 1:1-5	—	Prologue equates "the Word" with God, and life with "the Light" from God	Gnostic-style Hellenistic ideas mixed with Pauline theology
John 1:6-8	John the Baptist sent from God	To testify that God was coming into the world	Elaboration by "Later John"
John 1:9-18	—	Explains that the Word (ie God) became Flesh and dwelt on Earth. Jesus is the only Son of God	Gnostic-style Hellenistic ideas mixed with Pauline theology

Chapter and Verse	Inferred "Early John" Text	"Later John" Changes and Additions	Comments
John 1:19-23	Interviewed by priests and Levites from Jerusalem, John denies being Messiah, Elijah or "the Prophet"	—	Concise and cryptic. Focuses on John's inferiority. Expresses concern of Temple authorities about John.
John 1:24	—	"It was the Pharisees who had sent them."	Insert by "Later John" shifts responsibility to Pharisees.
John 1:25-27	Explains himself as inferior to Jesus "But among you stands one whom you do not know . . . the thong of whose sandal I am not worthy to untie."	—	Focuses on superiority of Jesus. Implies that Jesus may be a priest or Levite. Source for Mark 1:7
John 1:28	—	"This took place in Bethany, beyond the Jordan where John was baptizing."	Insert by "Later John" added perhaps to direct attention away from probable location at Bethany near Jerusalem.

Chapter and Verse	Inferred "Early John" Text	"Later John" Changes and Additions	Comments
John 1:29-31	John says: "Behold the Lamb of God . . . I myself did not know him, but for this I came baptizing with water, that he might be revealed to Israel."	"who takes away the sin of the world" and "after me comes a man who ranks before me, for he was before me."	"Early John" quotes John the Baptist as prophesying Passover death of Jesus, envisaged as sacrificed by God as a sign to Israel. "Later John" adds theological elaboration.
John 1:32-33	John says: "I saw the Spirit descend as a dove from heaven, and it remained on him . . . he who baptizes with the Holy Spirit."	—	Source for Mark 1:8,10, but here no direct mention of baptism of Jesus by John.
John 1:34	—	"I have seen . . . that this is the Son of God."	Addition by "Later John."

Chapter and Verse	Inferred "Early John" Text	"Later John" Changes and Additions	Comments
John 1:35-42	Recruitment of Andrew, Simon and unnamed person as disciples by Jesus on referral by John. Andrew says: "we have found the Messiah."	Rabbi (which means Teacher), Messiah (which means Christ), Cephas (which means Peter)	"Later John" explains "Early John" terminology to his readers. NOTE: Andrew and the unnamed person are jointly the first to find the Messiah. Partial source for Mark 1:16-20.
John 1:43	—	Jesus decides to go to Galilee.	—
John 1:43-44	Jesus recruits Philip, "Follow me"	Philip comes from Bethsaida	Partial source for Mark 1:17. NOTE: Philip, a Greek, shares same hometown as Andrew and Peter.
John 1:45-49	Jesus recruits Nathaniel	—	Jesus terms Nathaniel a true Israelite (without guile) even though Samaritan or Greek. Nathaniel terms Jesus true King of Israel, even though from Nazareth in Galilee.
John 1:49	—	Nathaniel says to Jesus "You are the Son of God."	Insert by "Later John."

Chapter and Verse	Inferred "Early John" Text	"Later John" Changes and Additions	Comments
John 1:50-51	—	Jesus tells Nathaniel he will see greater things.	Addition by "Later John," referring to ascent and descent from God.
John 2:1-11	—	Marriage at Cana and miracle of water changed into wine.	Addition by "Later John" of an opening symbolic "sign" by Jesus "you have kept the good wine till now."
John 2:12-13	—	Jesus goes to Capernaum with mother, brothers and disciples, and thence to Jerusalem for Passover Feast.	The Cana-Capernaum sequence suggests locational derivation from "Early John'" version of John 4:46-54, which may have included mention of mother, brothers and wedding.
John 2:14-16	Cleansing of the Temple	—	"Early John" demonstration of dual messianic and Temple authority in Jesus. "Later John" transfers from Feast of Tabernacles scenario, and suppresses reaction of Temple officials. Source for Mark 11:15-17.

Chapter and Verse	Inferred "Early John" Text	"Later John" Changes and Additions	Comments
John 2:17-22	—	Explanation by Jesus of his action.	However explained by "Early John," "Later John" reinterprets symbolically as metaphor for destruction of Jesus' body and resurrection in three days.
John 2:23-24	—	Jesus understands fickleness of new eyewitness believers and "didn't trust himself to them."	"Later John'" reference to multiple "signs" at Feast confirms his transfer of this event from Feast of Tabernacles to Passover Feast.
John 3:1-6	Jesus explains to Pharisee Nicodemus that baptism by water and by Spirit are both prerequisites for entry into Kingdom of God.	—	Endorsement of Jesus by leading Pharisee, with explanation that both water baptism and spiritual rebirth necessary for Kingdom of God on earth.
John 3:1	—	"a leader of the Jews"	Insert by "Later John"

Chapter and Verse	Inferred "Early John" Text	"Later John" Changes and Additions	Comments
John 3:7-21	—	Conversation between Jesus and Nicodemus "God so loved the world that he gave his only Son" etc.	—
John 3:22-30	John the Baptist re-endorses Jesus when he starts baptizing (presumably with the Spirit) in Judea. "He must increase, but I must decrease."	—	Implies competition between Jesus and John the Baptist, accompanied by "dispute over purification."
John 3:24	—	"For John had not yet been put in prison."	Insert by "Later John"
John 3:31-36	—	Further elaboration of superiority of Jesus, and of eternal life of believers in Him.	Additional interpretation of divinity of Jesus by "Later John."

Chapter and Verse	Inferred "Early John" Text	"Later John" Changes and Additions	Comments
John 4:1-3	Jesus leaves Judea for Galilee.	"because the Pharisees had heard that Jesus was . . . baptizing more disciples than John, although Jesus himself did not baptize, but only his disciples."	Probability that "Later John" suppresses "Early John" statement that Jesus goes to Galilee when John the Baptist is arrested.
John 4:3-42	Perhaps an endorsement of Jesus by Simon Magus of Samaria.	The Samaritan woman at the well. Jesus reveals himself as the Messiah to the woman, and recruits many Samaritans as believers.	"Later John" replacement shows empathy of Jesus to lowly women and despised Samaritans and their positive response to him. Seems intended to contrast with Jesus' inability "to trust himself" to fickle Judeans and Galileans (see John 2:23-24).
John 4:43-44	"A prophet has no honour in his own country."	—	—

Chapter and Verse	Inferred "Early John" Text	"Later John" Changes and Additions	Comments
John 4:45-46	Galileans welcome Jesus although Nazareth rejects him.	Galileans welcome Jesus because of earlier feats in Jerusalem and Cana.	Probability that "Later John" suppresses "Early John's" rejection of Jesus by people of Nazareth, and changes scene to Cana.
John 4:46-53	Healing of official's son at a distance.	—	Probably presented by "Early John" as contrast to rejection of Jesus by people of Nazareth.
John 4:48	"Unless you see signs and wonders you will not believe."	—	Probably applied by "Early John" to rejecting people of Nazareth. Switched by "Later John" to apply to official from Capernaum.
John 4:54	—	Second sign of Jesus in Galilee.	"Early John" may have initiated a Nazareth–Capernaum sequence, modified later by "Later John" as Cana scenario for two separate "signs" by Jesus.

Chapter and Verse	Inferred "Early John" Text	"Later John" Changes and Additions	Comments
John 5:1-9	Healing of paralytic in Jerusalem.	—	Story transferred by "Later John" from Feast of Tabernacles to an earlier feast attended by Jesus.
John 5:10-18	—	Controversy over healing on the Sabbath day.	Added by "Later John" to contrast foolish attitude of Judeans to Sabbath with Jesus' teaching about himself.
John 5:19-46	—	Monologue: son and father.	—
John 6:1-15	Feeding of the multitude.	—	Probability that "Later John" suppressed the story of the execution of John the Baptist by King Herod, which may have immediately preceded the "Feeding of the multitude" story.
John 6:16-21	Jesus walks on water.	—	—
John 6:22-71	—	Discourse by Jesus on himself as the bread of life.	Explanation of the Eucharist placed here because it doesn't fit into "Early John's" Last Supper story.

Chapter and Verse	Inferred "Early John" Text	"Later John" Changes and Additions	Comments
John 7:1-13	—	Secret visit by Jesus to Jerusalem for the Feast of Tabernacles.	Replacement by "Later John" of earlier story of Jesus going up to Jerusalem. "Entry into Jerusalem" and Cleansing of the Temple" stories are transferred to earlier and later Passover feasts respectively.
John 7:1	—	Jesus moves around Galilee.	Effort by "Later John" to separate "feeding of the multitude" from trip to Jerusalem.
John 7:2-5	Brothers urge Jesus to go to Jerusalem.	—	Perhaps because death of John the Baptist causing turbulence and despair.
John 7:6-13	Jesus undertakes public trip to Jerusalem.	Jesus rejects advice of his brothers, but goes up to Jerusalem privately.	"Later John" is replacing public trip to Jerusalem with an alternative story.

Chapter and Verse	Inferred "Early John" Text	"Later John" Changes and Additions	Comments
John 7:14-43	—	Lectures in the Temple by Jesus.	A replacement for earlier material, most of which has been suppressed. "Later John" describes a mixed-up crowd, both friendly and hostile to Jesus. The authorities fail to challenge Jesus, but try unsuccessfully to arrest him.
John 7:37-38	Jesus invites audience in Temple to believe in *his* mission "He who believes in me . . . out of his heart shall flow rivers of living water."	—	Refers to Temple ritual reminding Jews of the water from the rock in the desert (Num. 20,2-13), symbol of hope for messianic deliverance (ie don't give up hope despite the execution of John the Baptist).
John 7:39	—	Explains that Jesus is referring to Holy Spirit to be given to believers after crucifixion and resurrection of Jesus.	This later doctrine is inconsistent with "Early John" who describes Jesus as baptizing with the Spirit on an ongoing basis.

Chapter and Verse	Inferred "Early John" Text	"Later John" Changes and Additions	Comments
John 7:40-43	The Temple crowd argue whether Jesus is Messiah. One group says he can't be because he's from Galilee, and not Bethlehem as required by scripture "so there was division among the people over him."	—	"Early John" seems to be describing the divisions between Jerusalem traditionalists and the various supporters of Jesus.
John 7:44-49	Temple officers report to Temple authorities (Sanhedrin?) that they can't arrest Jesus because of crowd support, and Jesus' eloquence. Some curse the crowd as ignorant of Mosaic Law.	Probable substitution of term "chief priests and Pharisees."	"Later John" focuses on Pharisees and chief priests as opponents of Jesus, perhaps to offset support of Jesus by the Pharisee Nicodemus.

Chapter and Verse	Inferred "Early John" Text	"Later John" Changes and Additions	Comments
John 7:50-52	Nicodemus says the issue is what a man does rather than where he comes from, while others continue to insist that "no prophet is to rise from Galilee."	—	"Early John" continues the debate between Nicodemus the Pharisee and the traditionalists. Perhaps the insurrection occurs next, but is omitted by "Later John."
John 8:1-11	—	Episode of Jesus and the woman taken in adultery "Let him who is without sin among you be the first to throw a stone at her."	Reiteration of empathy of Jesus for lowly women and sinners, contrasting with the hypocrisy of the scribes and Pharisees.
John 8:12-58	—	A long discussion between Jesus and the Pharisees: "I am the light of the world" ending in their attempt to stone him to death.	This long review of "Later John's" message contains many clues and themes of "Later John."
John 9:1-41	The core story probably written by "Early John."	Story of cure of blind man on the Sabbath Day.	Another health miracle used as vehicle for "Later John's" ideas.

Chapter and Verse	Inferred "Early John" Text	"Later John" Changes and Additions	Comments
John 10:1-21	—	Jesus continues his teaching: "I am the good shepherd. The good shepherd lays down his life for his sheep."	More beautiful poetry on the theme of love of God for all who believe in his Son.
John 10:22-39	—	More teaching: "I and the Father are one." Jews try to stone and arrest Jesus.	More about eternal life for all the sheep "My sheep hear my voice, and I know them, and they follow me."
John 10:40-42	Jesus leaves Jerusalem going "across the Jordan to the place where John at first baptized and there he remained." Reiteration of John the Baptist's support for Jesus "And many believed in him there."	—	John the Baptist is now dead. Jesus appears to be linking up with his supporters, and putting more distance between himself and the Jerusalem Temple establishment. Insurrection has occurred.

Chapter and Verse	Inferred "Early John" Text	"Later John" Changes and Additions	Comments
John 11:1	"Now a certain man was ill, Lazarus of Bethany, the village of Mary and her sister Martha."	—	Concise initial statement impersonal. NOTE: relationship of Lazarus is ambiguous suggesting cover-up.
John 11:2	—	"It was Mary who anointed the Lord with ointment and wiped his feet with her hair, whose brother Lazarus was ill."	"Later John" seems anxious to clarify that Mary is *not* Mary of Magdala and that Lazarus is her *brother*. NOTE how referral to a later event in text points to authorship by "Later John."
John 11:3	"So the sisters sent to him, saying Lord, he whom you love is ill."	—	Note that "Early John" implies a special relationship. Lazarus is either a close relative or friend.
John 11:4	—	Jesus says illness will not lead to final death, so that Son of God may be glorified by it.	A typical explanatory elaboration by "Later John."

Chapter and Verse	Inferred "Early John" Text	"Later John" Changes and Additions	Comments
John 11:5	—	"Now Jesus loved Martha and her sister and Lazarus."	"Later John" seems to be clarifying (in contrast to "Early John") that Jesus has a special relationship with two sisters and Lazarus equally—so reader won't get the wrong implication.
John 11:6,7	"So when he heard that he was ill, he stayed two days longer in the place where he was. Then after this he said to the disciples 'Let us go into Judea again.'"	—	A factual statement designed to assure that Lazarus had time to die. But also implies some pre-knowledge or even a pre-planned situation. NOTE how inconsistent such a stay is with "Later John's" statement in verse 5. There *must* be two different writers.
John 11:8-10	—	Disciples argue against going back to Judea, but Jesus persists.	"Later John" continues to reiterate hostility of Judeans.

Chapter and Verse	Inferred "Early John" Text	"Later John" Changes and Additions	Comments
John 11:11	Then he said to them "Our friend Lazarus has fallen asleep, but I go to awake him out of sleep."	—	"Early John" again shows Jesus' intuitive knowledge at a physical distance. But also may indicate a pre-planned situation. Moreover, may imply that Lazarus not really dead—only seems to be dead.
John 11:12-16	—	Jesus explains that Lazarus really is dead and Thomas says "Let us also go that we may die with him."	"Later John" believes that Jesus really meant death, and confirms this by having Jesus change his statement. Thomas thinks they should all die, so that they too can be raised up.
John 11:17	"Now when Jesus came, he found that he had already been in the tomb four days."	—	This sentence relates directly to John 11:11.

Chapter and Verse	Inferred "Early John" Text	"Later John" Changes and Additions	Comments
John 11:18-37	—	Martha goes out to meet Jesus, criticizes him for not coming sooner. Jesus says "I am the resurrection and the life" etc. Martha confesses her belief in him as Son of God, returns to tell Mary who comes with accompanying friends. Again criticizes Jesus, who weeps, and proceeds to the tomb.	Typical "Later John" elaboration shows: grief of Martha and Mary; compassion of Jesus for them; difficulty they had in believing in him, Jesus saying "he who believes in me, though he die, yet shall he live, and whoever lives and believes in me shall never die." Lazarus story as a perfect demonstration that belief in Christ means eternal life.
John 11:38	"Then Jesus came to the tomb; it was a cave and a stone lay upon it."	"deeply moved again"	"Early John" tells his stories in straightforward cryptic fashion, does not include details, theological speeches and emotions of Jesus.

Chapter and Verse	Inferred "Early John" Text	"Later John" Changes and Additions	Comments
John 11:39-40	—	Martha still objects that Lazarus is dead, but Jesus says "if you would believe you would see the glory of God."	"Later John" heightens the tension, keeps pointing out the inability of even Martha to believe (note the earlier passage: not even his brothers believed in him).
John 11:41	"So they took away the stone. And Jesus lifted up his eyes and said 'Father, I thank thee that thou hast heard me.'"	—	"Early John" continues with his description of the "sign."
John 11:42	—	"I know that thou hearest me always, but I have said this on account of the people standing by, that they may believe that thou didst send me."	"Later John" feels compelled to explain why Jesus would need to thank God for hearing him, thus implying the possibility that God might not listen to him in some circumstances.

Chapter and Verse	Inferred "Early John" Text	"Later John" Changes and Additions	Comments
John 11:43-44	"When he had said this, he cried with a loud voice 'Lazarus come out.'"	"The dead man came out, his hands and feet bound with bandages, and his face wrapped with a cloth. Jesus said to them 'Unbind him and let him go.'"	"Later John" describes signs and miracles unrealistically (ie pure magic). How can a moving man be described as dead? How can he move if his feet are bound with bandages? See also descriptions of earlier "signs."
John 11:45-47	Meeting of Sanhedrin probably connected to insurrection story.	Some Judeans report raising of Lazarus to Pharisees who convene meeting of Sanhedrin.	"Later John" connects raising of Lazarus story to anti-Jesus response of Temple establishment.

Chapter and Verse	Inferred "Early John" Text	"Later John" Changes and Additions	Comments
John 11:48-52	"If we let him go on thus, everyone will believe in him, and the Romans will come and destroy both our place and our nation" . . . Caiphas said: "You know nothing at all; you do not understand that it is expedient for you that one man should die for the people, and that the whole nation should not perish" . . . he prophesied that Jesus should die for the nation, and to gather into one the children of God scattered abroad.	—	"Later John" transfers these statements from the Feast of Tabernacles meeting to an invented later meeting. Clues to their "Early John" origin include reference to the "many signs" performed by Jesus, and the Caiphas prophecy of the martyrdom of Jesus to save Israel and to restore the unity of all Jews. This seems to belong with John 7:44-52.

Chapter and Verse	Inferred "Early John" Text	"Later John" Changes and Additions	Comments
John 11:53	—	"So from that day on they took counsel how to put him to death."	Repetitive theme of "Later John."
John 11:54	After the Lazarus event Jesus withdraws again "to the country near the wilderness" with his disciples.	—	—
John 11:55-57	—	Country people come for Passover, look for Jesus, authorities want information in order to arrest him.	"Later John" sets stage for entry into Jerusalem, and betrayal by Judas Iscariot.

Chapter and Verse	Inferred "Early John" Text	"Later John" Changes and Additions	Comments
John 12:1-8	Describes Bethany Last Supper prior to Passover Feast, including anointment of Jesus' feet by Mary of Bethany, objections by Judas Thomas, and answer by Jesus "Let her keep it for the day of my burial. The poor you always have with you, but you do not always have me."	Specifies "six days before Passover." Attributes "objections" to Judas Iscariot who wants to sell the ointment and steal the money.	"Early John" provides motive for Mary of Magdala's later visit to the Empty Tomb (two names for same person). He also puts down Judas Thomas for misunderstanding events to come. "Later John" separates Bethany meal from Last Supper, and uses the Judas objections to point out the avarice of Judas Iscariot.

Chapter and Verse	Inferred "Early John" Text	"Later John" Changes and Additions	Comments
John 12:9-11	—	Great crowd comes to Bethany to see Lazarus. Chief priests plan death of Lazarus.	"Later John" uses public miracle of Lazarus to explain new crowd support for Jesus. No later explanation as to whether Lazarus dies or not. Lazarus disappears from story, and seems to be replaced by "other disciple" ("Early John") or "disciple that Jesus loved" ("Later John").
John 12:12-15	Probably crowd arrives with Jesus as in Mark's version. Otherwise mainly same as "Later John," except it is Feast of Tabernacles and located circa John 7:10-13.	Great crowd welcomes Jesus to Jerusalem with palm tree branches hailing him as King of Israel, as he arrives sitting on a young ass.	"Later John" transfers "entry into Jerusalem" scenario from Feast of Tabernacles to Passover, and explains crowd differently from "Early John."

Chapter and Verse	Inferred "Early John" Text	"Later John" Changes and Additions	Comments
John 12:16-19	—	Explains that disciples failed to understand this event until after glorification of Jesus. Reiterates that Lazarus event explains welcome by crowd. Pharisees complain.	—
John 12:20-50	Visit by Hellenists may have been mentioned.	Speech by Jesus to Greeks (Hellenists) who had come to the Feast. Explains himself as Light of the World, his own destiny, and reasons for unbelief of the Jews, despite his many "signs."	—
John 12:36	Jesus goes into hiding.	—	"Later John" places this after Passover "entry into Jerusalem." Transferred from "Early John," who must have placed it after Feast of Tabernacles events.

Chapter and Verse	Inferred "Early John" Text	"Later John" Changes and Additions	Comments
John 13:1-38	Foot washing as part of the Bethany supper.	Jesus has supper with his disciples, washes their feet, announces denial and betrayal, making clear to "beloved disciple" who will betray him after Peter's request, announces disciples cannot come where he is going, commands them to love one another.	Appears to be a complete substitution for whatever "Early John" may have written on this supper, as part of the Bethany supper.
John 13:27	"What you are going to do, do quickly."	—	May come from "Early John" text relating to Judas Thomas.
John 14:1-31	—	Explanation by Jesus of the Holy Trinity doctrine, that the Father can be reached only through Jesus, and that Holy Spirit will be sent after Jesus is gone "to teach you all things and bring to your remembrance all that I have said to you."	Beautiful departure discourse to bolster faith of disciples after Jesus is gone.

Chapter and Verse	Inferred "Early John" Text	"Later John" Changes and Additions	Comments
John 15:1-27; 16:1-33; 17:1-26	—	Jesus the true vine, why the world hates him and his followers, because his coming puts them in sin, "I have said all this to keep you from falling away." Explains the Christian's relation to the world. Comforts his disciples, temporary sorrow will yield to joy over his abiding presence. Promise of eternal life. Prayers to God.	Continuation of "pep talk" by Jesus.
John 18:1	"When Jesus had spoken these words, he went forth with his disciples across the Kidron valley, where there was a garden which he and his disciples entered."	—	We do not know "Early John's" version of what Jesus said to his disciples.

Chapter and Verse	Inferred "Early John" Text	"Later John" Changes and Additions	Comments
John 18:2	—	"Now Judas, who betrayed him, also knew the place; for Jesus often met there with his disciples."	—
John 18:4-5	"Then Jesus, knowing all that was to befall him, came forward and said to them 'Whom do you seek?' They answered him, 'Jesus of Nazareth.' Jesus said to them 'I am he.'"	"Judas, who betrayed him, was standing with them."	As usual, "Early John" indicates foreknowledge of Jesus in a way that can mean either special intuition, or preplanning.
John 18:6	"When he said to them 'I am he,' they drew back and fell to the ground."	—	"Early John" continues to show acknowledgement of Kingship of Jesus even by soldiers and Temple officers.

Chapter and Verse	Inferred "Early John" Text	"Later John" Changes and Additions	Comments
John 18:7-9	—	"Again he asked them 'Whom do you seek?' And they said 'Jesus of Nazareth.' Jesus answered 'I told you I am he, so if you seek me, let these men go.' This was to fulfill the word which he had spoken, 'Of those whom thou gavest me I lost not one.'"	Seems to be replacement for "Early John's" explanation for the deal which involved no arrest of Jesus' disciples by Pilate.
John 18:10-11	Peter strikes Malchus, the High Priest's slave, but Jesus commands him to put his sword away. "Shall I not drink the cup which the Father has given me?"	—	Transposed by "Later John." Ought to follow 18:12. It seems more logical that Peter strikes Malchus after Malchus treats Jesus roughly.

Chapter and Verse	Inferred "Early John" Text	"Later John" Changes and Additions	Comments
John 18:12-13	So the band of soldiers and their captain and the officers seized Jesus and bound him. First they led him to Annas; for he was the father-in-law of Caiphas	—	—
John 18:14	—	who was High Priest that year. It was Caiphas who had given counsel to the Jews that it was expedient that one man should die for the people.	Another reference back by "Later John" (to John 11:50) with rewording in his own style.

Chapter and Verse	Inferred "Early John" Text	"Later John" Changes and Additions	Comments
John 18:15-18	Peter and "another disciple known to the High Priest" follow Jesus, and enter court with him. At request of other disciple maid keeping the door brings Peter in, and asks if he is "not also one of this man's disciples." He said "I am not."	—	Implication that unnamed disciple as well as Peter are allowed within court even though known as disciples of Jesus. It doesn't matter to High Priest. The maid assumes this, but Peter denies it when asked because of fear since he wounded Malchus.

Chapter and Verse	Inferred "Early John" Text	"Later John" Changes and Additions	Comments
John 18:19-24	Annas questions Jesus "about his disciples and his teaching." Jesus responds that he has taught openly in synagogues and temple (and nothing secretly), and suggests they question those who heard him. An officer slaps him for impudence. Annas then sent him bound to Caiphas the High Priest.	—	Annas seems to be giving Jesus opportunity to explain himself in front of Roman observers. This is not a trial. Jesus declines the opportunity at this time. Annas may simply be curious. He does not pursue questioning. It is late in the evening. Caiphas apparently is otherwise occupied. There is an impression of pre-arrangement.

Chapter and Verse	Inferred "Early John" Text	"Later John" Changes and Additions	Comments
John 18:25-27	—	Simon Peter's three denials of Jesus, and the crowing of the cock.	An evident interpolation by "Later John" which changes the meaning of John 18:17. The question recorded by "Early John" from the doorkeeper maid was innocent confirmation that Peter was a fellow disciple of the "other disciple." NOTE significance of the word "also."

Chapter and Verse	Inferred "Early John" Text	"Later John" Changes and Additions	Comments
John 18:28-29	Then they led Jesus from the house of Caiphas to the praetorium. It was early. They themselves did not enter the praetorium so that they might not be defiled, but might eat the Passover. So Pilate went out and said "What accusation do you bring against this man?"	—	The reference to "they" appears to refer to prior sentences by "Early John" replaced by "Later John." As to what has been replaced, see Mark 15:1. NOTE: authenticity of inability of "they" to enter praetorium for religious scruples.

Chapter and Verse	Inferred "Early John" Text	"Later John" Changes and Additions	Comments
John 18:30-32	—	They answered him: "If this man were not an evildoer, we would not have handed him over." Pilate said to them "Take him yourself and judge him by your own law." The Jews said to him "It is not lawful for us to put any man to death." This was to fulfill the word which Jesus had spoken to show by what death he was to die.	NOTE: inauthentic impudent response of Jews. A more likely response would be "This man is behaving as if he believes himself to be our King." Further inauthentic response has Jews reminding Pilate that they are not allowed to impose death penalty. But if the crime was sedition, Pilate could not have asked them to judge him by Jewish law. This is an obvious cover-up.
John 18:33	Pilate entered the praetorium again and called Jesus and said to him "Are you the King of the Jews?"	—	This sentence follows logically from the presumed missing "Early John" text, and does not fit with "Later John's" replacement, John 18:30-32.

Chapter and Verse	Inferred "Early John" Text	"Later John" Changes and Additions	Comments
John 18:34-38	—	Dialogue between uncomprehending Pilate and Jesus who explains that his kingdom is not of this world, and that he has come to proclaim the truth. Pilate said to him "What is truth?"	Probably replaces missing "Early John" response of Jesus perhaps as in Mark 15:2 "And he answered him, 'You have said so,'" which could be consistent with "Early John" approach of having even Pilate acknowledge kingship.
John 18:38-39	—	Pilate "finds no crime in him" and advises them of *their* custom that *he* release one man at Passover.	An invention by "Later John." Seems to replace a dialogue that may be inferred from Mark 15:6-13.
John 18:39-40	"Will you have me release for you the King of the Jews?"	—	Extract from "Early John" in another context. See Mark 15.
John 18:40	They cried out again, "Not this man, but Barabbas."	Now Barabbas was a robber.	New cover-up explanation to replace "Early John" indication that Barabbas was a Zealot rebel. See Mark 15:6.

Chapter and Verse	Inferred "Early John" Text	"Later John" Changes and Additions	Comments
John 19:1-3	Then Pilate took Jesus and scourged him. And the soldiers plaited a crown of thorns, and put it on his head, and arrayed him in a purple robe; they came up to him saying "Hail, King of the Jews!" and struck him with their hands.	—	This was a punishment relevant to political insurrection.
John 19:4-16	—	Further dialogue between Pilate, Jesus and Jews with Pilate wanting to release him, and Jews forcing him to crucify him by threatening "you are not Caesar's friend." Pilate hands Jesus over to Jews to be crucified.	Completely inauthentic, relentlessly unrealistic. Overstatement of Jewish responsibility, and whitewash of Pilate. Replaces lost "Early John" version in which Pilate turns him over to soldiers for crucifixion. See Mark 15.

Chapter and Verse	Inferred "Early John" Text	"Later John" Changes and Additions	Comments
John 19:17-25	—	Jesus taken to Golgotha. Crucified with two others. Inscription King of the Jews. Division of garments among soldiers.	Rewritten, but probably substantially similar to "Early John" with elaboration. Omits carrying of cross by Simon of Cyrene and offer of wine mingled with myrrh.
John 19:25-27	—	Episode of Mary, two other women and the beloved disciple standing near cross "Behold your mother," "Behold your son."	Designed to emphasize pre-eminence of "beloved disciple."
John 19:28-30	Jesus takes the sponge of vinegar and dies peacefully.	—	Sounds like matter-of-fact "Early John."

Chapter and Verse	Inferred "Early John" Text	"Later John" Changes and Additions	Comments
John 19:31-33	"Since it was the day of preparation in order to prevent the bodies from remaining on the cross on the Sabbath (for that Sabbath was a High Day), the Jews asked Pilate that their legs might be broken and that they might be taken away. So the soldiers came and broke the legs of the first and of the other who had been crucified with him; but when they came to Jesus and saw that he was already dead, they did not break his legs."	—	All this suggests prior agreement by Pilate and High Priest that Jesus was not intended to die, but that God had decided otherwise.

Chapter and Verse	Inferred "Early John" Text	"Later John" Changes and Additions	Comments
John 19:34-37	—	Piercing of Jesus' body with spear by soldier, and special plea by eyewitness that it was true that blood and water came out, thus confirming humanity of Jesus.	This also seems to confirm that Jesus really died, but inadvertently suggests he was not already dead. Purpose may be to show that he was truly human, and not only a god.
John 19:38-42	Joseph of Arimathea and Nicodemus, with permission from Pilate, take body of Jesus, bind it in linen cloths with spices, and place it in a new tomb, close at hand, where no-one had ever been laid.	—	Seems authentic. Temporariness of tomb implies they were not expecting his death at that time.
John 20:1-10	Story of Mary coming early to tomb, finding it empty, informing Simon Peter and other disciple, etc.	—	Sounds very much like authentic "Early John."

Chapter and Verse	Inferred "Early John" Text	"Later John" Changes and Additions	Comments
John 20:2	—	the other disciple, the one whom Jesus loved.	"the one whom Jesus loved" added by "Later John."
John 20:11-30; 21:1-25	—	—	Substituted by "Later John" as his own version to replace what "Early John" wrote.

SELECTED
BIBLIOGRAPHY

Akenson, Donald Harman, *Surpassing Wonder: The Invention of the Bible and the Talmuds*, Montreal: McGill-Queen's University Press, 1998.

Akenson, Donald Harman, *Saint Saul: A Skeleton Key to the Historical Jesus*, Montreal: McGill-Queen's University Press, 2000.

Armstrong, Karen, *The First Christian*, London: Pan Books Ltd., 1983.

Armstrong, Karen, *A History of God*, New York: Alfred A Knopf, 1993.

Aron, Robert, *Les années obscures de Jésus*, Paris: Éditions Bernard Grasset, 1960.

Bible: *The New Oxford Annotated Bible, Revised Standard Version*, New York: Oxford University Press, 1973.

Brandon, S.G.F., *The Trial of Jesus of Nazareth*, New York: Dorset Press, 1968.

Breech, James, *The Silence of Jesus*, Toronto: Doubleday Canada Limited, 1971.

Cahill, Thomas, *The Gifts of the Jews*, New York: Harper Collins, 1998.

Charlesworth, James H., Editor, *Jesus and the Dead Sea Scrolls*, New York: Doubleday, 1992.

Crossan, John Dominic, *The Historical Jesus: The Life of a Mediterranean Jewish Peasant*, New York: Harper Collins, 1991.

Crossan, John Dominic, *Jesus: A Revolutionary Biography*, San Francisco: Harper Collins, 1994.

Crossan, John Dominic, *Who Killed Jesus?* San Francisco: Harper Collins, 1995.

Crossan, John Dominic, *The Birth of Christianity*, San Francisco: Harper Collins, 1998.

Dart, John, *The Jesus of Heresy and History*, San Francisco: Harper and Row, 1988.

Ehrman, Bart D., *Jesus, Apocalyptic Prophet of the New Millenium*, New York: Oxford University Press, 1999.

Ehrman, Bart D., *Lost Christianities*, New York: Oxford University Press, 2003.

Eisenman, Robert, *James, the Brother of Jesus*, New York: Penguin Books, 1997.

Fredriksen, Paula, *From Jesus to Christ*, New Haven: Yale University Press, 1988.

Fredriksen, Paula, *Jesus of Nazareth: King of the Jews*, New York: Alfred A. Knopf, 2000.

Fuller, R.H., *The Foundations of New Testament Christology*, London: Collins, 1965.

Funk, Robert W. and the Jesus Seminar, *The Five Gospels: What Did Jesus Really Say?* New York: Polebridge Press, MacMillan Publishing Company, 1993.

Funk, Robert W., *Honest to Jesus: Jesus for a New Millennium*, San Francisco: Harper, 1996.

Funk, Robert W. and the Jesus Seminar, *The Acts of Jesus: What Did Jesus Really Do?* San Francisco: Harper Collins, 1998.

Grant, Michael, *Jesus, An Historian's Review of the Gospels*, New York: Charles Scribner's Sons, 1977.

Grant, Michael, *A History of Ancient Israel*, New York: Charles Scribner's Sons, 1984.

Harpur, Tom, *The Pagan Christ*, Toronto: Thomas Allen Publishers, 2004.

Harvey, A.E., *Jesus and the Constraints of History*, London: Gerald Duckworth & Co. Ltd., 1982.

Holroyd, Stuart, *The Elements of Gnosticism*, New York: Element, Inc., 1994.

Johnson, Paul, *A History of Christianity*, New York: Atheneum, 1979.

Josephus, Flavius, *The Jewish War and Other Selections from Flavius Josephus*, edited by Moses I. Finley, New York: Washington Square Press, 1965.

Kasser, Rodolphe, Meyer, Marvin W., and Wurst, Gregor (editors), *The Gospel of Judas*, Washington, D.C., National Geographic Society, 2006.

Koester, Helmut, *Ancient Christian Gospels: Their History and Development*, Philadelphia: Trinity Press International, 1990.

Mack, Burton L., *The Lost Gospel, The Book of Q*, New York: Harper Collins, 1993.

Mack, Burton L., *Who Wrote the New Testament?* New York: Harper Collins, 1995.

Meier, John P., *A Marginal Jew: Rethinking the Historical Jesus*, New York: Doubleday, 1991.

Messadié, Gerald, *L'Homme qui devint Dieu, 1: Le récit, 2: Les sources*, Paris : Éditions Robert Laffont, 1988, 1989.

Messadié, Gerald, *L'Incendiaire: Vie de Saul, Apôtre*, Paris : Éditions Robert Laffont, 1991.

Meyer, Marvin W., *The Gospel of Thomas, The Hidden Sayings of Jesus*, New York: Harper Collins, 1992.

Pagels, Elaine, *The Gnostic Gospels*, New York: Random House, 1979.

Pagels, Elaine, *Adam, Eve and the Serpent*, New York: Random House, 1988.

Pagels, Elaine, *The Origin of Satan*, New York: Random House, 1995.

Pagels, Elaine, *Beyond Belief. The Secret Gospel of Thomas*, New York: Random House, 2003.

Sanders, E.P., *Jesus and Judaism*, Philadelphia: Fortress Press, 1985.

Schonfield, Hugh J., *The Passover Plot: New Light on the History of Jesus*, London: Hutchison, 1965.

Segal, Alan F., *Paul the Convert*, New Haven and London: Yale University Press, 1990.

Shanks, Hershel, Editor, *Understanding the Dead Sea Scrolls*, New York: Random House, 1992.

Shanks, Hershel, and Ben Witherington, *The Brother of Jesus*, New York: Harper Collins, 2003.

Sheehan, Thomas, *The First Coming*, New York: Random House, 1997.

Shorto, Russell, *Gospel Truth*, New York: Riverhead Books, 1997.

Smith, Morton, *The Secret Gospel: The Discovery and Interpretation of the Secret Gospel According to Mark*, New York: Harper and Row, 1973.

Smith, Morton, *Jesus the Magician*, New York: Harper and Row, 1978.

Spong, John Shelby, *Rescuing the Bible from Fundamentalism*, New York: Harper Collins, 1991.

Spong, John Shelby, *Born of a Woman*, New York: Harper Collins, 1992.

Spong, John Shelby, *Resurrection: Myth or Reality*, New York: Harper Collins, 1994.

Spong, John Shelby, *Reading the Bible with Jewish Eyes*, New York: Harper Collins, 1996.

Tarnas, Richard, *The Passion of the Western Mind*, New York: Ballantine Books, 1991.

Thich Nhat Hanh, *Living Buddha, Living Christ*, New York: Riverhead Books, 1995.

Vermes, G., *The Dead Sea Scrolls in English*, London: Penguin Books, 1962.

Vermes, Geza, *Jesus in His Jewish Context*, Minneapolis: Fortress Press, 2003.

Warner, Marina, *Alone of All Her Sex, The Myth and Cult of the Virgin Mary*, New York: Alfred A. Knopf, 1976.

Wilson, A.N., *Jesus*, London: Sinclair Stevenson Limited, 1992.

INDEX OF KEY EVENTS

A

Anointment of Jesus' feet:
    in Gospel of "Early John", 48-49,
        181-82, 202
    in Gospel of "Later John", 127
    in Gospel of Luke, 109
    in Gospel of Mark, 84
Appearances of Jesus, post-crucifixion,
    Chapter 19 (192-200)
    in Gospel of "Early John", 40, 52-
        60, 74-75, 107, 110, 153, 209,
        212-23
    in Gospel of "Later John", 74, 118,
        124-25
    in Gospel of Luke, 75, 107, 110-
        13, 230
    in Gospel of Mark, 71-72, 74-77,
        87, 90, 226
    in Gospel of Matthew, 100-101, 228
    to Mary of Magdala, 53-54, 71, 101,
        124, 190-191, 204, 211, 228
    in Epistles of Paul, 54-56, 59, 66-
        67, 75-76, 100-101, 107, 111-
        12, 125, 159, 161, 213, 223
    as retrojections by Mark to the

lifetime of Jesus, 54-56, 72,
    74-76, 87, 90, 110, 153, 226-
    27. *See also* Appointment of
    Apostles; Emmaeus, appearance
    of Jesus on road to; Feeding
    of the multitude (second);
    Recruitment of disciples;
    Transfiguration
Appointment of Apostles, 197-99
    in Gospel of "Early John", 56-58, 160
    in Gospel of "Later John", 125-26
    in Gospel of Luke, 56-57, 75,
        112-13
    in Gospel of Mark, 54, 56, 72, 75,
        87, 153, 226
    in Gospel of Thomas, 26
Apostles, appointment of, *See* Appointment
    of Apostles
Apostles, in early church, Chapter 20 (201-
    207); Chapter 21 (208-218)
Arrest of Jesus, 16, 160, 202-203, Chapter
    17 (180-185)
    in Gospel of "Early John", 38,
        47-50, 59
    in Gospel of "Later John", 123, 127
    in Gospel of Mark, 82-84

INDEX OF NAMES

Z

LaVergne, TN USA
31 December 2009
168665LV00001B/32/P